I0054655

# Active Directory Disaster Recovery

Expert guidance on planning and implementing Active Directory disaster recovery plans

**Florian Rommel**

[PACKT] PUBLISHING

BIRMINGHAM - MUMBAI

# Active Directory Disaster Recovery

Copyright © 2008 Packt Publishing

All rights reserved. No part of this book may be reproduced, stored in a retrieval system, or transmitted in any form or by any means, without the prior written permission of the publisher, except in the case of brief quotations embedded in critical articles or reviews.

Every effort has been made in the preparation of this book to ensure the accuracy of the information presented. However, the information contained in this book is sold without warranty, either express or implied. Neither the author, Packt Publishing, nor its dealers or distributors will be held liable for any damages caused or alleged to be caused directly or indirectly by this book.

Packt Publishing has endeavored to provide trademark information about all the companies and products mentioned in this book by the appropriate use of capitals. However, Packt Publishing cannot guarantee the accuracy of this information.

First published: June 2008

Production Reference: 1130608

Published by Packt Publishing Ltd.
32 Lincoln Road
Olton
Birmingham, B27 6PA, UK.

ISBN 978-1-847193-27-8

www.packtpub.com

Cover Image by Vinay Nihalani (sinless.photography@rediffmail.com)

# Credits

**Author**

Florian Rommel

**Reviewers**

James Eaton-Lee

Nathan Yocom

**Senior Acquisition Editor**

Douglas Paterson

**Development Editor**

Nikhil Bangera

**Technical Editor**

Ajay Shanker

**Copy Editor**

Sumathi Sridhar

**Editorial Team Leader**

Mithil Kulkarni

**Project Manager**

Abhijeet Deobhakta

**Indexer**

Rekha Nair

**Proofreader**

Dirk Manuel

**Production Coordinators**

Aparna Bhagat

Shantanu Zagade

**Cover Work**

Shantanu Zagade

# About the Author

**Florian Rommel** was born and raised in his native Germany until the age of 15, when he moved with this family to Central America and then the US. He has worked in the IT industry for more than 15 years and has gained a wealth of experience in many different IT environments. He also has a long and personal interest in Information Security.

His certifications include CISSP, SANS GIAC:GCUX, MCSE, MCSA , MCDBA, and several others. Together with his extensive experience, he is a qualified and recognized expert in the area of Information Security. After writing several Disaster Recovery guides for Windows 2003 and Active Directory environments in large blue chip and manufacturing companies, he now brings you this unique publication, which he hopes will become a key title in the collection of many Windows Server Administrators.

Florian is currently working in the IT Management department at a large global manufacturing corporation in Finland where he has lived for the past ten years. His responsibility includes the Active Directory and the global security infrastructure.

This book is the result of long hours of research and not having time for the people around me. For that reason, I would like to thank and dedicate this book to my wife Kaisa and my daughter Sofia as well as my parents, and Neil. Without them and their support, as well as support from all of the other people involved in my career over the years, I would have never been able to start and complete this project. I would also like to give special thanks to the people at Microsoft Finland who helped me with questions and solutions, and Guido Grillenmeier who helped me by providing a lot of input and knowledge on the subject.

# About the Reviewers

**James Eaton-Lee** works as a Consultant specializing in Infrastructure Security. He has worked with clients ranging from small businesses with a handful of employees to multinational banks. He has a varied background, including experience working with IT in ISPs, manufacturing firms, and call centers. James has been involved in the integration of a range of systems, from analogue and VOIP telephony systems to NT and AD domains in mission-critical environments with thousands of hosts, as well as UNIX & LINUX servers in a variety of roles. James is a strong advocate of the use of appropriate technology, and the need to make technology more approachable and flexible for businesses of all sizes, especially in the SME marketplace in which technology is often forgotten or avoided. James has been a strong believer in the relevancy and merit of Open Source and Free Software for a number of years and — wherever appropriate — uses it for himself and his clients, seamlessly integrating it with other technologies.

**Nathan Yocom** is an accomplished software engineer specializing in network security, identity, access control, and data integrity applications. With years of experience working at the system level, his involvement in the industry has ranged from creation of software such as the open source Windows authentication project pGina (`http://www.pgina.org`), to Bynari Inc's Linux/Outlook integration suite (`http://www.bynari.net`), to working on Centrify Corporation's ground breaking Active Directory integration and auditing products (`http://www.centrify.com`).

Nathan's publications have included several articles in trade journals such as SysAdmin Magazine, and co-authoring the Apress book "The Definitive Guide to Linux Network Programming" (ISBN: 1590593227). Additionally, Nathan served as technical reviewer for ExtremeTech's "RFID Toys: 11 Cool Projects for Home, Office and Entertainment" by Amal Graafstra, an early RFID proponent and pioneer.

When not hacking at code, Nathan enjoys spending time at home in the Seattle, WA area with his wife Katie, daughter Sydney, and son Ethan. He swears it does not rain in Seattle as much as people claim, but neither is it exactly Bermuda. Nathan can be contacted via email at: `nate@yocom.org`.

# Table of Contents

# Preface

Murphy's Law states that anything that can go wrong will go wrong. In relation to Information Systems and Technology, this could mean an incident that completely destroys data, slows down productivity, or causes any other major interruption to your operations or your business. How bad can it get? — "Most large companies spend between 2% and 4% of their IT budget on disaster recovery planning; this is intended to avoid larger losses. Of companies that had a major loss of computerized data, 43% never reopen, 51% close within two years, and only 6% will survive long-term." *Hoffer, Jim." Backing Up Business - Industry Trend or Event.*

Active Directory (AD) is a great system but it is also very delicate. If you encounter a problem, you will need to know how to recover from it as quickly and completely as possible. You will need to know about Disaster Recovery and be prepared with a business continuity plan. If Active Directory is a part of the backbone of your network and infrastructure, the guide to bring it back online in case of an incident needs to be as clear and concise as possible. If it happens or if you want to avoid all of this happening, this is the book for you.

Recovering Active Directory from any kind of disaster is trickier than most people think. If you do not understand the processes associated with recovery, you can cause more damage than you fix.

This is why you need this book. This book has a unique approach - the first half of the book focuses on planning and shows you how to configure your AD to be resilient. The second half of the book is response-focused and is meant as a reference where we discuss different disaster scenarios and how to recover from them. We follow a Symptom-Cause- Recovery approach – so all you have to do is follow along and get back on track.

This book describes the most common disaster scenarios and how to properly recover your infrastructure from them. It contains commands and steps for each process, and also contains information on how to plan for disaster and how to leverage technologies in your favour in the event of a disaster.

You will encounter the following types of disaster or incident in this book, and learn how to recover from each of them.

- Recovery of deleted objects
- Single domain controller hardware failure
- Single domain controller AD corruption
- Site AD corruption
- Site hardware failure
- Corporate AD corruption
- Complete corporate hardware failure

# What This Book Covers

*Chapter 1* provides an Overview of Active Directory Disaster Recovery.

*Chapter 2* discusses some of the key elements in Active Directory and then over to the actual design work. A few design models are dissected, which will give you a good starting point for your own design.

*Chapter 3* takes a look at all the steps and processes you should go through in order to have a DRP successfully implemented.

*Chapter 4* discusses directly (implementations) and indirectly (processes) related subjects that will help you make your AD environment stronger against events that can impact in a negative way.

*Chapter 5* looks at the different options and approaches for how to recover a DC that has a database corruption.

*Chapter 6* takes a look at the steps necessary to completely recover from a failed domain controller.

*Chapter 7* goes through the different methods of restoring deleted objects, and also looks at how to minimize the impact that such a deletion can have on your business.

*Chapter 8* provides a step-by-step guide to forest recovery.

*Chapter 9* discusses site AD infrastructure failure.

*Chapter 10* describes through a few tools and utilities that will help you monitor and diagnose your AD.

*Appendix A* provides an example of Business Continuity plan.

*Bibliography*

# What you need for this book

This book is oriented towards Windows 2003 Server R2 and Active Directory used in that release. Notes identify where commands vary from older Windows 2003 versions, and provide the equivalent commands in these older versions. As Microsoft is phasing out Windows 2000, we are omitting it entirely. However, the disaster recovery guidelines outlined in this book are applicable to any Active Directory environment, because they haven't changed that much. Please note that in order to get the most out of this book you should be running Windows 2003.

# Conventions

In this book you will find a number of styles of text that distinguish between different kinds of information. Here are some examples of these styles, and an explanation of their meaning.

Any command-line input and output is written as follows:

```
>seize domain naming master
>seize schema master
>seize infrastructure master
>seize pdc
```

**New terms** and **important words** are introduced in a bold-type font. Words that you see on the screen, in menus or dialog boxes for example, appear as follows: "clicking the **Next** button moves you to the next screen".

[ Warnings or important notes appear like this. ]

[ Tips and tricks appear like this. ]

## Reader Feedback

Feedback from our readers is always welcome. Let us know what you think about this book: what you like and what you may dislike. Reader feedback is important for us to develop titles that you really get the most out of.

To send us general feedback, simply drop an email to feedback@packtpub.com, mentioning the book title in the subject of your message.

If there is a book that you need and would like to see us publish, please send us a note via the **SUGGEST A TITLE** form on www.packtpub.com or email your suggestion to suggest@packtpub.com.

If there is a topic in which you have expertise and for which you are interested in either writing or contributing to a book, please see our author guide on www.packtpub.com/authors.

## Customer Support

Now that you are the proud owner of a Packt book, we have a number of things to help you to get the most from your purchase.

# Errata

Although we have taken every care to ensure the accuracy of our contents, mistakes do happen. If you find a mistake in one of our books—maybe a mistake in the text or in the sample code—we would be grateful if you would report this to us. By doing so you can save other readers from frustration, and help to improve subsequent versions of this book. If you find any errata, you can report them by visiting http://www.packtpub.com/support, selecting your book, clicking on the **Submit Errata** link, and entering the details of your errata. Once your errata are verified, your submission will be accepted and the errata are added to the list of existing errata. The existing errata can be viewed by selecting your title from http://www.packtpub.com/support.

# Questions

You can contact us at questions@packtpub.com if you are having a problem with some aspect of the book, and we will do our best to address it.

# 1
# An Overview of Active Directory Disaster Recovery

When Microsoft introduced Active Directory (AD) with Windows 2000, it was a huge step forward compared to the aged NT 4.0 domain model. AD has since evolved even more and emerged as almost the de-facto standard for corporate directory services.

Today, if an organization is running a Windows Server based infrastructure, then they are almost certainly running AD. There are still some organizations that have NT 4.0 DCs, though that is quickly changing.

AD is often used as THE authentication database even for non-Windows-based systems because of its stability and flexibility. There are many network-based applications relying on AD without its users being aware of it. For example, an HR application can use AD as a directory for personnel information such as name, phone number, email address, location in the company, and even the computer of the user. Yet the HR personnel may not be aware that the same information directory is used to fetch all the information for the global address book in the email system, and to authenticate the user when he or she logs on to his or her workstation.

Due to the strong integration between applications and AD, an event that could cause an outage could have quite a huge impact on systems, from sales to human resources, all the way to payroll and even logistics in manufacturing companies.

In most cases where AD is used for more than just authentication, it quickly becomes the  IT infrastructures' lifeline, which, if interrupted or stopped, causes chain reactions of failures that can bring a company to a halt, and stop production, communications, and delivery of goods.

Of course, once you have an AD running, a logical step is to have Exchange as your email and collaboration system. If you have both systems, then you know how critical AD is for Exchange. Without an AD, the email and collaboration systems will not function. For many companies, being without email functionality for even a day can be catastrophic. If email is your main method of communication within the organization, then picture having your preferred method of communicating taken away for an entire day (or more) within your entire organization. This applies to receiving as well as sending, and access to your mailbox and related functions.

As you might have noted by now, a proper Disaster Recovery (DR) plan is a necessity, and a proper DR is just as critical. You need to cut the possible downtime of your mission-critical systems to a minimum.

# What is Disaster Recovery?

Disaster Recovery (DR) is, or should be part of your Business Continuity plan. It is defined as the way of recovering from a disturbance to, or a destructive incident in, your daily operations. In the context of Information Systems and Technology, this means that if an incident completely destroys data, slows down productivity, or causes any other major interruptions of your operations or your business, the process of reverting to normal operations with minimum outage from that incident is called Business Continuity. Disaster Recovery is, or should be, a part of that process.

You could say that Business Continuity and Disaster Recovery go hand in hand, but they do vary depending on the area and subject. For example, if your WAN connection goes offline, it means that your business units can no longer communicate via email or share documents with each other, although each local unit can still operate and continue to work. This scenario would definitely be outlined in your Business Continuity Plan. However, if your server room burns down in one location, the rebuilding of the server room and the data housed in it would be Disaster Recovery.

The problem with Disaster Recovery is that the approach varies for different domains and applications. Also, the urgency and criticality vary across areas and subjects. A lot of companies have a very superficial Business Continuity plan, if they have any plan at all, and have Disaster Recovery plans that are just as superficial. A visual outline of a sample Business Continuity plan is shown below:

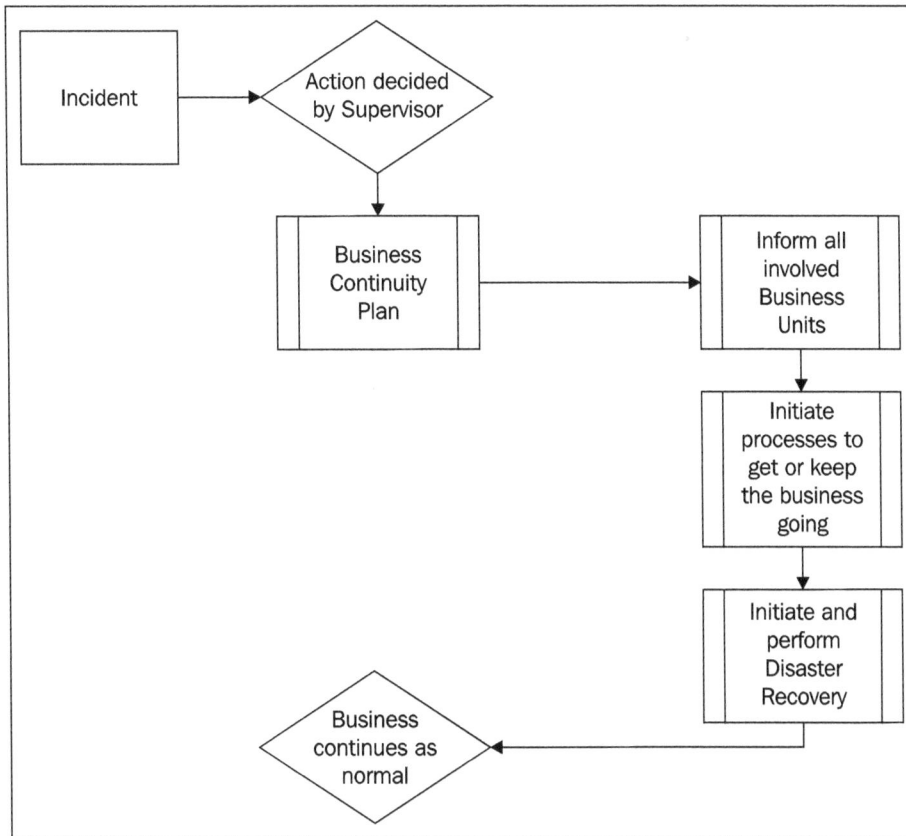

As you can see, DR is only a part of the greater picture. It is, however, one of the most crucial parts that many IT departments forget, or decide to overlook. Some even seem to think that DR is not an important step at all.

# Why is Disaster Recovery Needed?

A lot of people may ask themselves: "Why would we need a 'guide' for Disaster Recovery? If a Domain Controller (DC) has a critical failure, we just install another one". This might seem to work at first, and even for a longer period in small organizations, but in the long run, there would be problems, and a lot of error messages. Correct recovery is crucial to ensure a stable AD environment. The speed at which problems appear, grows exponentially if there are multiple locations of various sizes across different time zones and countries. For example, let's say a company called Nail Corporation (www.nailcorp.com) has its headquarters in Los Angeles, California, and branch offices with several hundred employees in Munich, and Germany, in addition to branch offices in Brazil and India.

NailCorp has one big AD domain and a data center in Brazil having a 512 kilobit link to the headquarters. Let's suppose that the data center in Brazil is partially destroyed due to an earthquake. Network connectivity is restored fairly quickly, but both DCs are physically broken and have therefore become non-functional. The company has around 10,000 employees and, according to Microsoft's AD Sizer software, the space requirement for each Global Catalog server is about 5GB.

As you have to start the rebuild process from scratch, and you have no other DC at the site, you have to replicate 5GB over a 512 kilobit link. Assuming that you get maximum connectivity speed, and no other traffic is flowing at the same time, which is nearly impossible because your users will inadvertently boot their machines and want to start working, you would need over a day to replicate the database. This will increase your restoration time even further-in this case, by at least a day.

In the event of a disastrous event for a company such as NailCorp, you would want to replicate and rebuild as fast as possible. During that time, since you have machines authenticating against the other domain controllers in your company — assuming your DNS service is globally configured to support failover — your replication will be much slower. In this case, you should have different plans in place than just installing another DC.

> To learn more about how DNS and authentication (DC selection) for Windows XP clients work, please read Microsoft's Knowledgebase article 314861 (http://support.microsoft.com/kb/314861).

Another good example is an application that authenticates against a specific DC, or pulls specific information from one. If that DC breaks, the DC will have to be rebuilt with the same name. If you do not do this the right way, you may see strange things happening This is not very far fetched especially in, for example, a software development company.

The need for Disaster Recovery is ever-increasing, and there are several books that touch upon the subject. But none of them are dedicated to different scenarios, and certainly none of them explain the entire process.

Recovering AD from any kind of disaster is trickier then most people think. If you do not understand the processes associated with recovery, you can damage more than you fix.

In order to prevent any kind of major interruptions, and to speed up recovery in the event of an disaster, there are several things that can be done.

For example, AD relies extremely heavily on DNSes. So you need to make sure that if you use AD Integrated (ADI) DNS zones, you should have a standard backup DNS server that has a complete copy of your zones in a non-integrated form. This DNS server should be on an isolated network, and should contain only the records and zones relating to AD, and not all existing dynamic updates.

You should also have a Delayed Replication Site (DRS), also called a lag site . This is a standard part of your AD domain. This should have one or two DCs, maybe a DNS server, and even a standby Exchange server in case one is needed. However, the AD replication is set up with a high link cost in order to prevent replication for a longer time period. Or, you can make it a completely isolated site with a firewall and force a replicate once every one to three months only. This will allow you to have a stable infrastructure. This state may be three months old, but if anything happens you can have a running AD within a few hours, instead of days.

Virtualization can be a boon, especially in this case. Buying a server is fairly cheap nowadays, and as for a DRS, you only need a lot of memory in the machine. VMWare server (http://vmware.com/products/server/) and Microsoft Virtual Server (http://www.microsoft.com/windowsserversystem/virtualserver/) can be downloaded and used for free nowadays. Both of these systems allow the DRS to be run in a virtualized, isolated environment.

Having a DRS can reduce restore time tremendously because, even if there is a global failure, the old DCs can be removed and new ones installed to replicate the DRS.

# Conventions Used in This Book

To avoid repetition, acronyms have been used wherever possible in this book. The following is a list of acronyms, with their respective explanations, used in this book:

- **DC**: Domain Controller (the server that acts as an authentication and directory authority within a domain).
- **OS**: Operating System (Windows 2000 and all 2003 Server varieties).
- **IP Address**: Internet Protocol Address. (This is the address that a computer uses to uniquely identify itself in a network.)
- **AD**: Active Directory (Microsoft Directory Service used for authentication and domain related information).
- **DNS**: Domain Name Service (This is a crucial service that AD relies on map IP addresses to domain names, and vice versa.)
- **FSMO** Roles: The roles that each DC holds within a domain.

- **NTDSA** and **NTDS** NT Data Storage and Architecture: In AD, the data store contains database files and processes that store and manage directory information for users, services, and applications. Basically, this is the back-end of AD.
- **FRS** (File Replication Services): These are services necessary to replicate AD.

# Disaster Recovery for Active Directory

We have established that DR is an important part of a Business Continuity plan. But now, we can go further and say that, DR for AD is only a part of a Disaster Recovery plan, and not the whole plan by itself.

You are correct if you think that you should have different DR guides for different things. While writing good DR documentation, it is important to take the standpoint that the person who performs the recovery has little or no knowledge of the system. If you roll out your own hardened and customized version of Windows 2003, some things might differ during the installation and someone who has no clear guide will install a system that differs from your actual DC install guidelines. This can cause incompatibility or result in an improperly-functioning system, later on. This happens say, when you have specific policies that are applied to DCs, and during an install process, the selection of policies is called in a manner different from the dictats of the DC policy.

You might think that this situation will never arise, but hurricane Katrina in the U.S., and the tsunami that struck Thailand, India, and others, proves that it can. Situations may arise when a knowledgeable person is not around at the time of crisis, so the guide needs to be as clear as possible. It may also be possible that the person doing the actual recovery is an external IT consultant or junior IT staff member because the senior and trained staff are not available. In this case, the person handling the recovery may not at familiar with your environment all be.

AD is a great system, but it is also very complex. Performing correct DR is therefore crucial. If AD forms a part of, or is the backbone of, your network and IT infrastructure, a proper guide to bringing it back online in the event of an incident needs to be as clear and concise as possible.

The Business Continuity plan, and the DR guides, especially the AD DR guides, should be practiced and tested at regular intervals. This effectively means that once a year or so, you need to test that your guides are working and that they will actually bring your business back online. In order to test all kinds of scenarios, building a test environment—preferably virtualized because it gives you much more flexibility such as rollbacks and snapshots—is a necessity.

Never test anything in your production environment. Rather, take a backup of your live AD database and restore it to an isolated (virtual) test AD. Make the test AD as close to your production AD as possible, and test there. This also goes for hotfixes and schema changes, even if it is just "a small change that won't affect anything". If it's a change, it will eventually affect something.

It may be difficult to convince the top management that your systems could actually fail, but replicating your systems, or even just a crucial portion of your server infrastructure, and testing that would definitely be acceptable to them.

# Disaster Types and Scenarios Covered by This Book

Since this book is meant as a reference, and we discuss different scenarios here, an overview of these scenarios is necessary. The following types of disasters or incidents are covered in this book. Illustrations and flowcharts are provided to visualize the disasters more easily, wherever necessary.

## Recovery of Deleted Objects

The most common scenario (more common than a single DC hardware failure) is the accidental deletion of objects, computer accounts, users or Organizational Units (OU) within the AD. This is a possible scenario where no proper change management controls are in place, or where testing is not done properly. The restore can take some time, even if the backup tapes are immediately at hand, because the object relationship in AD is quite complex, and simply restoring the deleted objects will not work.

The real fun starts when you have a "safe" replication schedule due to various time zones and other reasons, such as office locations and line speeds. There are, and have been, scenarios where the deletion or modification of a critical service account, such as the Exchange service group, gets replicated in the course of 12 hours to all locations within the organization. The service that uses the account then stops working, and as it is probably a mission-critical service, gets noticed, fixed, and force-replicated to the closest DC. If things proceed smoothly, all locations will have their service restored, one after another, to the point where one of the last locations starts replicating forward in the chain to the first DC again, before it gets the restored information applied. Then, a vicious circle forms, as shown in the following diagram, giving way to some interesting possibilities. One possibility is that the service in different locations goes from working to non-working and back within a few hours, or returns to step one while the account remains deleted. This addresses the need for proper restoration of lost objects, and the proper process of forced replication.

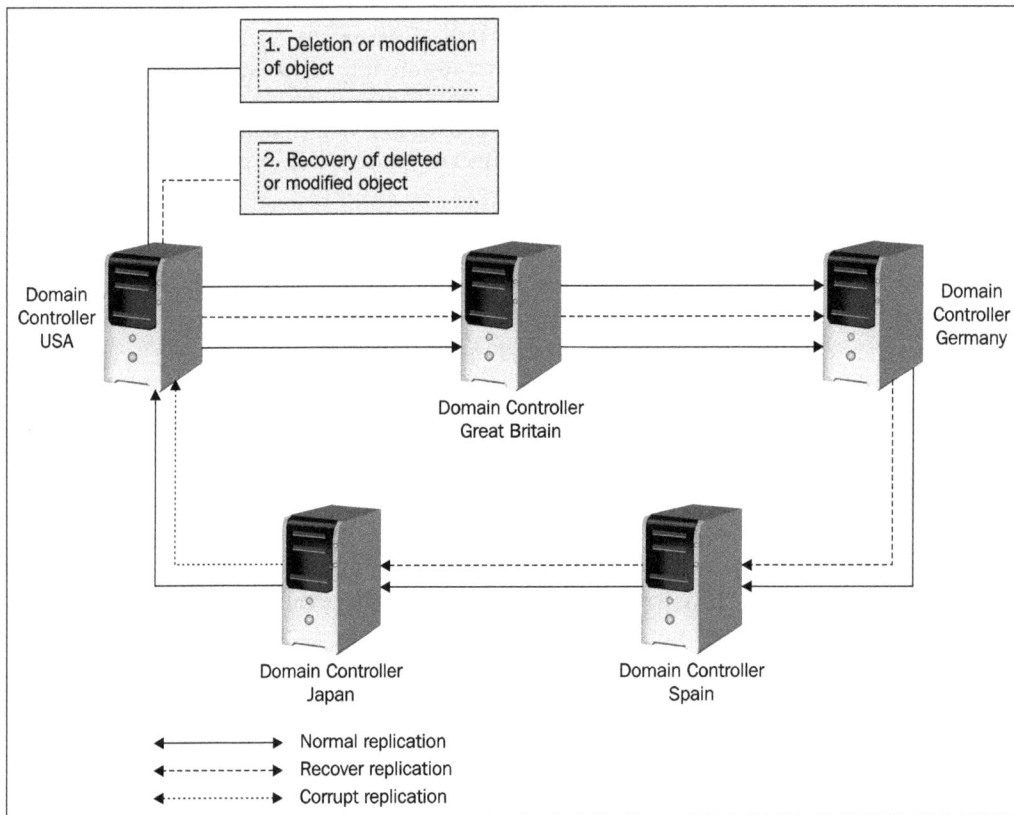

# Single DC Hardware Failure

This is another common scenario. You lose a DC due to a hardware or software failure. The reason for this can of course be failure of any of the hardware components caused by a faulty part, or an external event, such as water damage, a computer virus, or other reasons. At this stage, the DC is no longer operational and cannot be booted again.

If you have a small branch office with only one DC, this can be catastrophic and the need to bring the lost DC back online is critical because no-one at the location will be able to log in or use the directory service. Bringing a failed DC back is not very difficult, but there are steps that need to be taken to ensure that this does not affect the rest of your AD infrastructure. This incident might not be classified as extremely critical if you have two DCs at the site, but if some of these steps are not taken, and the DC has not been cleanly demoted, this can cause issues in the long term.

Some small offices also like to combine the file server, Exchange server, and DC onto one physical server so that more than just the authentication and the directory service is hosted on it. In the case of a file server, the recovery of the files is out of the scope of this book. However, if you run an Exchange server, and/or use the distributed file system service (DFS), or run services with domain accounts, such as Microsoft SQL, then the procedures outlined in this book will most definitely help you get your services back up and running.

# Single DC AD Corruption

The single DC AD corruption is also quite common, especially in smaller companies where the DC has more than one role, such as also being a file, Exchange, and print server. AD corruption essentially means that the Directory service cannot be initiated because the directory database is corrupted, and that no user can log on to this DC with domain authentication or use any of the AD services, such as a global address book in Exchange. It is also possible (though not very common) that during a write process or replication process, one of the DCs fails or interrupts the data stream for some reason. It then replicates the changes with its nearest DC, which is usually its failover, located in the same server room. Both AD databases are then corrupted, and essentially all Directory services for that site fail.

Owing to the nature of AD, DNS, and the client authentication process (mentioned earlier in this chapter), the clients may still try to authenticate against the corrupted DCs but may not get a valid response and may therefore have to rely on the cached login information on the client server. The users will be allowed to log in, but will not be able to access any file shares or other services in the domain, if the information on the servers has not been cached, or the cache has expired (on Windows 2003's Universal Group caching is for 8 hours).

# Site AD Corruption

If your AD gets corrupted on one DC in one site, the corrupted data is likely to replicate itself to other DCs within the same site very quickly. This leaves your entire site with a corrupted AD that makes it impossible for any users or services to use domain authentication. Basically, this is the same as the Single DC AD corruption, except that steps are outlined to recover an entire site, and not just a single DC.

# Corporate (Complete) AD Corruption

This scenario is very dramatic but it can happen faster than you would have thought possible. A corruption can be anything from failed forest preps to schema modifications that were either incomplete or wrong. Another possibility is denial of service attacks, or exploits of vulnerabilities by a disgruntled employee (maybe an administrator within the organization), although this is quite remote. Consider a situation where one DC has a corrupt AD due to a human error, such as making changes to the AD schema at a remote location on a Saturday night, and the remote person does not recognize his or her mistake. The chances are high that this mistake this mistake is replicated out to the other DCs before anyone notices it.

Now, this becomes something of a race condition with the clients or systems continuously authenticating against the AD. The DCs will replicate the corrupt AD one by one, while the clients don't notice anything, because if one DC gives no answer, the client continues to query the next one in the list and so on until the last DC receives the replication of the bad database and goes offline. Then, the alarm bells go off and the systems come to a grinding halt. In addition, you have a very decentralized organization, a lot of time will be spent in coordinating the restoration efforts as well.

Of course, there are steps to initiate and recover from this as well, but response time is very important in this situation, and effective and correct processes and steps are also necessary.

# Complete Site Hardware Failure

This scenario, describing an AD site and not necessarily a single physical site, is already quite drastic as it describes a total loss of AD service due to a complete hardware failure at a specific site. A site is a branch in your organization that is connected to your domain forest via a LAN or a WAN connection. This could also mean that a site includes two or more buildings, possibly distributed across an entire city. This scenario assumes that you have at least one other DC in your organization at another location that is unaffected. This scenario can be caused by anything that affects the whole server room, and is most likely to be physical. Fire and water, as well as storms or explosions, are very high on the probability list.

In this scenario, it is most likely that you have other servers that are also affected. This scenario will address the issue of how to get a complete site back up and running as quickly as possible. This is a critical scenario that needs to be fixed as soon as possible. You can, of course, re-route your users to another site for authentication if your WAN link gets backed up quickly, but if the links are not very fast, this can cause extreme slowness and precipitate incidents such as timeouts, and *domain controller not found* messages to the clients.

This is even worse if you have mission-critical systems authenticating against the AD as illustrated in the following diagram:

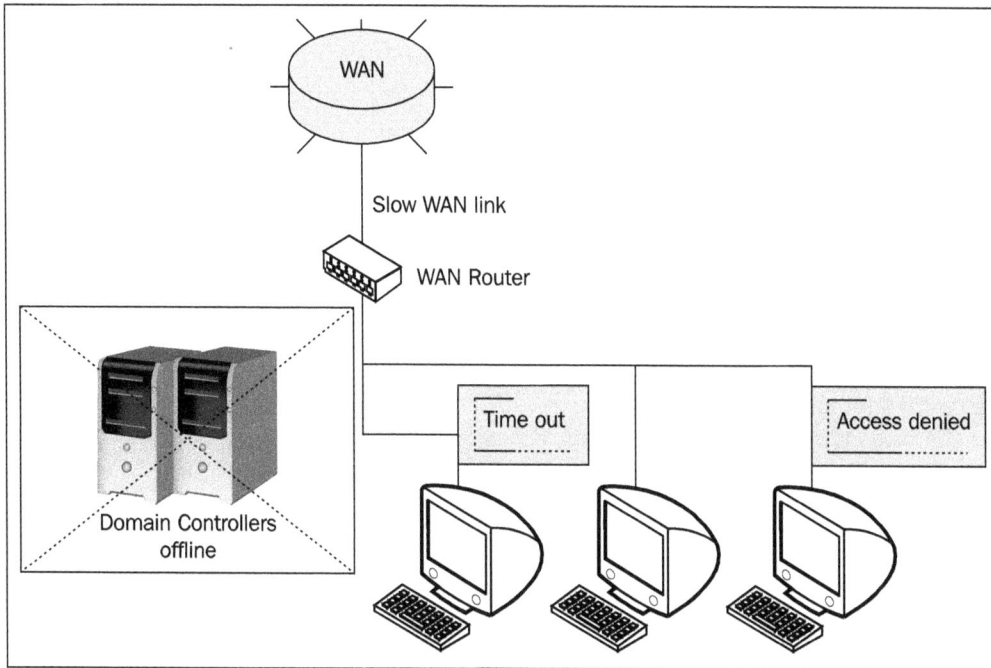

# Corporate (Complete) Hardware Failure

If your corporation or organization has their entire AD infrastructure in one location (which is not recommended, but neither is it unheard of in small organizations), and a disaster, such as fire, water, or any other destructive incident happens, you need to rebuild everything. Backups are valuable but will not do the work for you. The most crucial task, at that point, is to get the working system back so that users can start their work. Damage control is not part of your job, but bringing back the company's domain infrastructure is. This means that your first priority is to get the DCs back online, and restore the applications that rely on it. Don't waste valuable time trying to get the print server to work when your clients and applications cannot authenticate. You also need to be aware that just re-installing the DCs from scratch will not work as you have hundreds or even thousands of systems bound to your AD infrastructure. Some services depend on this structure very heavily, and re-configuring all the clients and services is definitely not an option once your organization grows to critical size.

Your client machines at this point have no way of getting any information out of the AD, and the only reason why most of them are still operating is because of cached logins. You might even have a Group Policy preventing cached logins in which case you will have quite a few users who cannot get anything done, and a Management team that is calculating the loss of revenue per hour.

# Summary

This chapter provided you with an overview of AD DR and how a DR guide fits into your organization's Business Continuity plan. It also provided you with a brief overview of the scenarios that will be addressed by this book. As you will have noticed by now, the subject of DR with an AD is much deeper and more crucial than you might think.

Microsoft's focus on pointing out the de-centralized architecture of AD is true, and it really does work for small incidents, for connection error, and so on. The picture is very different, however, when we look at how complex and devastating AD failure can be in some situations, and how crucial it is to have a proper recovery guide in place.

It is important to understand that the risks and threats discussed here exist in very real forms. In today's multi-platform environments and heterogeneous networks, there may be services and systems that authenticate against AD which probably didn't figure in your initial designs, but had to be added to the actual schema.

All these things make your infrastructure all the more mission-critical. If you want to use an analogy would you rather have insurance for your house that covers all your valuable items but not the house or one that covers the house as well?

# 2
# Active Directory Design Principles

In order to design a proper Active Directory infrastructure, knowledge of its workings, and what it is based on, is essential. The basis for Active Directory is the Lightweight Directory Access Protocol (LDAP), which is an X.500 standard (to read more about the X.500 standard please visit: http://en.wikipedia.org/wiki/x.500). LDAP defines that a directory is a tree of entries, with each entry containing a set of attributes. Each entry has a unique identifier and therefore cannot be duplicated. This way everything is an object in an LDAP-based directory.

There are many great books available for Active Directory design and some of them go into great detail. Compressing all this into a single chapter is just not possible, so in this chapter, we will stick to the basics and a high-level view, instead of too much detail. This will provide a good overview of how to design a proper Active Directory, with different strategies in mind, and tailor it best for your organization.

The one thing to keep in mind is that when designing your Active Directory, never go at it from a, present needs, point of view. Technology and systems are changing so fast nowadays that you have to design with the most open and future-proof concept that you can think of.

It was only a few years back when Windows 95 revolutionized the personal computing platform by pushing 32-bit addressing to the mainstream. Before that it was 14 years where everyone ran 16-bit programs on 16- or 32-bit processors. In April 2003, Microsoft launched the 64-bit version of its Server Operating System and in April 2005, the 64-bit version of its Desktop Operating System, Windows XP. These are less then a decade after the big Windows 95 push. Active Directory was introduced with Windows 2000, which is only Five years after Windows NT 4's "enhanced omain structure".

The trend is that new features and new technologies are constantly being invented and introduced. While there are quite a few companies that have a proper open and flexible design in their Active Directory structures, there are a lot more organizations that see Active Directory as the answer to all their prayers and just keep adding things to it and to the schema. To read more about the technical aspects of the AD schema, please refer to `http://msdn2.microsoft.com/en-us/library/ms675085.aspx`.

Software companies nowadays are pushing "Active Directory compatible" features more and more, and problems can arise when these packages need complete domain administrator rights in order to function (or modify the Active Directories' inner workings), which they usually do not advertise up-front.

The need for proper planning and design of the AD is extremely high in order to ensure that your DR strategies will work and are easy to implement. A properly designed AD is extremely resilient and still very flexible.

Whenever you intend to add new services, make sure that you test and re-test the things that are necessary for the service to function properly. As the IT department, you are responsible to keep the systems going and ensure business continuity. We will touch on this subject of becoming more involved in the chapter, "Design and implement a Disaster Recovery plan for your Organization".

# Active Directory Elements

When designing an Active Directory, you need to be completely clear of what each element or part actually means and how it fits into the overall design. The old saying goes: You can't see the forest because of the trees, and you can apply this to Active Directory as well. It is all about trees and forests and leaves and branches.

# The Active Directory Forest

The forest, in terms of Active Directory, basically means every domain, organizational unit, and any other object stored within its database. The forest is the absolute top level of your Active Directory infrastructure. Of course, you can have more than one forest in a company, which actually represent security boundaries, and can therefore improve security between different business units or companies belonging to a single organization. The point behind the forest is that you have all your domains and domain tree within your organization contained within it. It is designed so that you can have transitive trust-links between all of the trees within one forest.

> To read more about the technical layout of AD, please read Domains and Forests Technical Reference at: `http://technet2.microsoft.com/windowsserver/en/library/16a2bdb3-d0a3-4435-95fd-50116e300c571033.mspx`.

To visualize a forest with its parts, please see the following image.

# The Active Directory Tree

A tree in Active Directory refers to a domain and all of its objects that adhere to a single DNS name. For example, a tree of nailcorp.com would contain all other domains that end with "nailcorp.com". So, americas.nailcorp.com, europe.nailcorp.com, and asia.nailcorp.com all belong to the Active Directory tree of nailcorp.com. You cannot separate these unless you create a whole new forest for a sub-domain.

# Organizational Units and Leaf Objects

In Active Directory, Organizational Units (OU), which are also called Containers, and Leaf Objects, which are non-containing objects such as computer accounts and user accounts, are directly related and even though you could have objects that do not belong to an OU, it isn't recommended and isn't really feasible.

Organizational Units are comparable to folders in a filing cabinet, and objects are the files. You can move files between different folders, and classifications or properties are applied to the files within a folder. For example, if you move a file into a folder classified "Top Secret", the file will automatically fall under that classification. The same applies to objects within an OU, all properties or rules that apply to the OU apply to the objects within it. OUs, however, are mostly useful from an administrative point of view, not from an user's point of view. If you think of how your files are organized, for example, on your computer, they are most likely to be organized into different folders. You can go ahead and set different folder settings, such as permissions, and it will affect all of the files within that folder, but anything outside that folder won't have its permission affected. It is exactly the same principle with OUs. Any OU that will be created within an OU will contain all of the policy settings of the parent unless you change them. An object can also only belong to a single OU, just as a single file can only be contained within a single folder.

Leaf objects in Active Directory can be users, contacts, and computers. Or in short, any object that cannot contain other objects. They are called leaf objects because they are like leaves on a tree. And, as you can guess, they are the "lowest" class of objects within Active Directory. But if you now look at the forest-tree-branch-leaf concept, it is starting to make sense.

You can access the OUs and other objects through the Microsoft Management Console (MMC) or through the Users and Computers tool in the Administrative Tools. This second option actually just invokes the MMC with the correct view and is a lot quicker, as seen in the following screenshot:

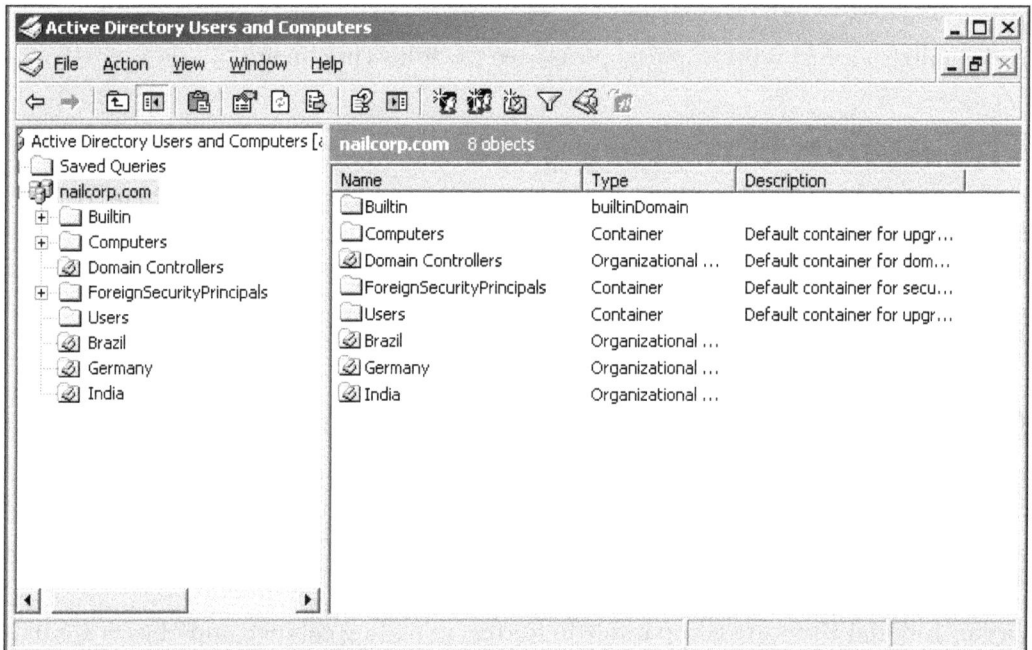

# Active Directory Sites

The Sites and Services MMC snap-in is a utility that a lot of Windows administrators, particularly in smaller organizations, completely overlook. This part of Active Directory, however, is one of the most crucial parts to understand and implement correctly.

If you have several locations in your organization, you need to know about Active Directory Sites. Sites give you a very unique and well-designed approach to separate specific locations within your Active Directory. As the principle of an Active Directory domain is global-meaning that it is meant to be the same anywhere-it could present a problem for users who move from office to office, or for offices with network connections that are slow. Active Directory sites allow you to specify the IP address spaces or subnets used within your organization and, therefore, bring the structure of your network into Active Directory. The usefulness of having properly organized and maintained Sites becomes more evident when you consider that any machine within an address space will use that Sites' DC to authenticate. This is a great feature of AD and reduces unnecessary traffic. However, it requires having Sites and subnets properly updated and maintained. This is also particularly useful for defining different replication schedules for different locations within the same domain, and also to support users who travel. Once they log on through the other location, they are assigned an IP address from that network. The Windows locator service will then look up which DC is the nearest one, and the user won't log on all the way to their usual DC (to read more about how the locator service works please refer to `http://support.microsoft.com/kb/314861`). This saves bandwidth and speeds up the authentication process.

Bandwidth nowadays is cheap, especially in developed countries such as the USA or most parts of Western Europe. But just because it is cheap in some parts, does not mean it is cheap in other parts of your organization. If you are primarily located within developed countries, but your then company decides to open 10 or 20 small sales offices within not-so-developed countries, where bandwidth is expensive, then you really need to start using AD sites. Of course, the problem then is that because you haven't used AD sites before, you need to make the appropriate changes to your infrastructure to accommodate them, and train staff appropriately in order to be able to implement, support, and manage them.

In this example, the argument might be brought up that each of these small branch offices has a local DC that also functions as a File and Print server where the local employees collaborate. This is great, but what about replication to and from your Hub site? Which is the data centre that hosts a critical part of your Active Directory backend? If changes to your AD are fairly frequent, for example, adding and removing users on a regular basis, then the Active Directory will replicate—if the Site links are properly configured—without compression every 15 minutes. Of course, depending on the size of your organization, this can be quite a strain on the link you have from that office. If the people at that office receive email and browse the Web over the same link, network performance will degrade significantly for users and cause unnecessary inconvenience.

To see what Sites look like in the Active Directory Sites and Services console, see the following screenshot:

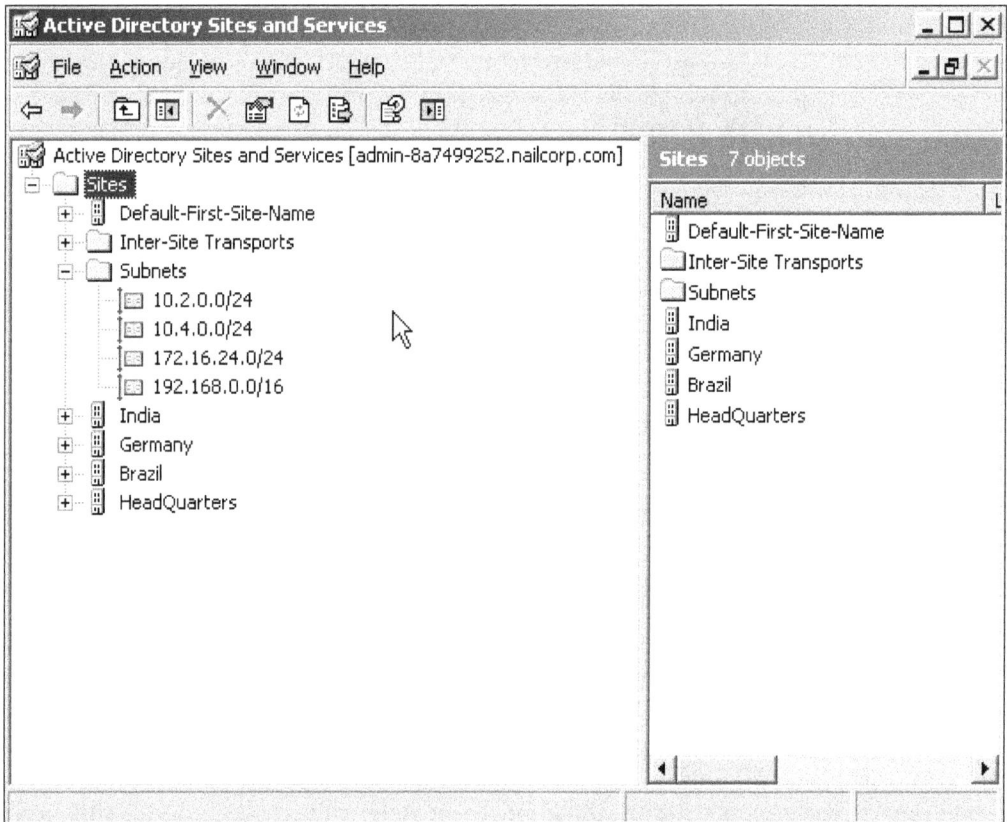

# Group Policy Objects

Group Policy Objects in Active Directory are a set of defined rules for settings about the user environment or the operating environment for a particular PC. They are treated as standalone objects because they can be linked to different OUs. This gives you the flexibility of creating one set of rules and applying it to different OUs in different OU structures, making settings deployment much easier and administratively quick.

The policy settings are quite extensive and if you want to get your hands dirty, you can create your own policy templates, giving you even more control over the machines and application settings located in your domain.

There are templates available for many settings, ready to use. The templates for these settings are called ADM templates and there are quite a few already included in the Windows 2003 installation. Some applications, such as Microsoft Office 2007, also provide ADM templates that can be loaded and modified (see `http://www.microsoft.com/downloads/details.aspx?displaylang=en&Fami lyID=92d8519a-e143-4aee-8f7a-e4bbaeba13e7` for Office 2007 ADM templates). Using ADM templates, you do not need to write anything by yourself, and so it is a quicker way apply to GPO settings. The following screenshot shows Office 2007 ADM templates loaded in the Group Policy Editor.

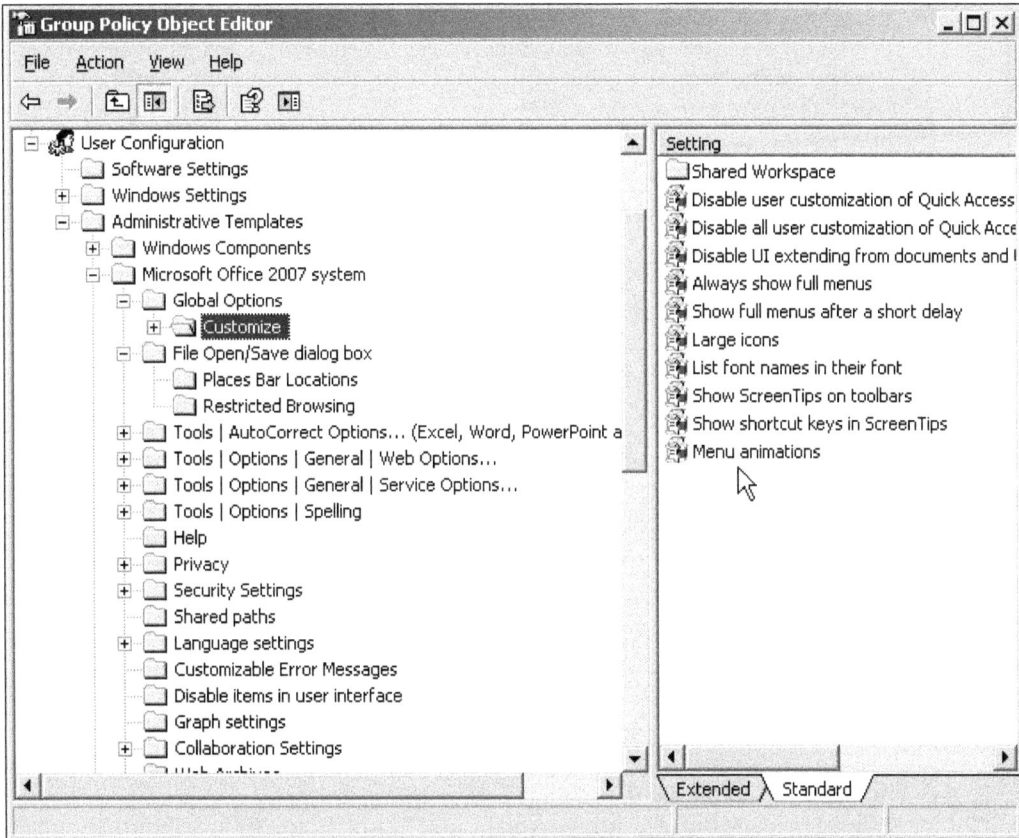

# Domain Design: Single Forest, Single Domain, and Star Shaped

A domain is not a security boundary within a forest. By default, all domains have transitive trust relationships within a forest and are therefore visible to each other. On top of that, all Global Catalogs contain the Security database and a rogue administrator can potentially gain access to different domains or even the entire forest. Please see `http://www.microsoft.com/technet/security/bulletin/MS02-001.mspx` for more details on such vulnerability. Even though this particular vulnerability no longer exists within Windows 2003, something causing similar effects can be a possibility.

This is the most common design version for small-and medium-size businesses, that have offices within one country or that are geographically close. It involves a single hub site and several small sites. A hub site is defined as a big data center where the majority of your infrastructure is housed. So if you have the headquarters and development for nailcorp.com taking place in Los Angeles where 40 servers are housed in a datacenter and 900 people work, then that would be a hub site. In short, a hub site is a location where a large part of your crucial infrastructure operates.

From the hub site, all changes are replicated out to smaller sites, which can be small branch offices, small development locations, or pretty much any office that warrants its own domain controller. This puts control firmly into the one major hub site and all the branch sites just replicate with that. The advantage of this set-up is that you can push out a forced replication to all branch sites at once (provided your bandwidth supports this) and do not have to wait for any delayed replication schedules due to time zones and so on. The drawback is that if you do have a problem, due to human error, for example, and this gets replicated, everyone gets it at once. If, for example, an administrator at NailCorp deletes or renames by accident a service account that is used by a certain service throughout the organization, and he does not notice it, then after the next replication the service stops working. If the replication was star shaped and went to everywhere at the same time, the service stops everywhere at the same time. If the service is something that does not get recognized immediately, such as an antivirus policy update or some automatic update service from a third-party application, this failure will not get noticed immediately and the service will stop and won't restart because it will be a logon failure. In this scenario, NailCorp could go on for days without anyone noticing.

As you can see in the following figure, in this design NailCorp would have a single hub site and three branch sites. Each site would have its own IP address range and would have, within Active Directory, its own site with DCs located inside it.

In this case, we only have a single forest and a single domain with different sites, but even in these sites all objects belong to the same forest and hence the same domain.

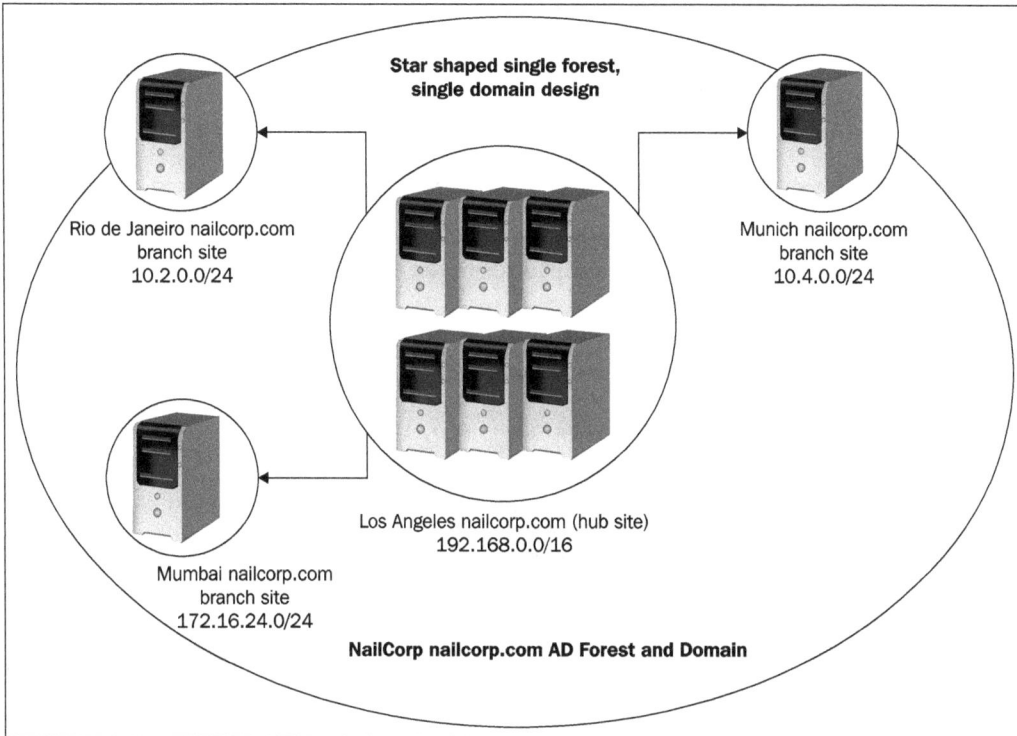

**Domain Design: Single Forest, Single Domain, Empty Root, Star Shaped**

Even though this architecture is no longer recommended, there are still quite a lot of companies that either use it or implement it. This is almost the same design as the previous one, except that it includes an empty root domain. Basically, it implies that the root of your forest is empty, meaning that there will be no computer accounts and no user accounts other than the Enterprise Administrators located in this domain. Within AD, a domain is not a security boundary. A forest, however is, so a multi-forest architecture would provide more security. An empty root domain has good and not-so-good points. The point is that this is a fairly safe design, which still adds layers of security. The other domain under the root domain - the child domain- will contain all of the user and computer accounts. This setup is beneficial from a security perspective in that the Enterprise and Schema Administrators groups are isolated from the other users and administrators. With this design, a few administrators can be selected to control the Enterprise and Schema Administrator groups, and all the other administrators reside in the child domains, configured to be Domain Administrators.

This will add a proper layer of security to the whole structure and will allow an easier structural change, should:

- New companies be acquired and need transitional access, or
- A separate AD be required for special access etc.

There has been some controversy about the necessity of an empty root domain. When Windows 2000 came out, the empty root was all the rage and everyone was doing it.

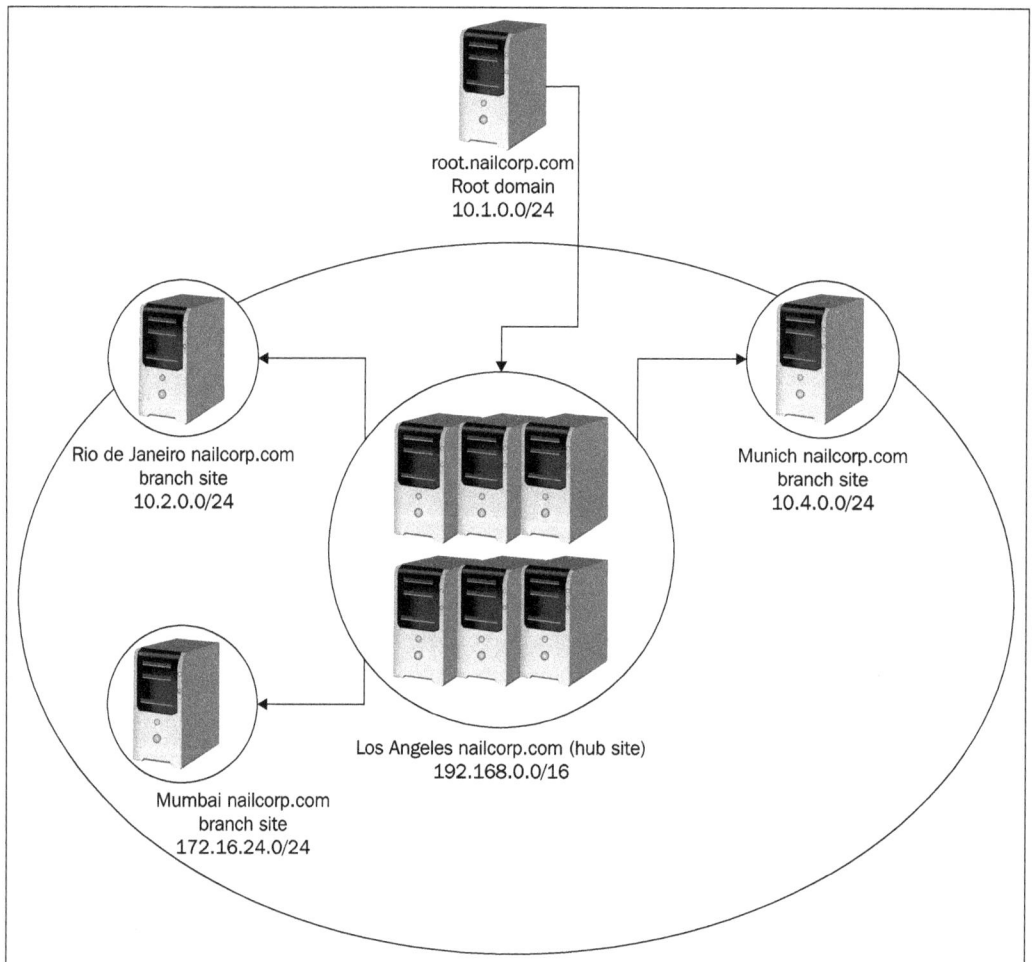

# Domain Design: Multi-Domain Forest

This design is used a lot in larger corporations and companies that do a lot of Quality Assurance testing for software, or software development. It has a forest and multiple trees under this. This is also very good if your company has expanded a lot through acquisitions and you need to ensure that the acquired companies can access cross-domain files.

This design approach needs to be designed from the beginning because you cannot create a new forest on top of an existing one. Windows 2003, however, makes moving domain information and migrating between two Active Directories easier, with the tools that it provides.

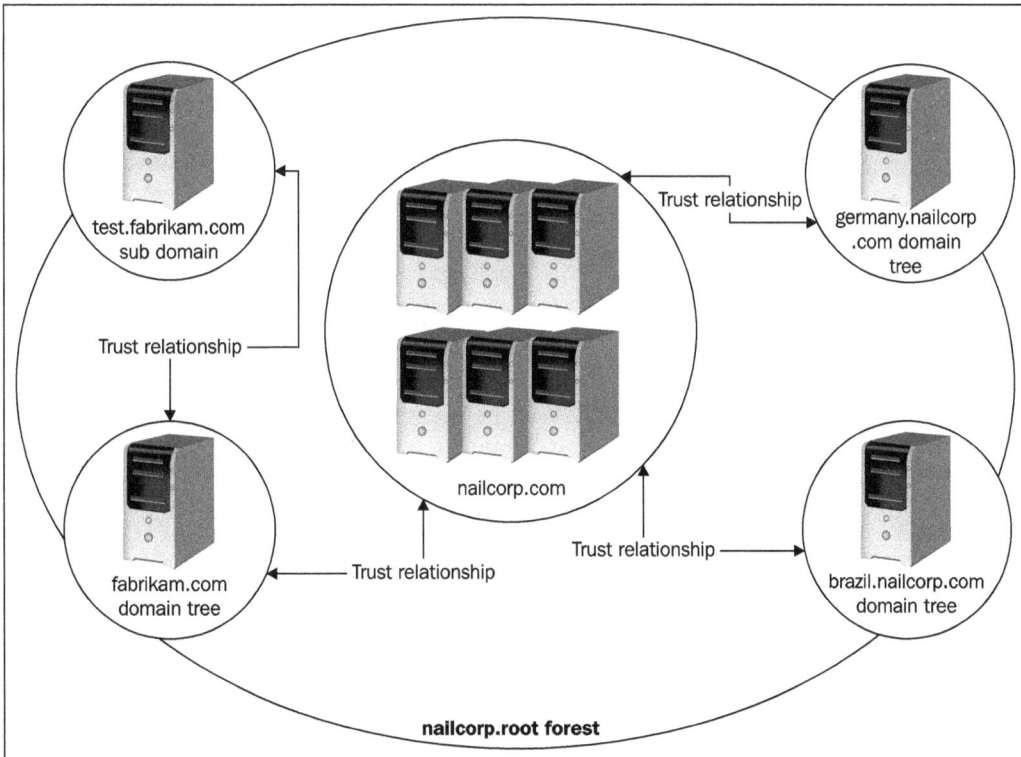

# Domain Design: Multi-Forest

This design, while administratively more complex, provides the best security. It also raises support costs and makes collaboration a little more difficult, but it definitely has its benefits. This design will have standalone forests for all of the business units or departments. This also means that by default they cannot see or access each other. Administrators then create trust relationships between the different domains that are within the forests. This will give the granularity needed. To visually understand this, please see the following image:

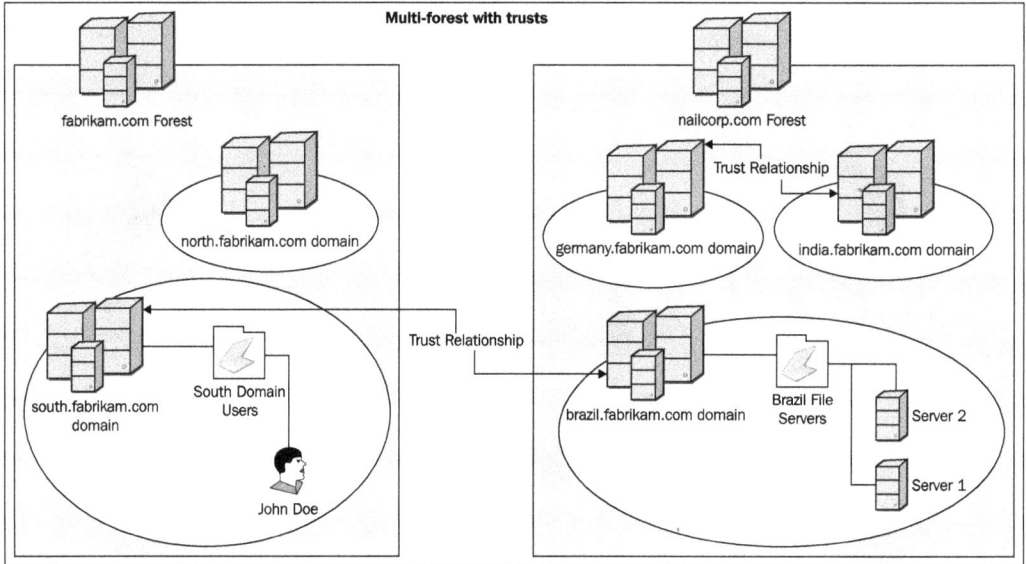

# LRS—Lag Replication Site

These sites are also often called RLS (Replication Lag Site), DRS (Delayed Replication Site), and just plain lag site. Officially, there really isn't a "correct" name as Microsoft and AD experts have referred to this concept in all four ways.

A lag site is a site in your AD that will contain at least one DC. This site is configured so that the replication only happens at a delayed schedule compared to all the other sites. This can be anything from one day to one week.

The purpose of lag sites is primarily to restore deleted objects quickly without having to go through the process of authoritative restores or even start working with tapes. If something gets inadvertently deleted, all that is needed is a replication in the opposite direction, from the lag site to the production DCs, and the deleted data is recovered. It is a clean, fast, and efficient way to recovery.

The other feature that is a natural by-product of a lag site, and used by quite a few organizations, is that in case of a disaster, it becomes easier, cleaner, and faster to recover a part of or your complete infrastructure. As lag sites are not used for authentication by users and DNS registration is disabled, they are considered stealth sites because they are not usable by any service or user.

Active Directory, as we have established, is a very complex infrastructure. There are a multitude of things that can go wrong at any given time, and human error, while the most common cause, is also the worst of the things that can happen if the changes are replicated out. Best practices generally include separating one or even two domain controllers per domain in your datacenter or somewhere else. (Create it in a new site in your Active Directory and make the link cost the highest possible. That means that it will only replicate the data with the main Active Directory once a week and the rest of the time just sit there. You can even design it so that there is no active replication going on by putting a firewall in front of the site and denying the traffic.)

Of course, you will get replication errors, but at least you have a working Active Directory in any event. If your infrastructure fails, all you need to do is complete an authoritative restore from the lag site, and activate the network link, meaning dropping the firewall if you have one, and promote or seize the roles of the domain controllers in the lag site. You will generally have a working infrastructure and since the lag site has an authoritative restore, all other DCs will replicate from it.

There are different approaches to lag sites and we will go through some of them in more detail in the next chapter, but if you want to keep your Active Directory even more redundant and safer, you should definitely consider establishing a lag site.

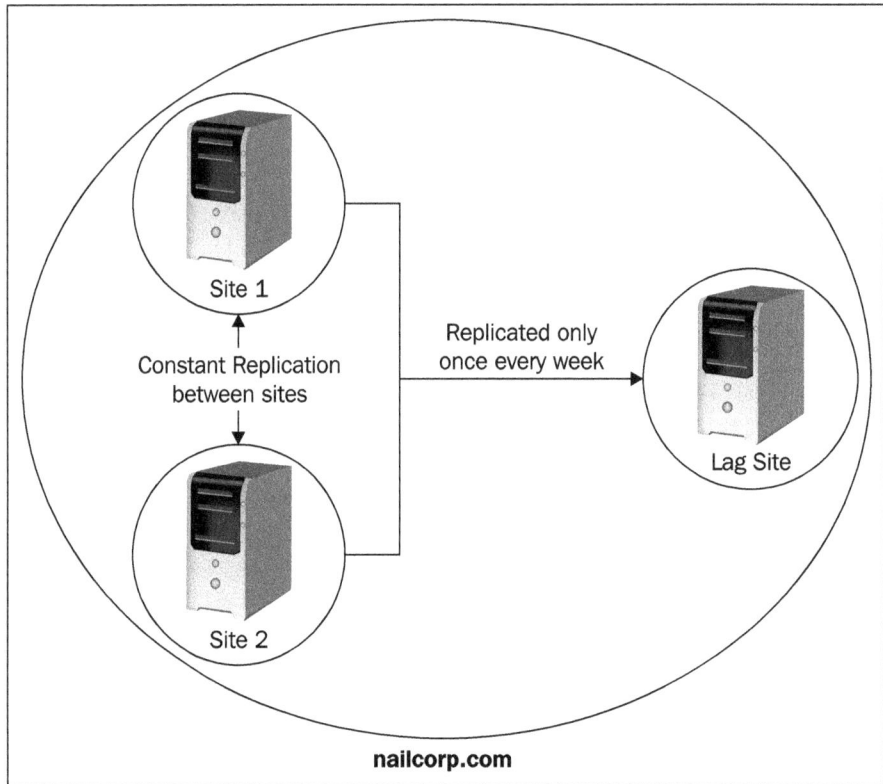

# Design Your Active Directory

In most corporations and large organizations, there are people with job titles such as "Network Architect", "Windows Server Configuration Owner" or "Network Designer". These people do not have these titles just for fun. In large organizations, there is an actual need for people whose sole purpose is to design or optimize the networking topology according to how technology progresses. This is also valid for people who work in the Security and the actual Business Solutions sections of large corporations.

There are always new ways of doing things and new designs surfacing in the IT world, and those people need to stay on top of their respective fields. If you are a medium to small-sized company, you can probably combine all of those roles into one person or have several roles distributed over few people.

This is especially true for Windows Server architecture and Active Directory. When designing your Active Directory, you need to really open your mind and focus on the future. A bit of clairvoyance doesn't hurt here. The problem with an Active Directory design for a medium to large-sized company is actually two-fold. One, you need to be able to make your design scalable in the future and two, you need to be able to migrate to your new architecture with the least user impact.

In order to make this a bit easier, here are two small checklists. The first one contains things to consider when designing a global AD, and the second one is a checklist of things to consider when finalizing the design, or when migrating. These points are not in any particular order as they should all be considered.

## Checklist When Designing a New AD

- Is the name future-proof (DNS)? Do you own the DNS name?
- How many users are in each office?
- What's the bandwidth available between offices?
    - Is it enough for smaller offices to authenticate in a central location?
- Who will administer the AD?
    - Who will perform day-to-day tasks (password resets, user and computer account creation)?
- Are there plans to build on the AD with additional services, such as Exchange, SharePoint etc.?
- Which DCs will be Global Catalog Servers?
- Where will the FSMO roles be located?
- Will the new design support all the current business functions?
    - If not at the beginning, will there be a transition period and if so how long?
    - Have you cleared this with business?
    - Will all the third-party applications still work with this design?

## Checklist When Finalizing the Design or When Migrating to an AD

- Have you chosen a design?
    - If yes, have you considered the model carefully, taking into account future growth?
- Is the DNS name available and is it future-proof?

- Have you calculated the appropriate number of DCs?

- Have you considered DC failover and the network strain?

- Is the number of administrators and their roles clearly defined?

- Do you have processes for change mangement in place?

  - If no, should you?

- Do you have back-up designs and solutions in place where it matters (hub sites and data centers)?

- Is your staff trained or will there be training to bring them up-to-date with the new methodologies?

- How significant will the user impact be?

  - Are mechanisms in place to inform the users of the coming changes?

- Are all networked applications accounted for?

- Have service accounts been assigned and possibly consolidated across the enterprise?

- Is a realistic implementation schedule in place?

  - Has it been approved and discussed?

# Naming Standards

Before you begin to design anything, you need to make sure that you have a naming standard for everything across your entire organization. If this is missing, and everyone just decides what to name the GPO and computers, how usernames are formatted, how service accounts are named, etc., then you will never have a proper structure.

# Username and Service Account Naming

There are endless ways of naming your user accounts and you probably already have one or another in place. If, however, you have a multitude of different ways because of acquisition, or autonomy of certain offices in the past, defining a universal way of naming user accounts is crucial. This will not only help you with administration, but also with deploying services across your organization. If you name the service accounts using a standard, every administrator knows exactly what the account is for. When you name the users in a standard way, processes regarding user administration can be very streamlined. You should also consider the lockdown of service accounts, for example by defining what machine they can authenticate from and what they can access. The same goes for user accounts.

# Group Policy Naming

A common thing for administrators to do is name group policies after what they see as the most logical thing at that moment. You should have clear guidelines of how to name GPO's so that they make sense even to a new person. "Internet Explorer Test 3" as a GPO name is not anything that you could guess what it includes, or to whom it applies. Naming conventions are overlooked a lot of the time, not only for GPOs but for many administrative things that do not seem to matter at the time. In short, the naming of the GPO is important so that you can immediately know what the policy does and who it applies to. This makes troubleshooting much easier. The following figure shows GPOs named with a little bit more sense, as it shows that the policy is global and that the settings that these policies set are for users and computers.

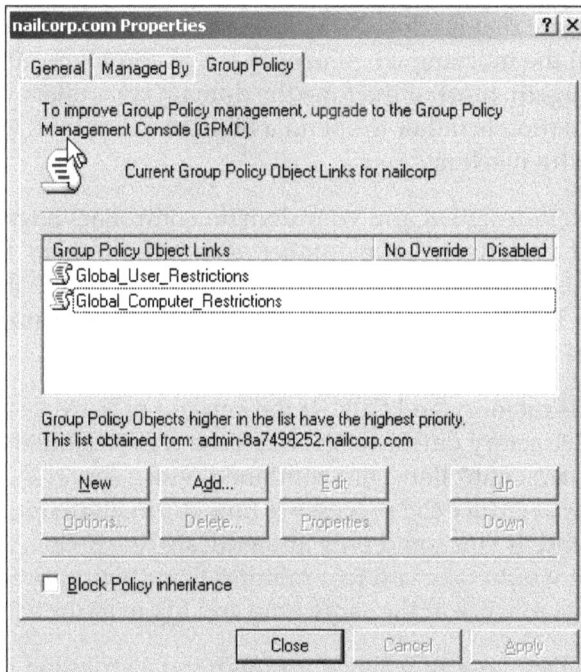

# Design with Scalability in Mind

Whenever you read books or white papers about Active Directory, they mention the amazing scalability of Active Directory, its security features, and the redundancy. Active Directory was coded from the ground up with mechanisms that make it easy to add or remove domain controllers. With this ability, features are built in to failover to the next domain controller in case of a failure in one of them. The client never really knows about this.

On paper, this is a great thing and reduces the administrative overhead. In practice, it is just as good. Large corporations can have Active Directory structures that work so perfectly that the administrators really do not have to worry about anything regarding stability. This applies even when there are more then 30,000 users over several countries and almost twice as many computer accounts. As the saying goes: "Behind every strong man stands a strong woman". The same goes for Active Directory: "Behind every perfectly working Active Directory, there is a good architect".

Microsoft's recommendation is to have 150 users per domain controller. This is a good recommendation yet you do not need to take it 100% verbatim. In any site with 150-200 users, you should have at least two domain controllers. This is not meant as an issue of scalability but more of a failover issue. In a case of 400 users for example, Microsoft recommends, according to their white paper, three domain controllers. For 400 users in a single site that is a lot. Considering that the heavy load on the domain controllers will be in the morning when people arrive and log in, and after lunch when people log in again, most of the time the domain controllers will sit idle. In this case, the recommendation is rather to spend a bit extra on more RAM and more CPU power than on an extra machine.

If your network is well-designed and your domain controllers have a little more power, you can load a relatively large number of users onto them. It is not unheard of to have over 600 users per domain controller in a large organization and the average load during the day is around 40%. It rises during peak hours of logon and logoff, as is expected, but quite a lot of time they are almost idle.

The key factor here is memory and CPU. If the amount of RAM you have is twice the size of your Active Directory database, the database will be loaded completely into memory by the domain controller. This, combined with a server-class CPU such as XEON or Opteron, will reduce the processing time during authentication per user to fractions of a second. If you could only authenticate five people per second on a domain controller, it would take you two minutes to authenticate 600 users. And 600 users do not all arrive at work at the same time and log in at the exact same time.

Scalability in Active Directory is achieved through the distributed model that it builds on. Every domain controller is writable in the AD and holds more-or-less a complete copy of the directory. When changes occur in one site on one DC, these changes are then replicated out to all the others. This architecture is radically different from Windows NT 4, where there was a primary domain controller and many backup domain controllers.

There is only one problem with this set-up, and this becomes apparent when you have a lot of distributed domain controllers and a lot of sites. If you do not invest time into the design of the sites and site links, you can cause a lot of damage and a lot of unnecessary traffic in a very short time. Site links are there to provide ways of controlling when and how the Active Directory is replicated to other domain controllers. You do not want to end up replicating a 2GB database during business hours over a 2 Mbit link. However, if you do not properly document and implement a good replication design, unnecessary delays will happen. You will then have the nice job of finding out where the replication went wrong, and depending on the number of sites you have, this can be a non-trivial task. The following figure shows different replication schedules and site links that make it quite normal for one site to have a six to eight hour delayed version of the Active Directory.

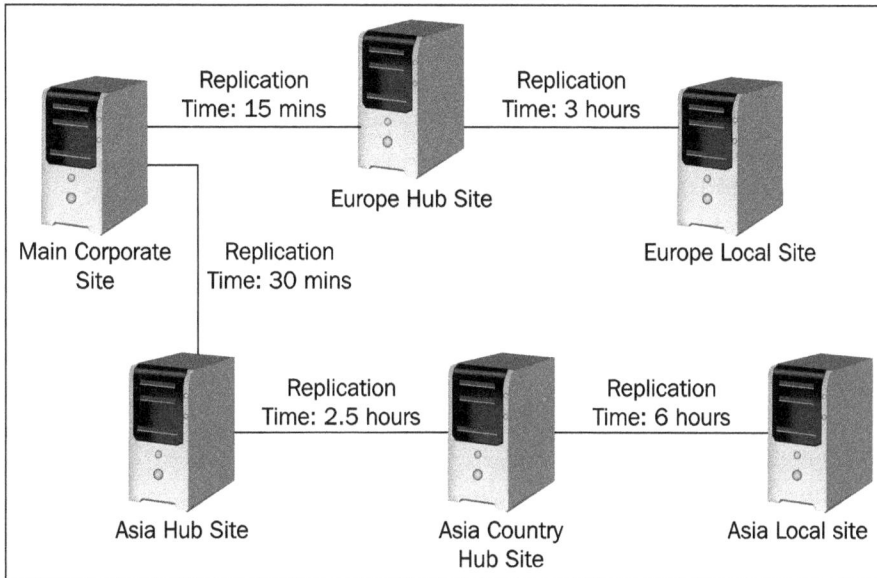

Replication schedules are not difficult to design and implement, but do require a bit of time and input from other sources. Remember, because Active Directory is so distributed, the site with the slowest site link and the slowest replication will have the most outdated version of Active Directory. It is recommended that in case something unexpected happens, such as dismissing an employee in a remote office, you force-replicate between the main site and that site-as soon as the changes are made. If the person is leaving in two week's time, set his or her account on the date they are scheduled to leave and then verify that the data has been replicated after this date.

# Flexible Single Master Operation Roles (FSMO)

When you design your topology, you have to be aware of the Flexible Single Master Operation Roles (FSMO) and place them accordingly.

FSMO roles are roles that only one server in an Active Directory can have. These roles, while not apparent immediately and not needed all the time, are very important, and some of them are very crucial.

There are five FSMO roles and they must be present in an Active Directory. Three of these roles are domain-specific, which means that in every domain in an AD forest, they have to be present. The other two are forest-specific and therefore one of each needs to be present in each of your AD forests. See the table below for a few summary of roles and where they belong:

| Name of the role | Where is it needed |
| --- | --- |
| RID Master (Relative ID Master) | In each domain |
| Infrastructure Master | In each domain |
| PDC Emulater | In each domain |
| Schema Master | In each forest |
| Domain name Master | In each forest |

Each role does different things and in order to understand the importance of the roles, a full description of each role, and the steps you need to take to see which server has what role, is given below:

## Relative ID Master (RID Master)

This role allocates security RIDs to DCs within a domain. The DCs use the allocated RIDs and in turn allocate them to security principals, such as users and computers, as they are added. The server that has this role also manages the movement of objects between domains. It monitors all of the pools allocated to all of the DCs within a domain and in doing so allocates more RIDs where needed, to prevent these pools from becoming exhausted, which would result in the inability to create new user or computer accounts.

## Infrastructure Manager

The server having this role maintains security Globally Unique Identifiers (GUIDs) and Distinguished Names (DNs) for all objects that are referenced across different domains. However, its most common task is to update user and group links.

# PDC Emulator

This is a crucial role, not only because it emulates a Primary Domain Controller for Windows NT, but because other DCs look at the PDC as the primary source for confirmation of authentication, and it is the most trusted source for time within a domain.

To change any of the three domain-specific roles, open Active Directory **Users and Computers**, right-click on the domain name and click on **Operations Masters**. You will then get the following screen where you can assign the roles in your domain.

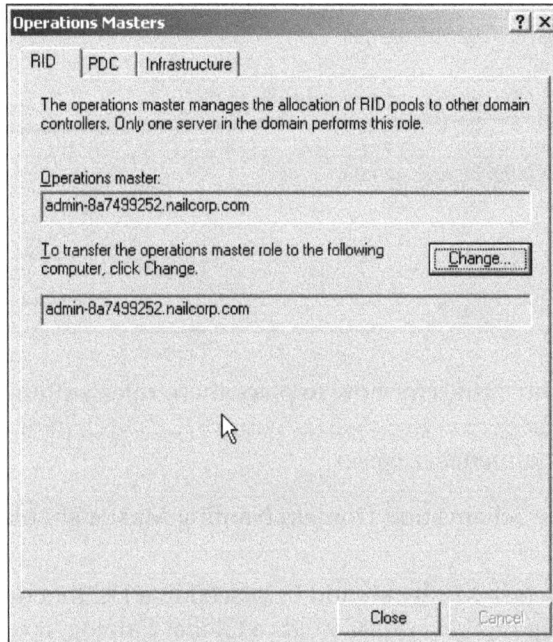

# Schema Master

The server having this role maintains all schema information and all modifications to the schema. The schema in a forest determines what types of objects are permitted and what types of attributes an object can have. A typical scenario for this role would be an installation or deployment of Exchange, or an upgrade from Windows 2000 to 2003, because these operations contain schema modifications.

# Domain Naming Master

The server having this role follows all of the names of the domains in a forest. This role is needed in order to add or remove domains.

To change the Domain Name Master, open **Active Directory Domains and Trusts**, right-click on **Active Directory Domains and Trusts** and then click on **Operations Master**. On the resulting screen, you can change the Domain Naming Master.

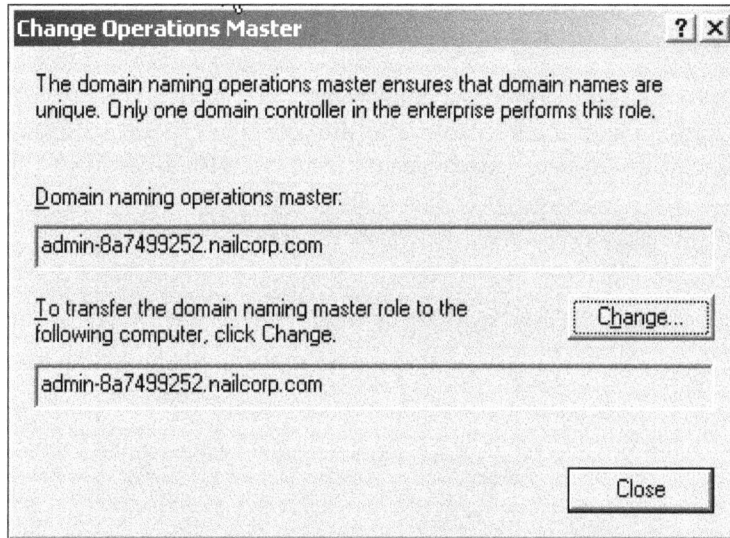

There are generally three rules for how to place these roles within an AD (outlined in `http://support.microsoft.com/kb/223346`), in order to make administration and maintenance easier.

1.  In a forest, the Schema and Domain Naming Master should be placed in the same DC.

2.  The Infrastructure Master should be placed in a DC that does not hold a Global Catalog or, if every DC holds a Global Catalog, it can be placed on any DC.

3.  The RID Master and PDC Emulator should reside on the same DC, which should have quite good hardware. If the load on this server calls for a separation, make sure that these two roles are located on DCs that are direct replication partners of each other in the same site.

Placement and maintenance of these roles is very important, and the next table shows each of the five FSMO roles and the consequence of a failure of these roles.

| Name of Role | Consequence of failure |
| --- | --- |
| Schema Master | No updates to the Active Directory schema will be possible. Since schema updates are rare (usually done by certain applications or possibly an administrator adding an attribute to an object), a malfunction of the server holding the Schema Master role will not pose a critical problem in the short term. |
| Domain Naming Master | The Domain Naming Master must be available when adding to or removing a domain from the forest (i.e. running DCPROMO). If it is not, then the domain cannot be added or removed. It is also needed when promoting or demoting a server to or from a Domain Controller. Like the Schema Master, this functionality is only used on occasion and is not critical unless you are modifying your domain or forest structure. |
| PDC Emulator | The server holding the PDC Emulator role will cause the most problems if it is unavailable. This would be most noticeable in a mixed mode domain where you are still running NT 4 BDCs and if you are using downlevel clients (NT and Win9x). Since the PDC Emulator acts as a NT 4 PDC, any actions that depend on the PDC would be affected (User Manager for Domains, Server Manager, changing passwords, browsing, and BDC replication). |
| | In a native-mode domain, the failure of the PDC Emulator isn't as critical because other domain controllers can assume most of the responsibilities of the PDC Emulator. |
| RID Master | The RID Master provides RIDs for security principles (users, groups, computer accounts). The failure of this FSMO server would have little impact unless you are adding a very large number of users or groups. |
| | Each DC in the domain has a pool of RIDs already, and a problem would occur only if the DC to which you are adding the users/groups on runs out of RIDs. |
| Infrastructure Master | This FSMO server is only relevant in a multi-domain environment. If you only have one domain, the Infrastructure Master is irrelevant. Failure of this server in a multi-domain environment would be a problem if you are trying to add objects from one domain to another. |

The other thing to consider is, of course, the future of the company and its strategy. If your business is in an industry or sector where fast organizational change, such as mergers or acquisitions, is quite possible or even likely, then you should adopt a design that will allow you to incorporate newcomers whilst maintaining the security of your own infrastructure.

The basic motto to follow when designing your Active Directory is to think of the future and not of the present.

# Migration from Other Authentication Services

Even though the time of Windows NT 4 is long gone, a lot of companies still have NT 4 domains running and are only now planning to migrate them to Active Directory. When you migrate from other domains, there is nothing more frustrating than installing a domain controller and, when prompted for the future NetBIOS name, it tells you that this name is already used in the network.

You have to do your research beforehand and make a decision as to what name to take. Then, scan your network and make sure no-one is using that name for some purpose at the time of installation. If your organization decides to use something that is already in use on the network, find out who is using it and explain to them that they have to change it due to company policy or, if it is used without authorization, have them remove it. Do not do this without proper approval from higher management.

Migration into Active Directory is, with the tools provided by Microsoft, not really a difficult task any more. The main issues you will face aren't the users and the fact that their logins might not work-this can be fixed fairly quickly by your helpdesk. The real challenge comes with applications that run on Service Accounts or authenticate against specific servers. Suppose NailCorp's accounting software is installed on a server and no one knows how it works any more, or the person who does know is unavailable. Suppose documentation, as it is often the case, is virtually non-existent. Then the machine is migrated to the new domain and the application stops working. After the migration is complete, the old domain controllers are turned off. As it happens, all of this was done during a weekend and the old machines have been removed and placed onto trolleys to be decommissioned or recycled. When the mistake eventually surfaces, things can become quite hectic in trying to get the application running again.

The key point in making a smooth migration is to properly plan it. This is especially true when you have a completely re-designed and very organized OU structure. Once you have policies in place, you don't want to migrate the wrong users or the wrong computers into the wrong OU.

# Keeping Up-To-Date and Safe

Now that we have gone through designing your Active Directory, and looked at some of the models available, we need to address security and documentation. These are both points that are just as vital as your design and migration. During the dot-com bubble, everyone that ever turned on a PC could call themselves a Systems Specialist or Systems Engineer. Crazy things, like Platform Designers, because they had a Windows 2000-based computer at home, were not unheard of either. The problems during the bubble were that people who really knew what they were doing were too expensive for a lot of companies to afford, and cheaper "specialists" were hired instead. These people then messed up most networks and network services and in the end were let go. The company then hired a more expensive person to fix the old issues, and so on. Because of this, and the rapid growth and changing markets during the bubble times, documentation was always ignored and backup solutions were bought and implemented—but 50% of them never really worked when push came to shove.

Those who survived the bubble and still work in IT have, to a big extent, adopted the 'no documentation and so-so backup' mentality. "Good enough is good enough" is what a lot of people say, but when it comes to a service that essentially is the lifeblood of your company, you do not want to go with 'just good enough'.

# Documentation

Documentation seems to be a problem in many companies and is usually the component in a project that is most often overlooked. Every time that either a new employee starts or an external contractor is hired for an AD related project, instead of getting a binder with proper documentation, he or she is assigned a mentor or a buddy who explains the systems and infrastructure. Then, the first new task is to write the documentation that has been missing for the last X years. However, after the first week he or she realizes there is not enough information and when they ask for it, they get some vague pointers on where to look.

Unfortunately, the usual circle is that documentation is left for later stages in the project, and over time gets forgotten or information is passed on by word of mouth, or as a collection of links to websites, instead. Over time, the missing or incomplete documentation becomes a costly burden to the organization knowledge is lost and, because of its non-existence, is impossible to back up. The eventual creation of this documentation, which wouldn't have taken that much time to begin with, is a lengthy and expensive process.

Documentation is not really that hard to do, but it can be hard to convince your project or program manager allocate the extra time in order to complete it. Usually, the questions will arise as to why this needs to be done now and cannot be done later. A good argument for this kind of questioning would be to explain to him or her that at a later time, information is no longer fresh and remembered, or that it is necessary for backtracking problems. I have found that both of these work very well and generally managers will give you time to document properly. If, however, you don't get the time, please make sure that you obtain written confirmation regarding the project or program managers acceptance that there is no way of knowing what has been done, and no time to write proper documentation.

Getting documentation done is actually quite easy. It comprises two steps, and once you have done this a couple of times, it will flow easily and you will produce documentation that your manager will actually be proud to show around.

First open notepad or any text editor and write, in short points, what you do, every step. In some cases, I just copy and paste the command, or the output, or both, into a line and keep going. Once you have completed the task, take a standard company template and format it into four sections. The outline is shown in the following table:

| Document part or section | Description |
| --- | --- |
| Presentation page | A plain page containing nothing but the title of the document, the department, and the name of the author. A version table at the bottom of the page is optional. |
| Index | A proper index table. This should be on its own page and will make it look more professional. |
| Purpose | This describes, in a short paragraph, what this document is about. |
| Content | All of the actions you took with detailed descriptions. Screenshots are a big winner here. Also make sure you separate different subjects with headers. |

If you stick to your template all the time when writing documentation, you will be the pride of your unit. Basically, should the need arise, you would be able to produce documentation where other people can't. It might look like a lot of extra work but as I mentioned already, it becomes very routine after a couple of times, and when you see a properly formatted document, it does make you proud. It also make your life easier when someone asks you how to do certain things,: you just open the document, print it, and point the person at the printer. A lot of time saved!

Of course, writing it is only one part of the equation. The other part is to keep it up-to-date. If you write a document about what group policies you are currently applying, then any change needs to be reflected in that document for it to be up-to-date.

Documentation plays a big part in disaster recovery, and sitting having a freshly-recovered domain, not knowing some of the settings that were applied earlier that now prevent things from working, dearly-it may even cost you even your job!

When writing your DR, please make sure that you have a printed copy in each location and at least one offsite copy per location. In some companies, it is standard practice for the domain or Enterprise admin at least to have a printed copy at home or on a USB key with him or her at all times. It is also good practice to have a printed copy or an electronic copy in the location's safe so that it can be retrieved very quickly.

Write your documents regarding your infrastructure as clearly as possible, and do not make any assumptions about who will be reading the documents. It could very well be a summer worker or a trainee, although very often companies rely on professional DR-specialized companies. Some of these companies not only do regular, twice a year, complete DR in an isolated environment, but also sometimes provide you with warm sites to get your infrastructure back up and running more quickly. However, you never know what the disaster situation will be and if it is bad, you will want to ensure that everything possible is provided in the instructions.

# Backups

I worked in a company once with a seasoned sysadmin who always said: Backups are like rumors, everyone talks about them but no one verifies that they are true. I found this to be correct a lot of times. Another good saying is: There are no backups, only restores, successful or unsuccessful ones. Everything else is just an activity leading to a restore.

Companies have backup strategies in place and the occasional repair or deleted file isn't a problem. But what happens if you have a catastrophic failure? What happens when the tapes that are in the server room neatly on a stacked, and labeled Monday through Friday, get water damaged or, worse, fall prey to an electrical fire?

Backups are one of the most crucial parts of your infrastructure and, next to documentation, probably the one taken for granted the most. It is not enough that you have a big nice tape drive or tape robot and that it backs up 100GB every night. What matters is how fast can you restore the data to a usable state. How fast can you recover a system state for a domain controller if your communications link is down and your network is being rebuilt after a natural disaster?

Testing is the key word. In some of the companies that I have worked for, testing of backups is a routine, weekly, event. This might sound like overkill but when the data contained on those tapes is highly sensitive and costs millions of dollars to replace, you will gladly invest half an hour to make sure that you can restore valid and complete files.

Backups, just like documentation, can be a pain but, in the end, you have to weigh the risk versus benefit, and unless you are backing up completely useless data, I guarantee you that your business people will always show you that it is worth keeping an eye on the backups.

# Summary

In this chapter, we went through some of the key elements in Active Directory and then over to the actual design work. A few design models were dissected, and this should give you a good starting point for your own design. There are more in-depth books available and the aim of this book is not to help your design your Active Directory but to give you some guidance along the way. Finally, we looked at some of the crucial points to consider with your infrastructure, which included scalability, security, and documentation.

This should give you a good running start and good points to discuss with your management, or at least bring to their attention because they need to be aware of all of this, and they need to see some benefit in your work. Short-term winnings or savings are not always the best and cannot be applied to everything, and the things discussed in this chapter are prime examples of this.

# 3

# Design and Implement a Disaster Recovery Plan for Your Organization

Implementing a Disaster Recovery guide in an organization that has never had one, or has had one that is outdated, may seem like an easy task. But it is not, as there are many hurdles that need to be overcome in the Disaster Recovery process. So, an accurate and proper method of implementation is very important. This chapter is designed to help you take that approach and get the whole process of Disaster Recovery implemented as fast as possible.

A lot of people assume that a Disaster Recovery guide (DRG) explains reasonably well what needs to be done to get systems back online. This is absolutely wrong. The first question that this assumption could raise is, why would one superficially touch the subject when you are writing a guide already? The second question could be that one never knows who will do the actual recovery. This statement is something that quite a few administrators that I know smiled over so at. The most compelling arguments, however are that someone technical is always around and that a non-technical person is unlikely to perform the recovery.

While both arguments have their validity, the risk of a non-technical person restoring one of the mission-critical systems and clicking the wrong button in the process, is just too high. Even if it takes a few more hours to write a proper guide, it can save days during system recovery.

The key to a successful and well-implemented DRG is motivation. If there is no motivation from the management and no motivation from the actual technical personnel, then it is not possible to develop a well-implemented and functional DRG. The all-too-common problem, though, is that the motivation usually comes in the form of an incident where a DRG would have helped but was not available.

# Analyze the Risks, Threats, and the Ways to Mitigate

In order to be able to analyze the risks and threats for our Active Directory (AD), we need to first understand what we are actually protecting. Active Directory is not exactly a physical entity that we are protecting. We are protecting the content and its function or service. The following things are the main points of an AD, that need protection and safe-keeping:

- The ability of a user to log on to the domain and access resources located in your network.
- The information for authentication and authorization, such as user names, passwords, and group memberships.
- Personal information within the AD.
- The ability of network-based services to start, authenticate, and function properly.
- Group policy application to the workstation, which may contain specific security settings.

A crucial step (the actual basis for proceeding forward), is to analyze the cost involved in an outage of a part of your AD backbone.

This is should be outlined in your Business Continuity Plan (BCP). The BCP describes the process how the business continues to operate in the event of a sustained outage of the asset, while the DRG describes the technical recovery of this asset. Included in Appendix A is a sample BCP that can be used as a foundation, and to get a good head start with our BCP.

Before we start analyzing risks, threats, and vulnerabilities, we need to understand what each of these terms really mean in conjunction with AD.

A threat is, in simple terms, the potential for something bad or unwanted to happen. For AD, this could be the potential of losing records by deletion. The threat would be accidentally deleting objects within AD.

To identify a threat, we need to analyze what is running on our DCs. For a small sales office, the number of services provided by a single server is much higher than in the corporate data centre. Each service poses a potential threat. The likelihood of a service becoming a threat by being exploited is a difficult question. In Table 1, there are examples of common services that run on a DC, and in Table 2, there is a sample list of things that can run on DCs offering more services. These tables also show the threat levels for each service. The values might differ across environments, but this is a good starting point.

| Service | Threat | Threat level |
|---|---|---|
| Kerberos Key Distribution Centre | DOS, malicious cookie insertion | 2 (low) |
| Net Logon | DOS | 2 (low) |
| Server | DOS, enumeration, buffer overflow, remote exploitation | 3 (moderate) |
| Terminal Services | Remote exploitation, brute force password cracking | 3 (moderate) |
| Security Accounts Manager | Difficult to exploit | 1 (very low) |
| DNS Server | DOS, recursion attacks | 2 (low) |
| **Average** | | **2.1** |

| Service | Threat | Threat level |
|---|---|---|
| Kerberos Key Distribution Centre | DOS, malicious cookie insertion | 2 (low) |
| Net Logon | DOS | 2 (low) |
| Server | DOS, enumeration, buffer overflow, remote exploitation | 3 (moderate) |
| Terminal Services | Remote exploitation, brute force password cracking | 3 (moderate) |
| Security Accounts Manager | Difficult to exploit | 1 (very low) |
| Print Spooler | DOS, remote exploit | 3 (moderate) |
| DNS Server | DOS, recursion attacks | 2 (low) |
| **Average** | | **2.3** |

Vulnerability is the characteristic of a system that can be exploited, and then pose a threat. For AD, this would be an unsecured AD, or ACLs that are not in place, which when used with the right tools can give someone full access to all or part of the AD or parts of it.

And lastly, A risk is the probability of an occurrence that would have a negative impact on an asset. In plain words, this means: what are the chances of a certain thing going wrong, and how likely is it for a specific thing to happen. For AD, an example could be–: what are the chances of the records getting deleted by an authorized or unauthorized person?

Identifying risks can be especially difficult when a monetary value has to be assigned to it. The value that a systems administrator assigns to his or her servers would be different to the value assigned by, say, a business controller or a marketing executive. Following the process of risk assessment, the risk values will be found to differ across people, especially since people outside the IT department would be unaware of the extent of dependence on Active Directory.

While planning for DR, analyzing the risks faced by the infrastructure is an extremely important step. Although going through this process is not as easy as it seems, we can loosely classify likely threats into the following categories, learning from the experiences of other organizations:

- Misuse of privileges by an Enterprise or Domain administrator
- Hardware failure
- Illegal cracking and hacking attempts
- Internal disgruntled employee attacks
- DOS attacks by sending many queries
- Crashing of other services hosted on the DC that render the DC non-functional

These are just a few examples of what could be classified as risks. Classifying any of the above as actual threats will however, be reduced by about half if the DC only hosts AD services.

Assessing the risk and assigning monetary values for a system being hacked, or a hardware failure occurring, may not be easy. Yet our calculations have to be accurate so that they can be presented to our peers. The formula for calculating the monetary value of risk, that is how much money it could cost us-according to Intel (see `http://www.intel.com/technology/itj/2007/v11i2/5-restricted-countries/5-methodology.htm`), MCI (see `http://www.computerworld.com/printthis/2006/0,4814,107647,00.html`), and others (see `http://www.computerworld.com/printthis/2006/0,4814,107647,00.html`) is:

```
RISK = THREAT x VULNERABILTY x VALUE
```

So, if we have a scale of classification that goes from 1 (very low) to 5(very high), and a threat probability of, for example, 1 in the event of a power supply failure (because we have it redundant), a vulnerability of 1 (because we do have everything redundant), and the cost of a new power supply of 400 USD, this formula gives us 1 x 1 x 4 = 400 USD. So the risk associated with losing the power supply is USD 400. This isn't so bad! However, doing the same equation for a slightly different scenario, say disks, increases the complexity levels and higher.

For example, say our server has a RAID 5 disk array where all our files are hosted, and also a tape drive. Two disks fail from the array and it breaks, and we lose all the files. The combined cost per hour that we would lose by losing these files is USD 20,000, because none of our developers and managers would be able to access important data. The USD 20,000 is an average because it's less in the beginning, but becomes more when the data is off for a longer period of time.

Now, the calculation looks like this:

Threat 4 (because disks do fail and our tape drive is slow and old; so it will take several hours to get the data back), vulnerability 1 (usually one disk fails at any given time), and a cost of 20,000. Or simply:

```
Risk = 4 x 1 x 20000, or 80000 USD.
```

So we risk losing 80,000 USD through just a simple disk failure. This should be justification enough to get a newer tape drive, which would mitigate (for example) our threat level to 1 or 2 and thereby reduce the risk by half.

However, reading the Microsoft Security Management Guide at `http://www.microsoft.com/technet/security/guidance/complianceandpolicies/secrisk/default.mspx` is highly recommended. Chapter 4 of this guide (`http://www.microsoft.com/technet/security/guidance/complianceandpolicies/secrisk/srsgch04.mspx`) is specifically on risk assessment.

It must be stated here that the easy way to mitigate threats and risks is to spend time securing the Domain Controllers. Though Windows 2003 provides very good default security templates that can be applied to a DC, it is definitely worth checking the high security settings, the Domain Controller Security template, and all the other templates that can be, and need to be, customized, but are already. A very strong and good baseline can be found in the Windows 2003 security guide (`http://www.microsoft.com/downloads/details.aspx?FamilyID=8A2643C1-0685-4D89-B655-521EA6C7B4DB&displaylang=en`). These settings lock down a DC quite heavily, and you can then open whatever you need at a smaller office. However, once we have an adequate setting, we should save the template, and then apply a GPO to all the other DCs in the same classification. The threat and risk levels for exploitation and brute force hacking or cracking diminish dramatically.

The risk of hardware failures can, of course, be lessened by having enough redundancy everywhere. A suggestion, for a small office DC, would be to spend a little more on those servers and get them to build in redundancy wherever possible. They generally will do fine with A RAID 5 setup, and a tape drive for tape backup in case of one or more disk failures, will generally be adequate.

While taking into account hardware failures, proper service contracts and SLAs from manufacturers can help a lot. Having a four hour or lower response time, 24x7, for a server does not cost much any more and is probably worth having, especially in smaller offices. Having a spare standby server per region,which can be quickly deployed as a DC and brought on location for fast recovery of the AD until the rest of the functions of the failed server(s) are restored, should also be considered.

# The Two-Part, 10 Step Implementation Guide

So now we know our risks and have an understanding of how to mitigate them. We know that we need a Disaster Recovery plan, and a Business Continuity Plan to go with it.

The following is a 10 step walk-through to easily implement a good Disaster Recovery plan in an organization. The first part, which describes the steps that should be taken during any disaster recovery implementation, is generic. The second part is oriented at Active Directory. For a quick overview, here is a listing of the steps:

## General Steps

1. Calculate and analyze
2. Create a Business Continuity Plan
3. Make a presentation to the Management (for Part 1 and Part 2 of this implementation guide)
4. Define roles and responsibilities
5. Train the staff
6. Test the Disaster Recovery plan frequently

## Active Directory oriented Steps

1. Writing it is not all
2. Ensure that everyone is aware of locations of the DRP
3. Define the order of restoration for different systems (root first in hub site, then add one server, and so on)
4. Go back to "Presentation to the Management".

# Part One: The Steps for General Implementation

In this part, we go through the steps that are needed to implement pretty much any Disaster Recovery plan, for any purpose. The first few steps are always the same, since every DRP is similar. Only certain sections, numbers, and risks differ.

# Calculate and Analyze

The first step is to calculate the risk associated with losing the Active Directory infrastructure, either partly or wholly. These numbers must be well-calculated and cannot be pulled out of thin air. It is best to include people from other business units into making this calculation. To calculate the numbers, always remember that:

- Threat is the possibility of a certain destructive event.

- Risk is the likelihood of a threat to occurring.

- Cost is the cost in real money terms, including the time of IT staff, hardware and so on.

- Vulnerability is a weakness in a system that can be exploited.

(please refer to `http://www.microsoft.com/technet/security/guidance/complianceandpolicies/secrisk/srsgch01.mspx` for more terms regarding risk management):

The calculation and analysis should also tale into account that if a site has two DCs and one fails, the other one will take the load and there won't be a break in service while the IT staff repairs the other DC.

# Create a Business Continuity Plan

Business Continuity Plans are, as mentioned earlier, high-level documents and procedures. These should always accompany Disaster Recovery guides. A BCP can be created for the Active Directory as well, and the sample in Appendix can help us get started. But in order to create one, we need to have a clear view of our infrastructure and what impact any outage has on our business. The key thing that needs to be done is to define the acceptable downtime and recovery time.

The communications department should also be involved in this process so that the right communications channels and responsibilities are used and defined. Communications, within the company and with external entities, can be crucial in the event of a disaster if an organization has responsibilities to investors or is in collaboration with partners. Setting and defining the right channels and processes for company personnel helps to mitigate the outage because users will then know that there is an issue and that the IT department is working on it. They won't bombard you with phone calls complaining that they cannot work properly.

The second important thing, though no less critical, is to define a call tree. We need to have a complete contact list and an escalation path clearly defined in our BCP. The communications department also needs to be involved in this.

The call tree is a diagram with different levels of escalation, with the responsible person and phone number listed. With this, it is easy for someone to follow the chain of command and understand who needs to give the go-ahead for a certain action.

The following diagram shows the call tree for NailCorp as an example:

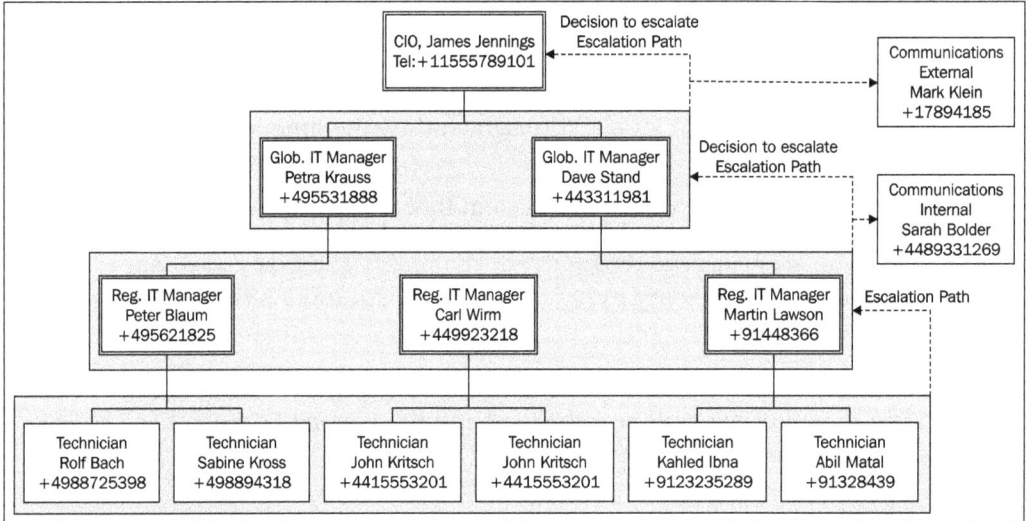

During an outage or disaster, the communications department should take responsibility for communicating the issue to the entire workforce, and not just the technical staff. For example, the information bulletin could state that the IT department is aware of the problem and is working on solving it, and also give a rough estimate of the time within which the problem is expected to be fixed and normal operations resumed.

The BCP needs to be clearly understandable and well written, because in the event of a disaster, confusing instructions can hardly be helpful. Once the final draft is ready, it would be best to have the communications department or technical writer(s) go over it to ensure an easily-readable yet professional-looking BCP.

# Present it to the Management (Part 1 and 2)

This is a step that should be done by someone who has good presentation skills and an in-depth knowledge of the BCP that was designed. It is also a "two-part step" because the project has to get going start before the final draft can be approved. In order to clear this process with the management, the importance and the consequences of the BCP have to be communicated to them in a non-threatening manner.

Often, people who were deeply involved in the design of the BCP and the DRP failed in making it official due to their lack of presentation skills and "social connectivity". Explaining in detail what we are trying to achieve and why it is crucial for the organization is essential. Once the process has been cleared and has received the go-ahead for creation of the BCP, we must proceed to the next step, and then come back to this step later.

Ultimately, it is in the best interest of the organization to have a proper DRP. Obtaining management clearance, and therefore being able to make the BCP and DRP an official standard in the organization, can open a lot of doors for you in the acceptance department. Whenever you hear complaints regarding the implementation, or disagreements in terms of content or testing, you can point to the directive and say: "take your complaints up to the next level". Nine times out of ten, the discussion ends at that point.

# Define Roles and Responsibilities

This step is an important one because the people who have been delegated responsibilities are also accountable for them. This might not be what some people want, so the roles and responsibilities have to be discussed with the staff to ensure that they understand the implications of them.

A clear list of contacts and their roles in the BCP and DRG should be drawn up. This is not a step to be rushed. Make sure that everyone involved, including the managers, know what they are supposed to be doing when push comes to shove.

Also important here is the on-call role. Someone from the IT department should always be contactable. Rotation of this role, as well as adequate compensation for this duty, need to be clearly defined. The on-call person needs to have a clear understanding of what steps to take when something happens, and how he or she can determine whether this needs to be escalated or not.

Once everyone is on board and clear with their responsibilities, we need to put this into a visual form, a call tree. Many people, especially a lot of technical staff, complain about presenting things visually. B lot of professionals agree that a visual representation helps immensely in understanding a process, a visual representation of that process helps immensely. When you then read the text regarding that representation, most likely you will understand and memorize the process steps easier.

To get a clear picture of what roles and responsibilities should be included in the BCP of NailCorp, see the following table. This example gives an overview of who should be included.

| Role/Title | Name | Email | Telephone |
| --- | --- | --- | --- |
| Chief Information Officer | | | Office phone and emergency number |
| Global IT Manager(s) | | | Office phone and emergency number |
| Regional IT Manager(s) | | | Office phone and emergency number |
| Regional Technicians or Specialist(s) | | | Office phone and emergency number |
| Global System specialist(s) | | | Office phone and emergency number |
| Regional System Specialist(s) | | | Office phone and emergency number |
| Internal Communications | | | Office phone and emergency number |
| External Communications | | | Office phone and emergency number |

# Train the Staff for DR

Training, it seems, is one of the things that is cut very frequently in an IT budget. In this case, you need to spend money on training your IT staff in disaster recovery. This can and should be part of the internal training sessions meant for your systems and your DRP. The IT staff, such as the help desk or first level support, must be trained in the procedures that involve them. This includes verification of a DC that no longer responds, or answering the phone and letting people know that things are already being investigated. The technical staff has to be aware of the correct steps for recovery, and the chain of command. Even if the work culture is very open and relaxed, it is very important to take the hierarchy and responsibility very seriously.

Testing a DRP for Active Directory is a fairly straightforward task. Today's virtualization products, such as VMWare Server or Microsoft's Virtual Server, form invaluable components for testing any kind of DRP. Especially for AD, testing the recovery process in an isolated environment with the production backup is possible.

Testing full recoveries, or even partial ones involves having at least two machines, acting as DCs, to test replication, and at least one for each of the application servers that you may have, to communicate with the AD. Also needed are a couple of clients who have accounts within your AD, whom you can use to test connectivity and recovery of computer accounts.

An example test would involve the following steps to test recovery and verify whether the recovery was successful. We are starting from a DC that is completely clean and not yet a fully-functioning DC.

**Prerequisites**:

- A virtual server with enough RAM and disk space to run multiple virtual machines.
- A virtual client machine that has a computer account in your current AD. Many organizations create a separate production OU specifically for machines like this and apply a generic GPO, which includes some specific settings, to it.
- A few blank virtual Windows 2003 server installations or pre-installation images. (The resealing option in the sysprep utility in your support tools can save a lot of time and hassle here.)
- Application server images to suit the needs of your organization.
- A current backup of the AD.

## Steps that Need to be Completed During Testing:

- Promote the DC to make it the first DC in the domain with the same DNS name as your AD.
- Restore the DNS database to the DC or to a separate server, if that is how your organization has set it up.
- Restore the AD database from a backup onto the DC.
- Verify that all the data in the AD is present, and that all the GPOs are linked to their respective OUs as they should be.
- Verify that the DNS is working properly, and that your DC is registered in it.
- Start one of the client VMs and make sure that it gets GPOs applied and can communicate with the DCs, say by accessing some arbitrary shares, or even just authenticating users on the machine.
- Start the application servers, and verify whether the applications can access or communicate with the AD.
- Verify that all these machines work perfectly with the isolated AD and can perform all the functions that they need to do.

The testing process should be documented, and only the DRP and its included documents should be used as guidance material. Any problems encountered on the way should be noted, and your DRP adjusted accordingly after the test.

Discipline during the whole process, and a clear understanding of the preventive measurements to be applied, when the technical staff start working overtime, will ensure a safe and speedy recovery without major inconvenience for other workers. The whole process of disaster recovery has to be as transparent to the user as possible, and proper training and implementation is the key to success.

## Test Your DRP Frequently

Many organizations write their Disaster Recovery Plan and get everything approved, yet over the course of a few years, it has become so outdated that they have to start from scratch again. The importance is to test, test, and re-test the DRP frequently.

This doesn't mean that it should be tested on a weekly or monthly basis, but at least a bi-annual test should be in your plans. The DRP test should be based on real-life scenarios. So you create a "disaster" at a testing facility, and start the whole process all the way to the recovery of a functional system. All this should be written down and then analyzed. You will be amazed at how much you can learn and improve during your first two tests.

Excuses for non-participation in the test from anyone involved in the process should be unacceptable because in real life you wouldn't be able to say: "Well you know, this emergency doesn't fit in with my weekend plans...". However, tests should be announced well in advance to everyone involved. A coordinated schedule is recommended. Some organizations have a bi-yearly test for which the date is published well in advance so that all parties involved can prepare themselves for participation.

# Part Two: Implementing a Disaster Recovery Plan for AD

These steps are Active Directory-oriented and geared for successful implementation to suit your AD environment. Going back to the management presentation in the last step means that you have to repeat the presentation in order to get a final "OK" from the top management and, in effect, make your DRP a standard in your organization.

# Writing is Not All

The flow of information to all parties involved, especially your staff, is very important. For example, they need to be aware of fundamental changes in the domain structure, new important corporate policies, and the steps required for system recovery.

The implementation, meaning the approval and standardization of this task in your organization, is the hardest part. Once it becomes a standard and is implemented, getting approval for things necessary to keep the DRP and BCP up-to-date and well-tested should be easier.

In case of a DRP for AD, the recovery process will really have to be communicated, trained, and tested well. This is a critical service for your organization and the better you have your process working, the faster the recovery of the service will be. This will ensure that the users feel the least impact of a disaster, or at least experience the shortest downtime possible.

# Ensure that Everyone is Aware of Locations of the DRP

This has happened twice in companies that I worked with. They had invested a lot of money into a DRP process and tested it once. They passed with flying colors, but the man in charge subsequently left the company. The DRP was put on ice because no one took the responsibility and even worse, the whole plan got "lost".

When I asked for the BCP and DRP, I got a blank face saying: "Well, we have it somewhere". Eventually, someone dug up a draft version from their archived inbox. After 2 weeks of searching, I found the actual plan in an obscure and forgotten place on their intranet. Not really a good thing.

> Please make sure that the location of the DRP is well known. Make a section in your IT pages in your intranet, print it out, and hand it to everyone, and always mail the latest version to the people involved. An off-site, updated, copy of the DRP and all its related documents, along with copies of software that is running in your organization, is absolutely critical. The process of keeping the DRP off-site in printed form and possibly also in electronic form is likely going to be an enormous time and money saver. This way, many copies will be around in case of an emergency.

## Define the Order of Restoration for Different Systems (Root First in Hub Site, then Add One Server etc.)

The contents to be recovered and their order of recovery should be clearly defined in the DRP and the BCP. (This means, first the root DC in the hub site, then the first Domain Controller, then the second, then one at a regional sites, and so on.) Also, if the Active Directory Application Mode (ADAM) is deployed in any way, issues, such as at what point it needs to be recovered, should also be considered. If you have deployed an application specific to a single department that relies on ADAM, you need to make sure that the ADAM gets restored properly before the application is recovered or re-installed. For more information on ADAM, please see `http://www.microsoft.com/windowsserver2003/techinfo/overview/adam.mspx`.

This is probably also one of the crucial steps to be taken, because mix-ups, replication errors, and bad timings can put you end up in the same situation as you were in before you started recovery, or an even worse situation if you have no coordination and communication.

## Go back to "Presentation to Management"

This is the final step. Once everything is implemented, documented, and tested, go back to the management and tell them that the task is complete. Show them numbers for recovery times, pie charts of possibilities, and maximum outage numbers. Once they are convinced that money was not wasted, get it all approved and standardized.

You should be well known by then as "the man" for disaster recovery and your job, in case of an emergency, just got much, much easier.

# Summary

In this chapter, we went through all the steps and processes required to get a DRP implemented successfully. Knowing the correct processes, even if it seems strange and out of place, and then applying these processes can save a lot of additional work, and possibly your job.

If you have a trained team and a plan that illustrates every step of the way, your downtime will be minimal and if the downtime is caused by something that you had no control over, such as a natural disaster or someone with a screwdriver in the wrong place, then your management and your company will know what they invested the time, effort and money into.

This is by no means a complete guide to implement a DRP but it should definitely point you in the right direction, and a good way there.

# 4

# Strengthening AD to Increase Resilience

Out of the box, Active Directory (AD) provides very good redundancy and failover features. Yet there are still quite a few things that can make it much more resistant to potential day-to-day operating mistakes, and other disruptive events.

In this chapter, we will go over both directly-related (implementations) and indirectly-related (processes) subjects that will help you make your AD environment stronger against events that can negatively impact it.

## Baseline Security

To ensure the same level of security in your AD-throughout your organization, you need to have a security baseline for your AD and your Domain Controllers (DC). Whilst the security baseline has to be in line with your organizational security policy, there are several things that you should consider implementing.

## Domain Policy

The default Domain Security Policy contains default values that are quite relaxed for most organizations. You should definitely change some of them.

As per Microsoft's recommendations (see: `http://technet2.microsoft.com/`
`windowsserver/en/library/cae0e49c-7929-4c94-be3a-ea6a63f09b6e1033.`
`mspx` for more information), you should at least change the password policy, the
**Account Lockout Policy**, and the **Kerberos Policy**, all of which can be found in
the **Default Domain Security Settings** under **Account Policies**, as shown in the
following screenshot:

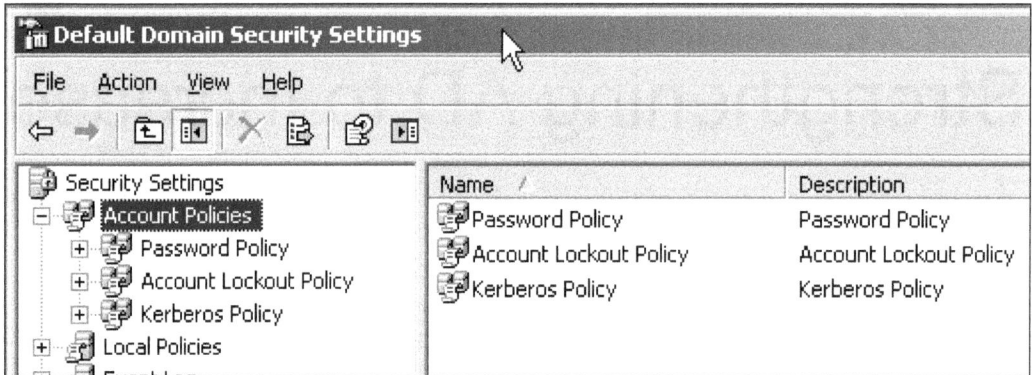

Strengthening an AD through password and Kerberos settings might not seem
directly related. However, with proper password, lockout, and expiry settings, you
can impair brute force cracking quite a bit, and therefore prevent administrative
access to your AD by unauthorized people.

# Domain Controller Security Policy

In order to maintain a unified and strong AD, every DC should have the same
security settings and much of the same configurations. Having multiple vendor
servers acting as DCs is an acceptable risk factor (considering the fact that you have
to trust multiple drivers in different scenarios). But you should always choose to use
the latest stable drivers—which does not mean necessarily the newest ones, from
your chosen vendor, in each location.

Another thing to ensure is that all DCs should have the same patch level and
the same Service Pack level throughout your domain. This ensures that no new
features are available on some DCs but others, and you won't run the risk of either
incompatibility, or other errors appearing in your Event Logs.

The Microsoft Windows 2003 Security guide, Chapter 5 (`http://www.microsoft.com/technet/security/prodtech/windowsserver2003/w2003hg/s3sgch05.mspx`), shows the recommended settings for policies, specifically for DCs, and you may want to use some of these, whilst adjusting others to suit your needs.

# Securing Your DNS Configuration

DNS represents AD's foundation, and all clients connected to an AD require a working and correct DNS in order to access resources. DNS has had several security flaws with significant impact. From an attacker's point of view, an unsecured or relaxed DNS environment is probably the best attack vector against an AD. Microsoft's TechNet white paper on securing an AD environment discusses best practices for securing DNS, in Chapter 6 (`http://technet2.microsoft.com/windowsserver/en/library/cc1eff0a-3a9e-46d2-8a7d-6b2e16461c711033.mspx`).

One DNS attack vector is a Denial of Service (DoS), which, by causing too much traffic for example, causes the DNS service to fail to respond to legitimate client queries. Another attack vector is DNS poisoning , which means that an attacker successfully modifies entries in the DNS database, which then causes client requests to resolve incorrectly. All traffic is then sent to the attacker's machine, which can cause a lot of problems. A good example would be password collection. If records that are used by clients to locate a DC are modified, then all authentication requests would go to the destinations that the attacker inserted. This type of attack is also called 'Man in the Middle' attack, because the traffic is sent somewhere else first, before reaching its intended destination. The attacker would be able to collect all the traffic with a network sniffer, which is a specific piece of software that lets you collect and analyze network traffic, and filter the encrypted passwords out, before moving on to brute force cracking them. This, of course, represents a very simple way in which the attacker would go about obtaining passwords, though the possibility does exist.

While this attack is not that easily accomplished, as the attacker will need access to your internal network, it is still a viable attack vector.

# Secure Updates

A simple yet very effective way to ensure that your DNS records are only updated by the client who owns the record is to make sure that the **Secure Only** option is used in the DNS console as shown in the following screenshot:

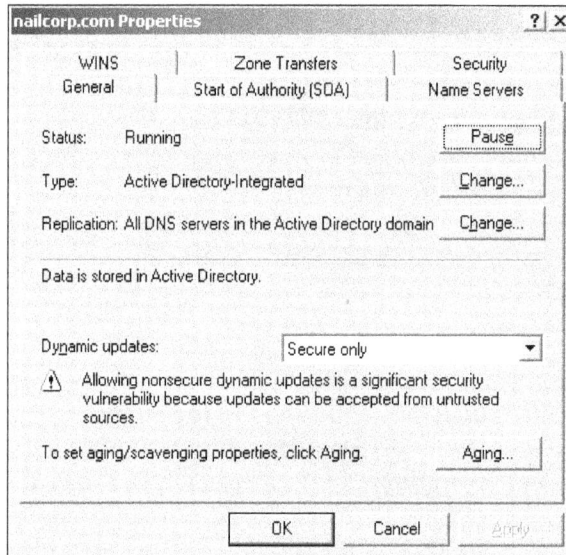

Secure Dynamic Updates is a mechanism where the DNS server does not register new IP addresses if a secret key, generated on first registration, does not match, or is missing from an update request.

Secure Dynamic Updates is the default in Windows 2000 and 2003, and unless you have a very specific reason for doing so, you should not change this option. By changing it to "None" or "Non-secure and Secure", you leave yourself open to the dummy creation of DNS records by clients who are not a part of your domain, resulting in a DoS, or DNS poisoning. If the DoS attack is aimed at exhausting disk space, then your replications will also become extremely slow as the Zone files become huge. This in turn can stop your AD data from being replicated. As you can see, a simple thing can turn into a chain reaction of negative events.

# Split Zone DNS

Split Zone DNS, also called split namespace DNS, is a way of separating your internal and external DNS records. If your company uses the same DNS name for the AD and the Internet presence (as is the case for nailcorp.com), you would have an internal DNS infrastructure that contains all of the internal records of the AD, and an external DNS that contains DNS entries only relevant to external users.

External records could be something like www.nailcorp.com, mail.nailcorp.com, and vpngateway.nailcorp.com, which would allow visitors to access the website and allow email to find its way, while remote users would have a friendlier name to access the VPN gateway. However, as these are the only records for the external nailcorp.com domain, it is impossible for someone outside to resolve, for example, intranet.nailcorp.com, dc01.nailcorp.com or any other internal name.

Exposing your internal DNS records will provide a wealth of information to anyone attempting to break into your network and your AD.

# Active Directory Integrated Zones

According to Microsoft's DNS best practices article (`http://technet2.microsoft.com/windowsserver/en/library/66add8fa-0348-4cc4-94d1-6d68127290881033.mspx`), you should, wherever possible, use AD integrated zones. For AD Disaster Recovery, this is the recommended DNS implementation strategy. It affords you full integration with AD, and is therefore just as distributed and replicated as your AD infrastructure. Integrated Zones put the DNS zone files within the AD replication and data files. Depending on the option you select, you can push to all DNS servers within the AD, to all the DCs, or both if your DCs are also DNS servers. You can move your zones to AD integrated, and remove them quite easily within the properties of the zone in the DNS console, as shown in the following screenshot:

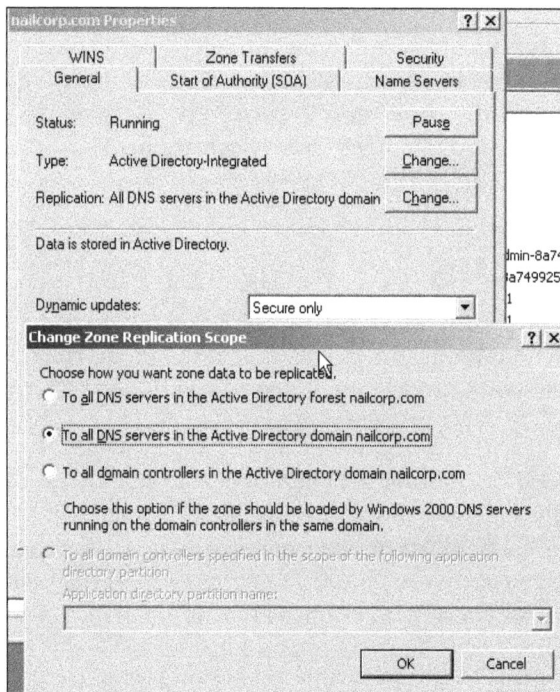

If you have adequate bandwidth between all the DNS servers, it is a good idea to push the zone files to all the DNS servers within the forest, in order to provide efficient trusts and lookups between all the domains in one forest, . If you have large locations with a lot of dynamic updates, such as through the DHCP updates, then you might consider just pointing stub zones to the main DNS server of the domain in question. This way, your clients will resolve all the client names, as the client looks them up from the correct DNS server, but you won't waste precious bandwidth by replicating all of the DNS data, to all of the servers, all of the time.

Consider, however, that for a good failover, a DNS server should have a partner or peer to which the zone gets replicated. This can be a secondary DNS server or an AD integrated DNS server, but it should be in a different location. Please be aware that a secondary DNS server here refers to the traditional DNS model, which is a single master with several slave or secondary servers. Updates, traditionally, could only be made to the single master, and were then replicated through requests to the slave servers.

AD Integrated Zones are actually stored within the AD data store, and are therefore part of the AD data replication. AD Integrated Zones are also multi-master, similar to AD itself. This means that changes can be made to each DC, and then replicated to all the other DCs in the infrastructure. This provides quite a few benefits, besides just allowing you to scale your network, by combining DNS replication with AD replication and compressing the traffic.

As DNS information is part of the AD, you can apply some of the AD security features , such as ACLs, to DNS records such as ACLs to secure them. Also, all of the records are automatically replicated to each new DC when records are added. Of course, in relation to Disaster Recovery, the zones are backed up with the AD data, and can be restored as such.

# Configuring DNS for Failover

Failover mechanisms are built into DNS right from the beginning, through the primary and secondary model. This means that if the primary DNS server is down, the secondary will answer and, possibly with a little delay, provide the result of the request to the client.

The problem begins with providing the client with the IP address of the secondary DNS server. Many times, the secondary or tertiary DNS server is located within the same network and the same location. This, of course, presents the problem of single point of failure. Whilst a hardware failure of one DNS server is easily covered by the secondary server, and the client won't notice anything, the loss of the entire server room will cause the clients to get nowhere and have no DNS server from which to query. If there are multiple locations within an organization, the secondary DNS server should always be located in another building, or even city. As long as the secondary server contains a frequently-updated zone file, which it will when using AD integrated DNS servers and primary or secondary DNS servers that all are part of the same DNS zones, the clients will query the secondary server when the primary is offline, and will receive an answer and therefore be able to authenticate. The AD SRV locators are given to the client for authentication servers. An example of this configuration can be seen in the following figure:

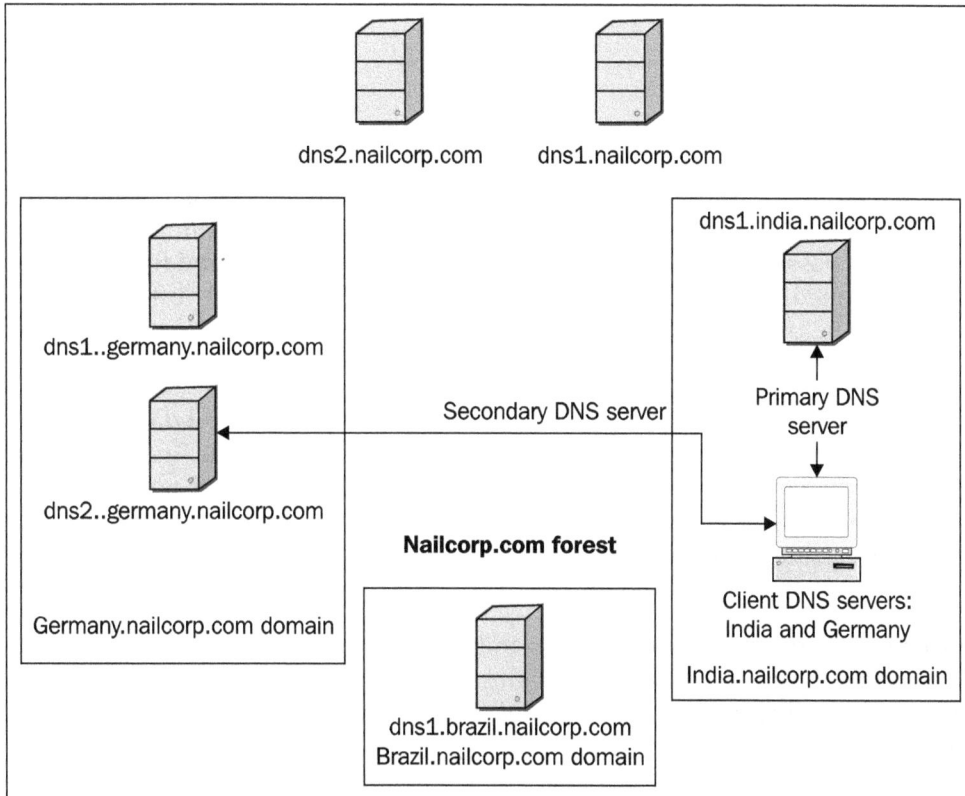

dns2.nailcorp.com    dns1.nailcorp.com

dns1.india.nailcorp.com

dns1..germany.nailcorp.com

Secondary DNS server

Primary DNS server

dns2..germany.nailcorp.com

**Nailcorp.com forest**

Client DNS servers: India and Germany

Germany.nailcorp.com domain

India.nailcorp.com domain

dns1.brazil.nailcorp.com
Brazil.nailcorp.com domain

# DHCP within AD

Dynamic Host Configuration Protocol (DHCP) has many functions and allows you to tell the clients on your network how to access the network. In AD, DHCP servers need to be authorized before they are allowed to serve IP addresses.

DHCP can be be tightly integrated with the DNS server, to update the DNS records as the IP addresses are given. Many times, a malfunction in the DHCP server, or misconfiguration, is the cause of problems within an AD infrastructure.

In order to make sure the DHCP server IP addresses is working and serving, make sure it has been properly authorized and that all of the configuration necessary for your network are in the scope of the DHCP servers. This way, your clients can always access the AD.

The DHCP server data, the address leases and so on, are not replicated within the AD. Details of which servers are the DHCP servers, however, is replicated and known in the AD. When talking about Disaster Recovery, it is necessary to ensure that when a machine is recovered, the DHCP service is configured correctly and authorized to serve again.

# Tight User Controls and Delegation

Having a medium or large -sized AD environment can involve a great deal of day-to-day maintenance work with respect to simple user or computer administrative tasks. This includes password resets, user creation, adding computers, and folder access controls. In a medium-sized organization, the technical staff usually off-loads these activities to a help desk, which is either staffed by the organization or bought as in a third-party service.

AD contains a few security groups that have the power to cause real damage. These are Enterprise Admins, Schema Admins, and Domain Admins. The first, Enterprise Admins comprises the administrators group that has full rights to the entire enterprise, meaning the whole forest. If you are part of this group, you can modify the schema, elevate account privileges in all domains within a forest, and generally have no restrictions on your actions.

The second group, Schema Admins, can modify the AD schema. While they do not have any other domain administrator rights, they can wreak havoc by modifying the schema to their advantage. Also, remember that schema changes generally cannot be undone.

The last group, Domain Admins, has full rights to everything, everywhere within a domain in a forest. This group also has the power to take ownership of files on any machine in this domain, and is generally the all-powerful account within a domain to which attackers want to be elevated.

These three groups should be restricted to a few, trusted administrators, depending upon the needs of the organization.

However, these groups are necessary, and they should contain a separate, unassigned user with a password that is located in a secure location. This will then ensure that not all domain admin privileges are lost in the event of a disaster, if the administrators are not available.

Every administrator should generally have two domain accounts: one for daily use, and one which is a part of the administrative group to which he or she needs to belong. When a task requires Enterprise Admin rights, for example establishing a Certificate Authority, the administrator should log in with the admin account and perform the task. This way, his or her day-to-day account will not cause any accidental actions within the domain or the forest, because it simply does not have the rights to do so.

All too often, support staff receive higher privileges than they actually need, and all too often, AD delegation is not used to assign privileges to accomplish common administrative tasks.

A good solution to that particular problem is to use Restricted Groups. Restricted Groups are part of the Group Policy, and allow you to define specific access for specific groups or accounts, for a specific node within the AD. You can find them within the Group Policy Editor, under **Computer Configuration**, **Windows Settings** and then **Security Settings**, as shown in the following screenshot:

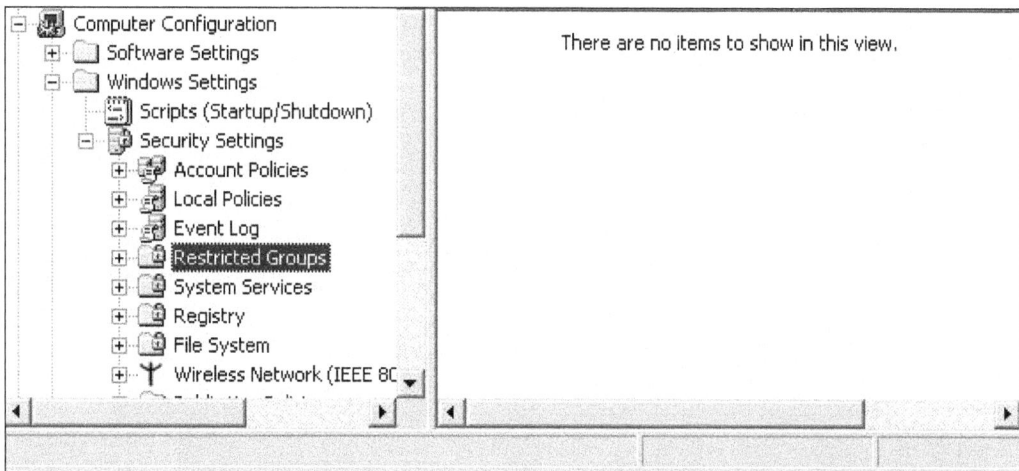

Delegation of administrative tasks within AD may be driven by organizational reasons, which means that parts of your organization require some kind of independence and right to administrate their own boundaries. Alternatively, it can be operational, which is one of the most common reasons, because it means that hosting services or other services require administrative rights to parts of the organization. Finally, it can be for legal reasons, for example because employees in certain countries or regions cannot have access to certain parts of your infrastructure.

There is a clear trade-off between autonomy and isolation when delegating duties and tasks. Microsoft considers a forest to be a Security Boundary (as you can read at Technet here: `http://technet2.microsoft.com/windowsserver/en/library/6f8a7c80-45fc-4916-80d9-16e6d46241f91033.mspx?mfr=true`) within AD. Therefore, if you want total and granular isolation, you should consider a multi-forest AD structure. With delegation, you are trying to achieve one of the two. Autonomy allows administrators to independently manage parts or all of AD or its objects. Isolation allows administrators to prevent other administrators from accessing or managing part or all of AD.

Autonomy, in many commercial organizations, is probably the most common type of delegation, while isolation is more often used in large and international corporations and military establishments. This does not mean that both types are not used in both groups, but the more common scenarios are within these groups.

Once you have established the tasks to be delegated, for example password resets for help desk personnel, you can easily accomplish this from the **Active Directory Users and Computers** console, by right-clicking on the specific OU, and selecting **Delegate Control**. The resulting wizard is quite simple, and allows you to give specific rights to specific users or groups of users, as you can see in the following screenshot:

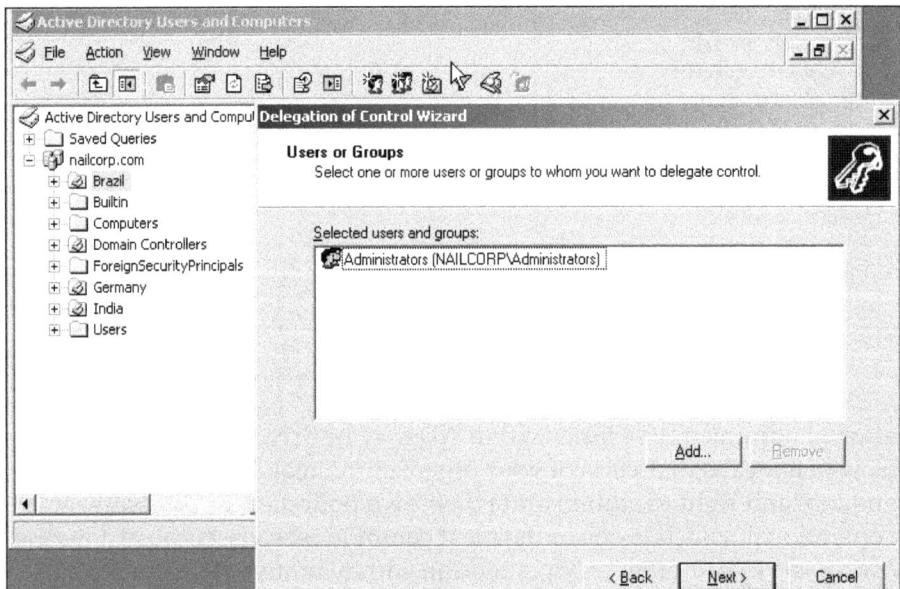

# Proper User Delegation

As discussed, proper User delegation is something that any medium to large organization needs to have. The all too common thing to do is, even when organizations use delegation, they usually just delegate full control of an entire OU to a group of people. This group is usually mixed and consists of the administrators and the support personnels. While the administrators usually have the proper training, the support personnels usually do not. Having too many rights then can cause the occasional deletion or moving of entire OUs. If you have specific Group Policies applied to certain OUs and others get moved into them without anyone noticing for a while, chaos and confusion can be caused and it might take a while before anyone gets to actually fixing it. The worst part is if an OU gets deleted and no one knows who it was. On a side note, common best practices conclude to never delete a user, just to disable them rather

We will now go through proper user rights delegation in order to achieve the following tasks: Allow a group, in this case DE_Admins in nailcorp.com, full control over an OU, allow a group of people, DE_PowerUsers, to create new users and add them to groups within the OU, and lastly, allowing a group of people, DE_Support, to just reset passwords of users. In sense, this would represent 3rd, 2nd, and 1st level support in an organization.

# Group Full control

To grant a group of users full control over an OU is quite straightforward, simply start the Delegate Control wizard from the context menu that appears when you right-click on an OU in the Active Directory Users and Computers console. After the welcome screen, select the group you want to give full control, **DE_Admins** in this case, and click **Next**. On the next screen, make sure you select a custom task to delegate (as shown in the following screenshot) and click **Next.**

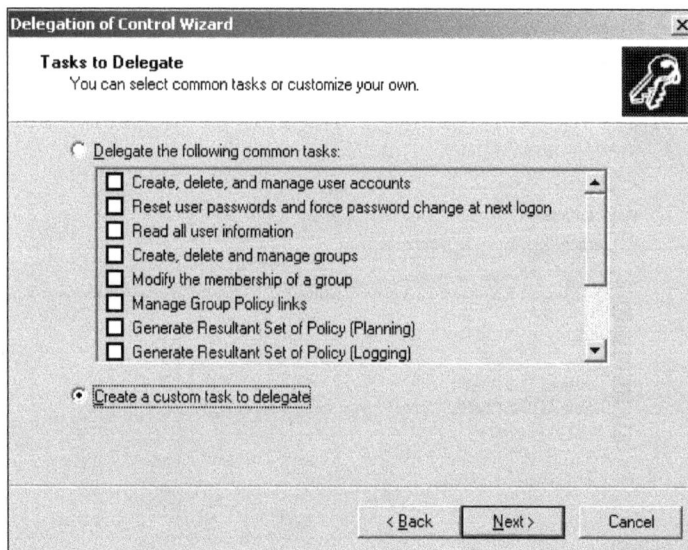

Next, make sure the selection is set to **This folder, exiting objects in this folder and creation of new objects in this folder** (shown in the following screenshot) and click **Next**.

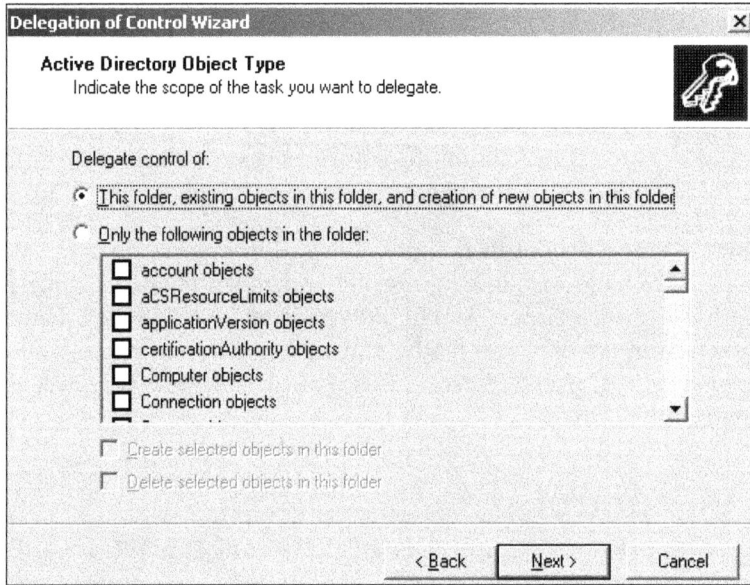

Next, select all three checkboxes, **General, Property-specific** and **Creation/deletion of specific child objects**. Also, click on **Full control** and click **Next** (shown in the following screenshot)

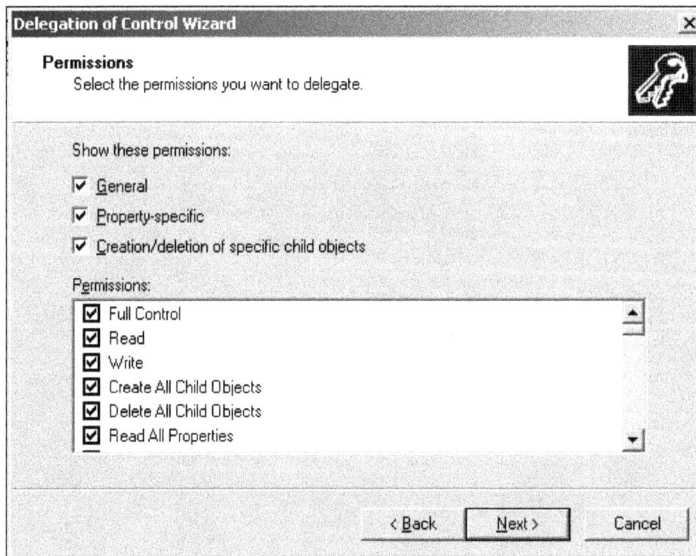

While granting permissions to a group, certain permissions can be done manually by selecting the **Advanced Features** from the **View** menu in Active Directory Users and computers and then selecting the properties of the OU in question and the **Security** tab and the **Advanced** button. We are using this step purely for verification that the actual delegation has taken place (shown in the following screenshot)

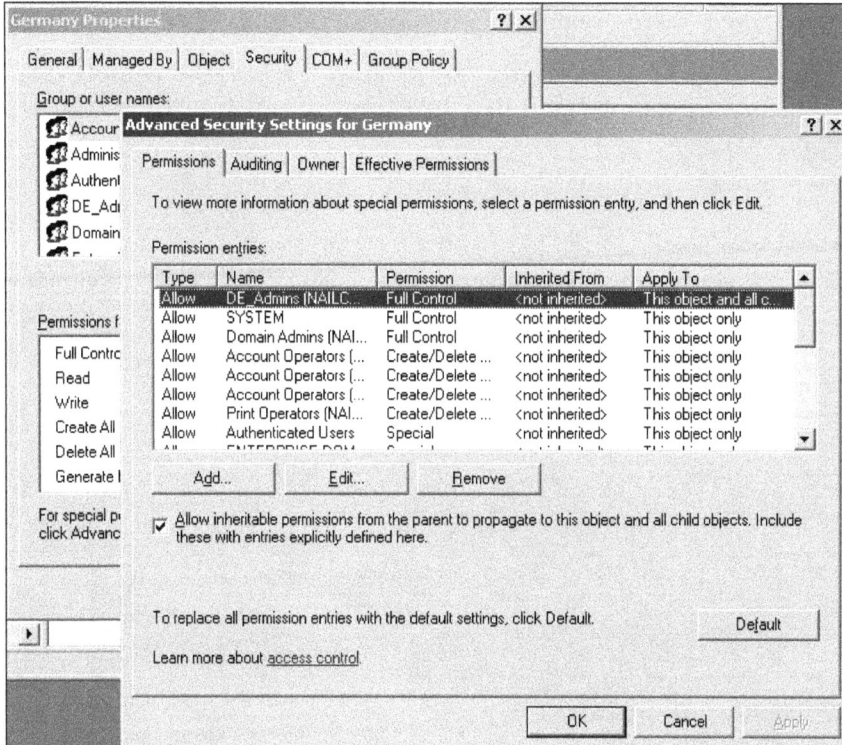

# Group with Less Control

Giving a group of people a little less control is already a bit trickier because if you don't give them full control, they have no rights at all by default. To delegate the full user administration to a group of people, follow the steps outlined before to open the delegation wizard. Now select the **DE_PowerUsers** group and click **Next**. At this point, you need to select **Delegate the following common tasks** and check the following tick boxes

- **Create, delete and manage user accounts**
- **Reset user passwords and force change at next logon**
- **Modify the membership of a group**
- **Create, delete and manage an inetOrgPerson account**

- **Reset inetOrgPerson passwords and force change password at next logon**
- **Read all inetOrgPerson information**

These six tasks ensure that the group can manage all aspects of the user accounts within the OU. The members of this group cannot, howeve, create any shared folders, modify or link to Group Policy Objects or anything else. Click **Next** and then **Finish** when these tasks are selected.

If you now follow the steps for verification again,you will see something like GROUPDELEGATE 5 and it shows that the appropriate permissions are given to the group DE_PowerUsers.

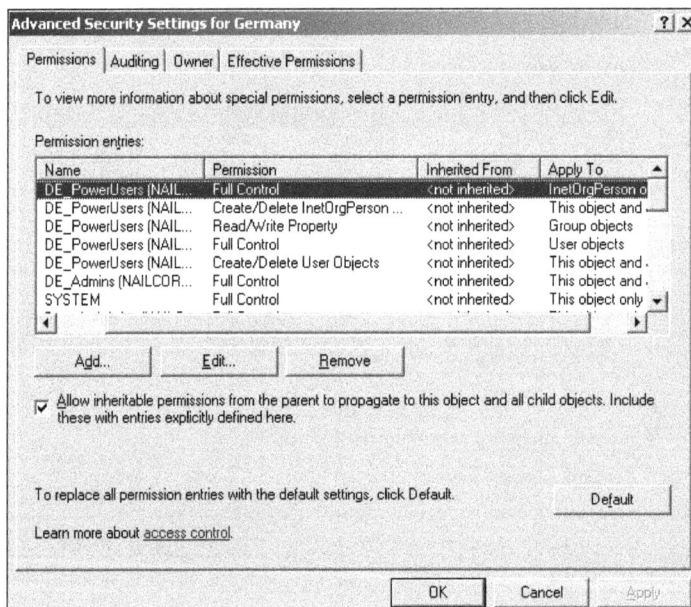

# Group to Allow Password Resets

The last and most restrictive option we will go through is aimed at mostly first level support personnel that should not be allowed to do anything else other than resetting users passwords. Everything else should be logged and assigned to second or third level support.

To delegate the resetting of passwords to the support personnel, follow the steps to open the delegation wizard and select the **DE_Support** group. At the **Common tasks to delegate** screen, only select the following two options:

- **Reset user passwords and force change at next logon**
- **Reset inetOrgPerson passwords and force change password at next logon**

Once selected, click **Next** and then **Finish** and verify once more that the permissions are set for the DE_Support group (GROUPDELEGATE 6).

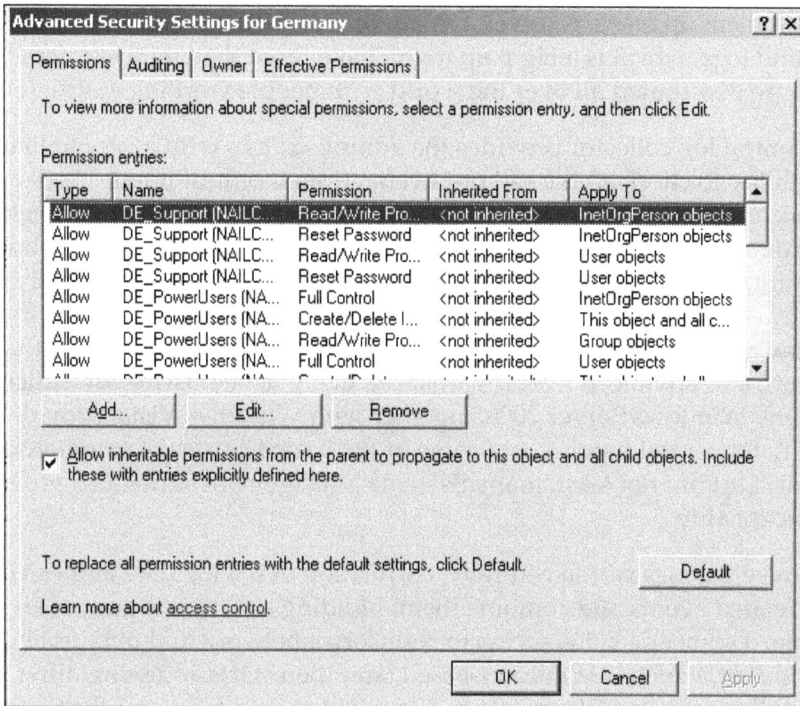

You can delegate very granular tasks and permissions with the custom tasks section. This, however, is very much out of the scope of this part as the options are so plentiful and sometimes named so confusing that it would merit a full chapter on its own, if not a whole book. This small section was merely geared towards showing that common tasks can easily be delegated and that it is a must to do so in a medium to large organization.

# Central Logging

The event log is an administrator's best friend when it comes to detecting and troubleshooting problems. Although some of the error messages are not quite as clear as they could be, Microsoft's Knowledgebase and eventid.net are valuable resources that shed light on the more cryptic messages.

Windows server 2003 allows you to audit and log a multitude of activities within the AD, from access to files, to access to objects. Your organization may require some of these, either by law or by policy. In that case, storing them is problematic, as you have to back them up on each server. On top of that, you have to check each server for issues and logs, which is a big pain if you have more than ten DCs, especially when they are distributed all over the world with people working at different hours.

Having a central log collector provides the administrators with a very valuable tool — the ability to check all the servers' events from a central point. There are many commercial, and pricey, solutions available that provide you with an immense amount of data and some excellent tools for correlation of events. If you choose to do so, creating (or finding on the Internet) a script written in VBScript will allow you to easily export the data in plain text, or any other format that can be imported into a central database and read easily. The drawback of this approach is that there is no support, and advanced features are more likely to be missing, or difficult to implement. Windows Server 2008, together with Windows Vista, provides functionality for central logging and some of the basic features of commercial log applications. Last but not least, many Systems Management suites also provide this kind of functionality.

Once you have the logs stored centrally, correlation of the log data allows you to search for related events and combine them, building a complete path of an incident. For example, if someone gains access to NailCorp's network and obtains an IP from the DHCP server, which is Windows-based, and then starts accessing different servers and files, tries to authenticate to some folders and fails, and then gains access to the AD and deletes a few records, the tools for correlation allow you to backtrack the entire process, and will give you a detailed list, including time stamps, of the actions taken. This provides you with a very powerful toolset for internal investigations, disaster recovery, action identification, or even for providing the law agencies in case of criminal investigations.

Of course, although these commercial solutions are expensive, in the long run they could be an immensely valuable thing to have when you consider the man-hours lost back-tracking an undocumented change, or trying to figure out from where a deletion of objects was made. LogLogic, one of the upper-level commercial products, is considered to be among the best, and this does not requires the installation of an agent on any of the DCs, which is quite good as you do not generally want to install additional software on your stable DCs. Splunk and Snare Client are other products available for free, but these require agents on the DCs. The price difference, however, is quite significant, even counting a server for logs which, depending on your infrastructure, will need vast amounts of disk space. From a purely AD point of view, an environment of about 15 DCs and 3,000 users might produce between 3 and 500MB of log data every day, which then needs to be compressed and stored.

In larger environments, however, this can scale up to tens of gigabytes per day. As this is plain text, it will compress very well, but you may still have to make sure you have the necessary environment to handle this amount of data.

# Proper Change Management

It seems to be quite common in small-or medium-sized organizations to let the IT department decide upon the changes to be implemented in the infrastructure. This can include application server upgrades and DCs.

Moreover, this process is usually done with an attitude of "inform the IT manager and that's it". Whenever administrators hear about Change Management, there is a lot of resistance because of the perceived additional bureaucracy.

To ensure full accountability and proper management of your IT infrastructure, however, Change Management is a necessity, and implementing it can save your infrastructure from accidents and unsupervised changes, which can cause problems with other parts of your AD of which the person implementing the change was not aware.

Generally, the process could be seen as shown in the following figure. Stakeholders are the parties who depend on the AD, such as heads of business units, the IT manager, and the CFO. It is important that the change is also communicated to the affected users.

Whilst using proper Change Management may appear to slow things down, as we get used to the process, this perception will disappear. Another point to be noted is that proper Change Management should make changes clearer to the staff.

Change Management also allows you to schedule changes at the most suitable time, which in turn allows you to mitigate the risk of conflict, such as other changes taking place, or in fact eliminate that risk entirely. Change Management allows the review of a change request by many technical people, and hidden impact zones, such as specific applications, can be found, and the RfC (Request for Change) adjusted accordingly to ensure a smooth implementation. It needs to be mentioned here that Change Records (CRs) or Change Management Records (CMRs) are the documented records of the change. These will allow you to retract or verify any changes made, and check who made them, and who approved them.

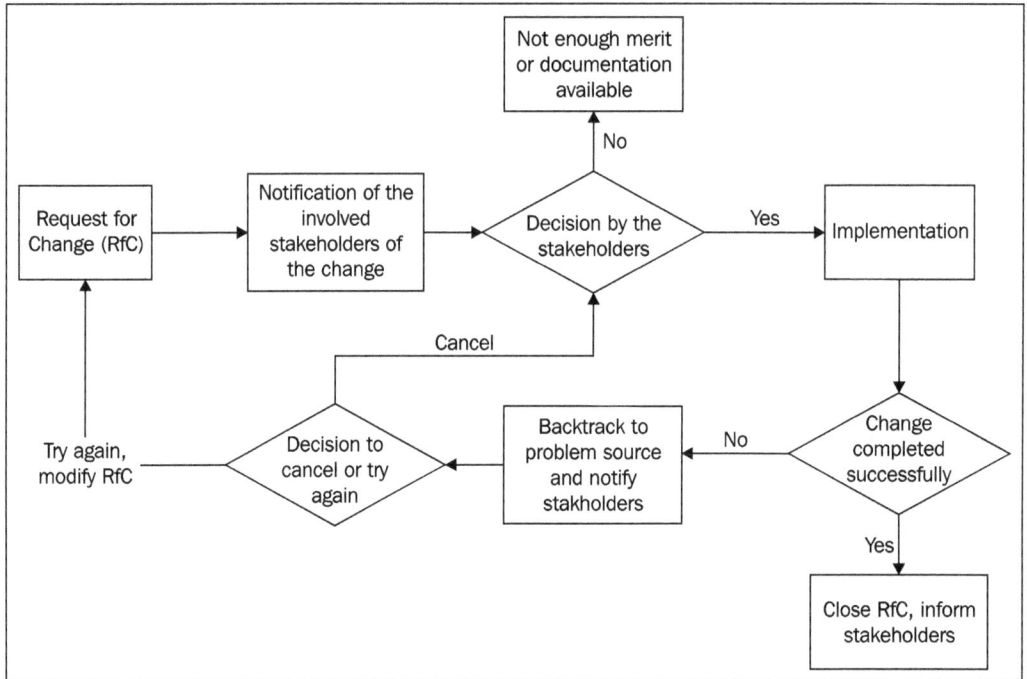

As you can see in the above figure,, the process of Change Management is fairly simple. The RfC usually includes documentation needed to explain the change request, and the stakeholders make the decision based on the level of detail in the RfC. It wouldn't make sense to add functionality while migrating servers or client computers from Windows NT to Windows XP for example, since you want a stable back-end while migrating.

# Virtualization and Lag Sites

The subject that everyone seems to talk about is virtualization—putting all of your servers in a virtual environment, which is hosted on 'big iron'-an, extremely stable server, or consolidating services that are provided by several servers in a branch office into a virtual environment. It also might not involve only one server, but several servers that host several virtual servers that each provide dedicated key services. Quite a few companies virtualize their DCs nowadays, and some of them have their entire AD infrastructure running on Virtual DCs. The reasons for doing so are valid, especially for smaller AD environments, and if you have the possibility it might be a good idea. However, it has to be said that this also needs to be evaluated for each organization. If the DC load is quite high, as it is normal in very large AD environments, then it would not be wise to virtualize the DCs since they will start fighting with other virtual machines for resources on the host system. However, if you have an environment where DCs are not heavily loaded, it would make sense to consolidate several servers into a virtual environment.

## Resource Assignment

When a DC is virtualized, the virtual server uses the host resources and dynamically adjusts the need for the virtual machine. In most virtualization products, you can specify the percentage of CPU and memory that a certain virtual machine can use, but these can be reduced and used differently if the machine is idle, or under a lesser load. This effectively gives you the system resources for the DC that you need to cope with load during peak times, such as morning logins and after-lunch logins.Yet, when the load is less on the server, its resources can be used on application servers, for example, the ones hosted in the same virtual environment.

## Backups and Snapshots

The next strong argument for virtualization is backups and snapshots. Backing up a virtual DC is as easy as backing up some files every night to tape or archive storage. You can schedule a hard risk shrink before the backup to optimize compression and space usage, and if one DC fails, all you have to do is to restore the previous backup, and the service is back online.

Snapshots allow you to take a picture of system's complete state, and save it as a file in a virtual environment. This is especially good for patching. Before patching a server, you take snapshots, and then patch. If something goes wrong, you revert to the snapshot and everything is back to the pre-patch state. This is very fast, and efficient recovery can make administrators' lives easier.

Moreover, upgrades of hardware are also much easier and can be performed with a lower risk of problems. Nowadays, virtual environments allow you to add several processors and increase memory as needed. You no longer have to keep creating new installation packages for different hardware platforms, because the virtual image of the DC can easily be moved to a new host server. As the lifetime of the OS is usually more than the lifetime of the hardware, this will make things much easier when upgrades are needed.

# Deployment

Deployment of servers within a virtual environment is faster than within a non-virtual environment. You can have ready images, resealed with the sysprep utility, having a certain patch level, with necessary customizations, and applications installed, just waiting to be copied and unpacked. You do not have to wait to order new hardware as long as your host continues to handle more virtual machines, and you can cut down on the time to deploy any server.

The drawbacks with virtualization are of course, the initial investment in hardware, and the expensive software licenses. However, VMWare Server and Virtual Server from Microsoft are both free of charge, and quite capable of running production environments. Each product has its downsides, for example support is not included in VMWare Server. For Microsoft Virtual Server, some support is available from Microsoft, but not yet for 64-bit operating systems.

# Sites and Services Explained

Active Directory Sites and Services, as mentioned in earlier chapters, will let you configure your AD's infrastructure from a usable interface. The AD infrastructure here refers to all the subnets within your organization and all your DCs.

In large organizations, the amount of subnets can grow out of proportion fast and turn into a mess where no one knows what subnet is. While this is more of a secondary or ternary function of AD Sites and Services, it does make things much more readable and manageable. This, however, is a by-product of its main feature— to manage your locations properly and assign DCs to them where the clients should log on to, to avoid unnecessary network traffic, and allow services to find the closest servers in locations if they are configured in the Sites and Services.

The way it works, if your DNS is set up correctly and everyone has the correct DNS servers assigned to them, is that the client gets an IP address and a DNS server assigned to it. It then looks up the site in DNS that corresponds to that IP and from that it will lookup the DC that it should authenticate to (shown in the following screenshot). This means that, if your subnets and sites are managed and assigned properly, authentication traffic should never leave the site, hence cutting down network traffic and delays in authentication.

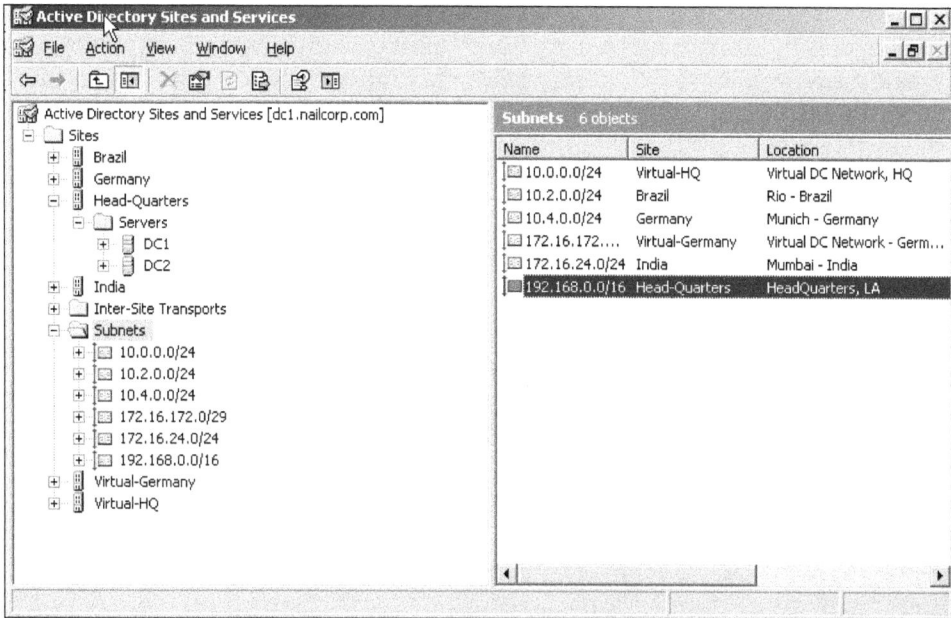

As shown, nailcorp.com has several subnets and each subnet is assigned to a site. In this case, the virtual networks are located in the headquarters and the German office.

Active Directory Sites and Services contain several components but the most crucial ones are the subnets, the Sites and the Site links.

The subnets are just that, they are all the subnets that are used in your organization and each one is assigned to a site.

The Sites are the locations that contain at least one DC. This DC is the one authentication point that will be used by all computers that are located in the subnets, which are assigned to the site of the DC. Should a site DC fail, the clients within this site will find another DC to authenticate, even if there is only a really slow connection to another site. This is completely transparent to the user.

The Site links refer to the replication direction that you want to use. In other words, from where to where does the AD replication go. If you have, for example, a headquarter like nailcorp.com and all replications come to and go from that data-centre, then you would have to create different site links from the headquarter to all of the locations. Should you then choose that a new sub office in Brazil should replicate from the Brazilian hub site, you would create a Site link that only contains the Brazilian hub site and the new office.

# Creating Sites, Subnets, and Site Links

The way the creation of sites, subnets, and site links works is that you first create a site, then a subnet and assign it to the site, and then a site link to which you add the replication sites. While this looks perfectly clear, it is confusing in the way that when you create a site, you are asked to select the Site Link, which you cannot create unless you have the site.

To create a new site, simply right click on the **SITES** container and select **New Site** (shown in the following screenshot).

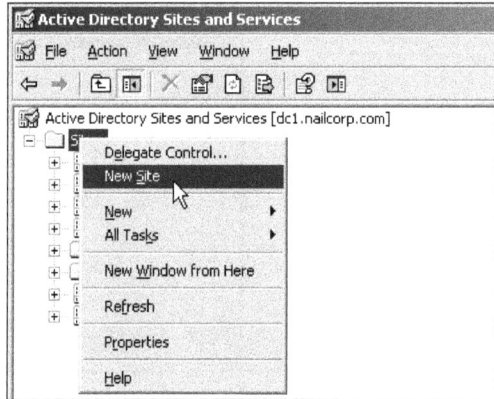

Next, select the site link you want to use. In the beginning, there is only one, which is the **DEFAULTSITEIPLINK**. In our case, we already have a few links, however, you cannot create a Site link before you create the site, so if in doubt, choose the **DEFAULTIPSITELINK** and click **OK** (shown in the following screenshot).

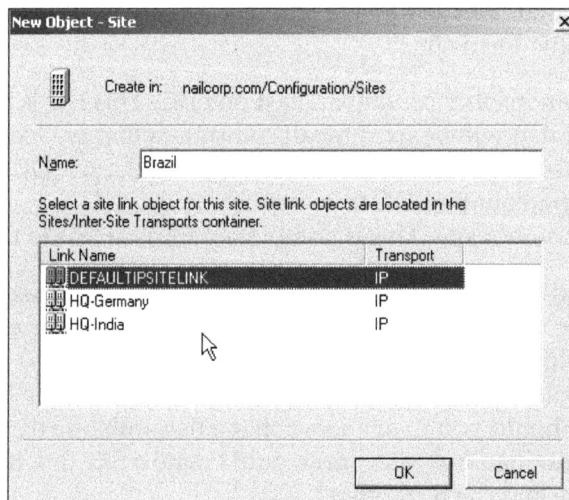

Once you click **OK**, you will have a site and can proceed to assigning it a subnet.

For that you need to create a subnet by right clicking on the **Subnets** container and selecting **New Subnet**. You will then be prompted to enter the subnet information and selecting the site you want to assign it to, and then click on **OK** (shown in the following screenshot).

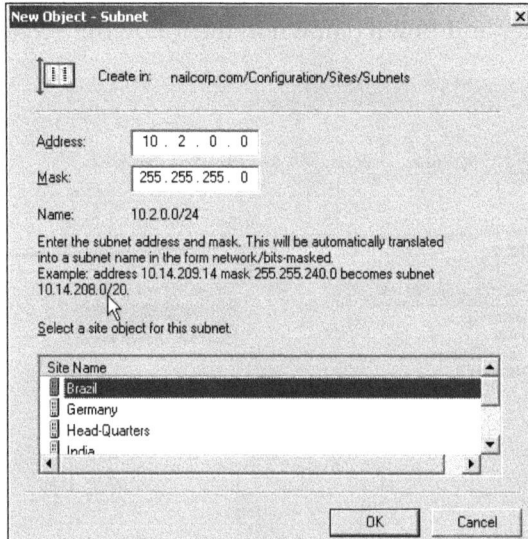

You now have the site created and assigned a subnet to it. You can assign as many subnets as you want to one site, and to avoid assigning one subnet to two sites, the subnet properties, which you can obtain by right clicking on the subnet and selecting **Properties**, allow site assignments only by drop down menu. This way you can only have one selected (shown in the following screenshot).

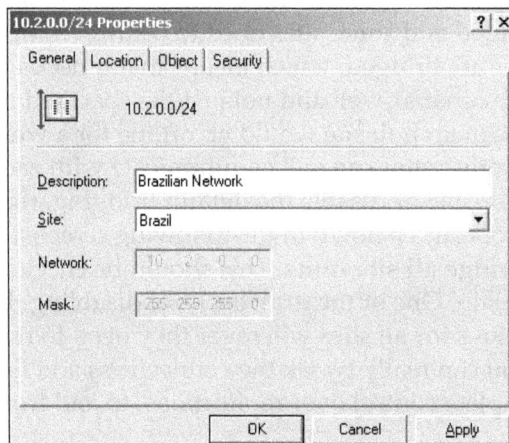

The last part of this procedure is the creation of a site link. As mentioned before, we have already a couple in nailcorp.com but we are missing the site link from headquarters to Brazil. You can have two different site links, an IP link, which uses standard IP transfers, or a SMTP link, which uses SMTP transmissions. The most common usage is the IP link. So, expand the **Inter-Site Transports** container and then right click on IP, where you select new site link. To create a new site link, simply give it a name and add the sites you want in the replication link and click **OK**. In our case, this is headquarter and Brazil (shown in the following screenshot).

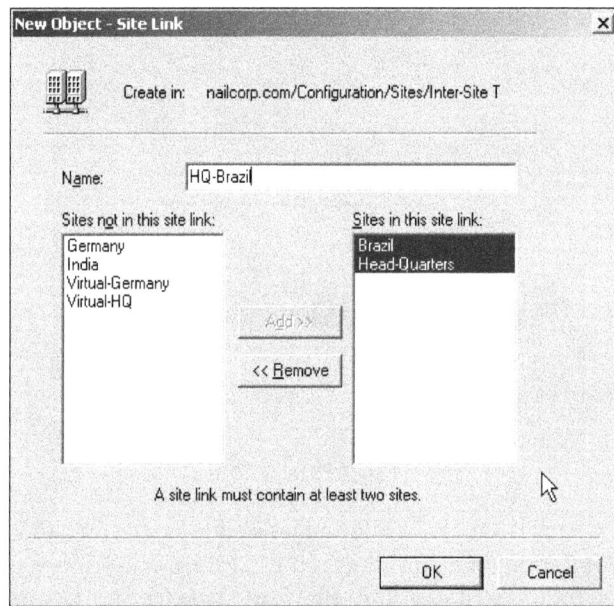

When selecting to create a site link, you can also select to create a new site link bridge. Site link bridges are used when you disable bridging of sites or if your network is not fully routed and some sites need to connect to through a specific link. By default, all sites are bridged, which means that if needs be the sites can communicate with each other as well and not just the specified links. This, for example, is useful if the main hub site would go offline for a while and replication would fail with it. The other sites can still communicate with each other though if they are bridged. To enable or disable the default bridging, right click on the IP container and select properties (shown in the following screenshot). You will see a checkbox that says **Bridge all site links**. This should be checked to make your network easier to maintain. One of the drawbacks of disabling this is that you have to then create specific links for all sites wherever they need to replicate to. Of course, on the positive side, you can really tweak the connections and link design for your network and have complete control over replications, to and from what site and even when they replicate.

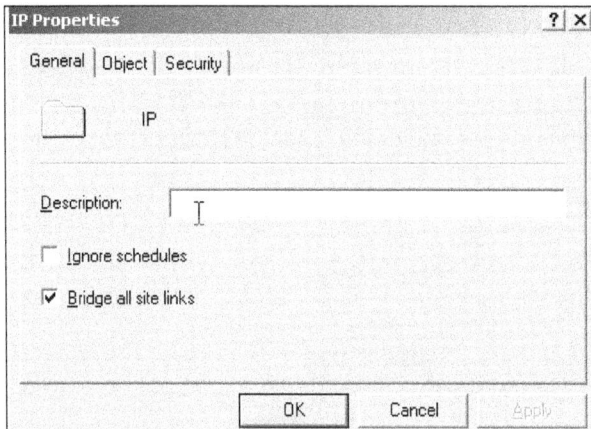

At this point, you have a site fully configured. All you need now is the DC. You can wait for a complete replication cycle and at that point, the DC should show up by itself under the Servers container, or you can move the DC from whatever site it is currently located and then wait for the replication cycle to finish for the replication links to be assigned. If you DNS and your sites are correctly configured, you shouldn't really have to do much in terms of configuring the DCs and the replication links.

If you create the sites before, you actually install a DC in a site, the DC will be moved immediately and automatically into the correct site and the replication links will be applied.

## Setting Replication Schedules and Costs

This is the section where a lot of administrators get confused and it is also the section that, if poorly implemented, can cause extremely high network traffic generated by excessive replication.

First off, in order to reduce traffic by users and allow more for replication, you will want to have at least one Global Catalog server in each site. The negative aspect of having one is that the server will consume more resources and the initial replication is bigger, The positive aspect, however, is that you speed up other communications especially concerning the whole forest and other domains.

Next, you need to spend some good amount of time to design the replication schedules between sites, especially for the sites connecting over a slower WAN link. This means that you actually have to define during which hours replication bandwidth is available and when it is not. Also, you need to then define how often the replication occurs if the bandwidth is available. This whole procedure divides the scheduling into three main points: cost, schedule, and availability.

# Cost

The cost of a link defines how favoured it is. This is particularly important when you have backup connections straight from the DC via VPN and Remote Access going through a modem line or, in some cases, even a wireless 3G connection.

If you have a permanent link, and each Site and only have a routing gateway with a gateway failover, this is pretty much irrelevant; but if you have Routing and Remote Access configured for DC direct connections, you will be able to assign costs to your backup links.

This cost then allows the DC to choose which way to go for replication. The links with the higher cost are not used unless the "cheap" links, meaning your permanent and normal WAN connections, are unavailable.

Should the normal link timeout, the DC will try to establish a connection over the more "costly" link, in this case, the VPN connection, still get the AD data replicated, and in doing so , keeping it up-to-date. This cannot always be implemented. In some organizations, the high cost of the backup lines, security policies or other reasons are posing too big of a challenge; however, if you can, this is a fairly secure way to keeping your DCs all up-to-date, especially if your organization is multinational. In order for the DCs to do this, you need to have routing and remote access implemented in each DC and a modem or second connection installed.

To assign the cost, simply right click on the **Site** link and select **properties** in the Active Directory Sites and Services console where you need to expand the **Inter-Site Transports** container and within it the IP container. You can set the cost much higher then the connection you want the DC usually to take, like the normal replication connection over the WAN and that way, AD will favour the WAN link unless it's not available (shown in the following screenshot)

# Scheduling

The schedule in AD Sites and Services refers to the replication time window. Replication schedules, however, are a two-part process. First, you can set the replication schedule for the site link and then you set the amounts of replications per hour in the actual site settings. The settings for the site allow you to choose the window when the replication can be used from the site, to all other sites. This applies to all site links and is site-specific. By default, this is once an hour. You can allow this up to four times per hour which means that once every 15 minutes the replication event will be created and initiated, depending on the allowance and the link setting.

In the site link properties, you can then set the schedule for when to run the replication between the sites and every how many minutes the replication event is initiated.

The best way to start a replication design is to actually draw the structure out on paper, or diagram software such as Microsoft Visio, and design the links and schedules visually. Once you have the diagram created, you can then use it in your documentation and even base the documentation on the picture. As long as you can keep the diagram clear and your schedules calculated properly, you will have a very smooth running replication cycle. You can see a small example of such a diagram in the following:.

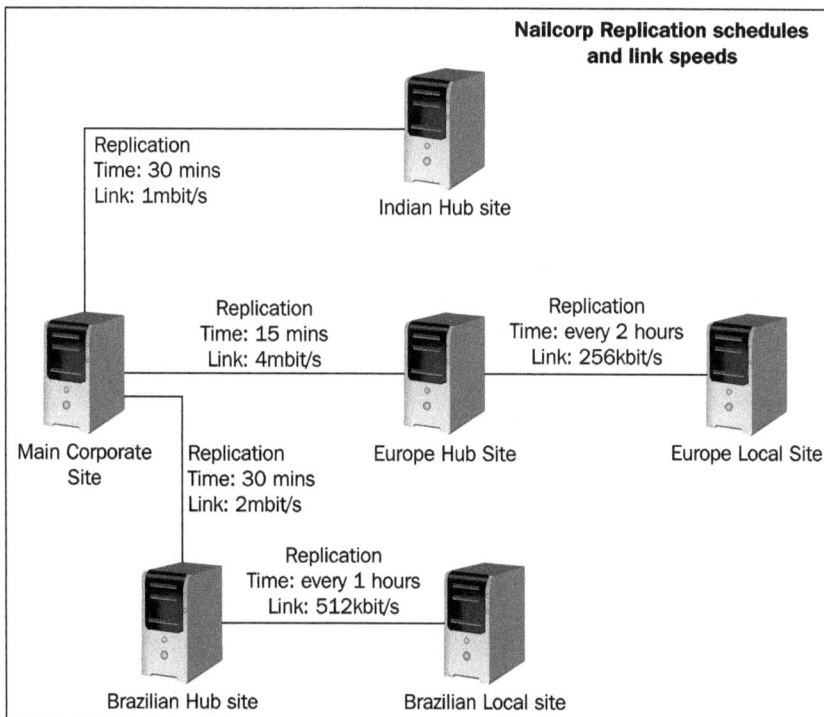

**Nailcorp Replication schedules and link speeds**

Replication Time: 30 mins Link: 1mbit/s — Indian Hub site

Replication Time: 15 mins Link: 4mbit/s

Replication Time: every 2 hours Link: 256kbit/s

Main Corporate Site

Replication Time: 30 mins Link: 2mbit/s — Europe Hub Site — Europe Local Site

Replication Time: every 1 hours Link: 512kbit/s

Brazilian Hub site — Brazilian Local site

The problem occurs when the replication schedules are done on-the-fly or just quickly or without leaving proper documentation. A small misconfiguration on a site with a slow link can cause constant replications, which will saturate the connection, and no one will know what is causing it until someone starts analyzing the replication schedules.

If you have WAN links that are not extremely high speed and mess up in the replication schedules, you can cause the exact opposite effect then their intended purpose and generate a lot of traffic and connections or none at all. The actual math way of how scheduling works is basically the time interval you set, in this case, 3 hours ($t$) plus the replication occurrence per hour ($n$). If you have then a replication window of 8 hours, from midnight to 8:00am, in order to prevent replication during peak hours, you will only get a maximum of 4 replications. The explanation is as follows: You have 8 hours as a replication window but you want to replicate every 3 hours, which means you can have only 3 replications within your window as the next replication would be after 9 hours and is outside your window.

In addition, you gave a occurrence of twice per hour. This means that when the replication starts, for example at 3:00am, during the hour of 3:00am to 4:00am it will replicate twice. The first replication is between 3:00:01am and 3:29:59. The second replication is anytime from 3:30 until 3:59:59. The same goes then for the next window at 6:00 am, which is then from 6:00:01 until 6:29:59 and 6:30 until 6:59:59.

The replication window count, in this case 3 hours, starts again from the beginning of the last replications, 3am. That way the next replication windows would start at 9:00am. As that is outside the allowed window, the next count will again start at 0:00:01 midnight the next day.

# Site Scheduling

The schedule per site actually only allows you to specify how many times per hour and during which window the replications can occur from the site. This does not affect the intra-site replications, which is the replication between the DCs located in the same site.

To open the schedule properties, open Active Directory Sites and Services, expand the site container of the site you want to modify, in our case Brazil, and then double click on the right hand window the NTDS Site Settings. A screen like the one shown in the following screenshot should appear.

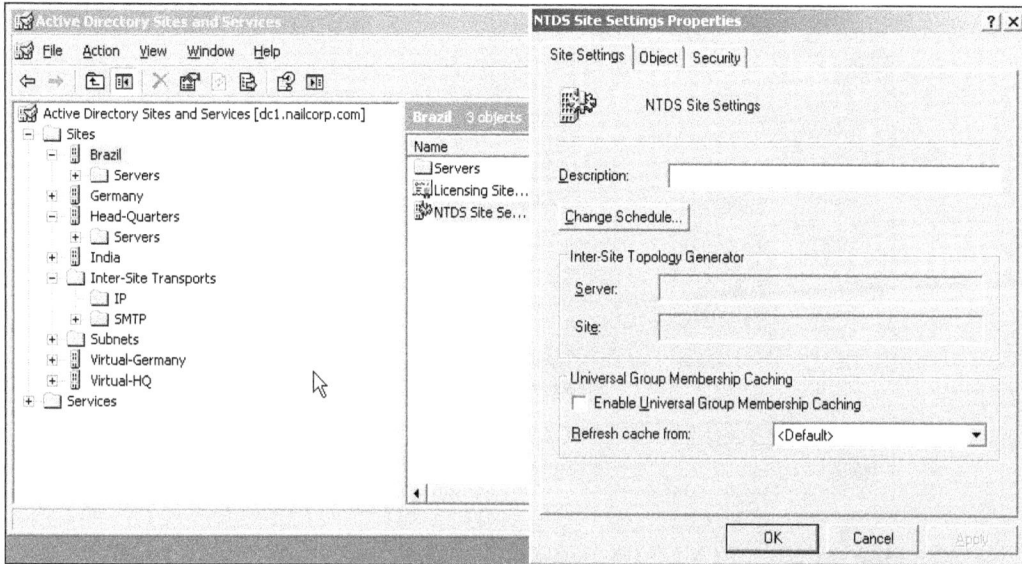

You can then simply click on the **Change Schedule** button and you will be prompted with a screen that contains a full weeks' view with all the hours and all the days. On the left-hand-side, you will see the radio buttons for how many times per hour the replication can be queued, ranging from **None** to **Four times per hour** as seen in the following screenshot.

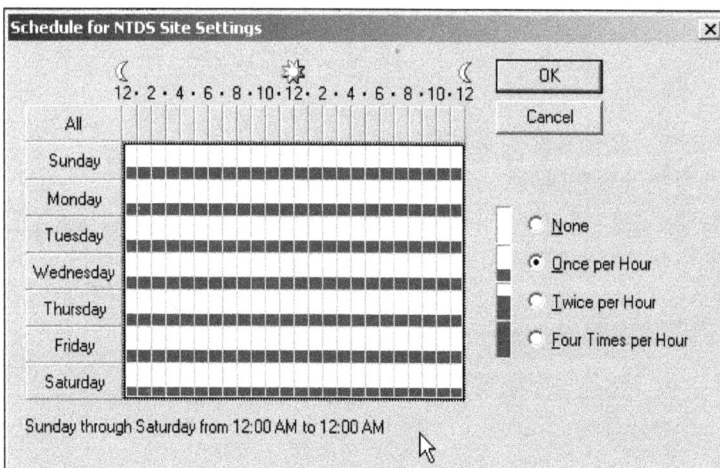

The trick is to select only a specific window of replication here. In our example, the replication from the Brazilian site cannot occur during business hours in Brazil from 8 am to 6pm, Monday through Friday, but all the other times twice per hour. To do this, first click the **ALL** button in the top left corner and then click on **Twice per hour** (shown in the following screenshot).

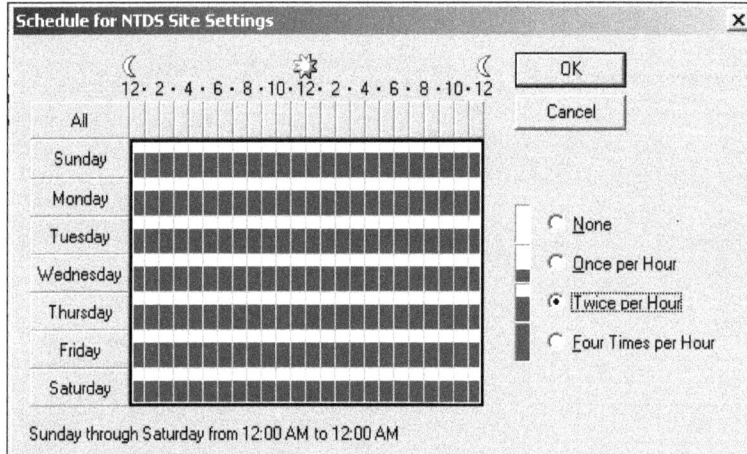

Now select the range from Monday between 8 am (to the left of the screen) until 6 pm (the right of the screen) all the way until Friday. Clicking and dragging a rectangle for the window can do this. When that rectangle is selected, simply click on **None** on the right-hand-side. This will clean the window out (as shown in the following screenshot). Then, click **OK** and in the NTDS Settings, **OK** again. You now have a schedule window defined for the time frame we wanted.

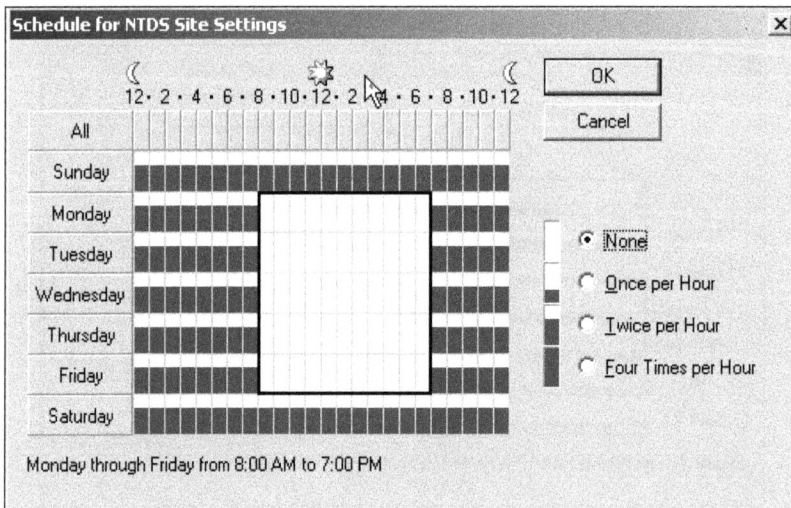

# Link Scheduling

Link schedules are done with an interface that looks fairly similar to the site schedules. As mentioned before, you can open the link schedule in the link properties, which you can open by right clicking the link in the Inter-Site Transports/IP container, by clicking on the **Change schedule** button. Here, you only have two options on the right-hand-side, **Replication is Available** and **Replication is not available**. The same principle then in the site properties works with selecting the replication window. By default, however, the schedule shows that replication is always available (shown in the following screenshot).

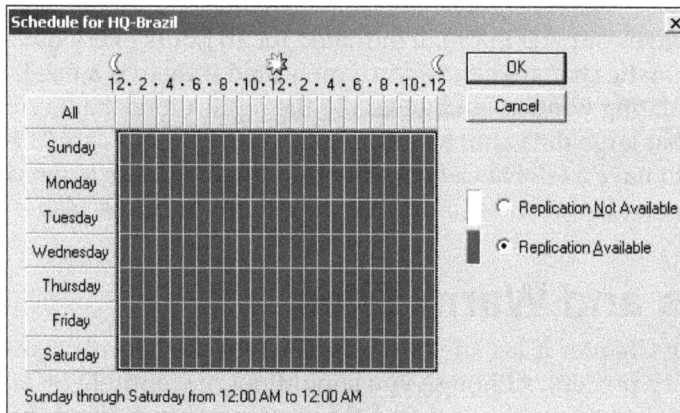

You need to change this for our Brazil site to reflect the actual availability that we chose for our site. To do this, simply drag again the selector window starting from Monday 8am to Friday 6pm and then on the right-hand-side click **Replication Not available** (shown in the following screenshot).

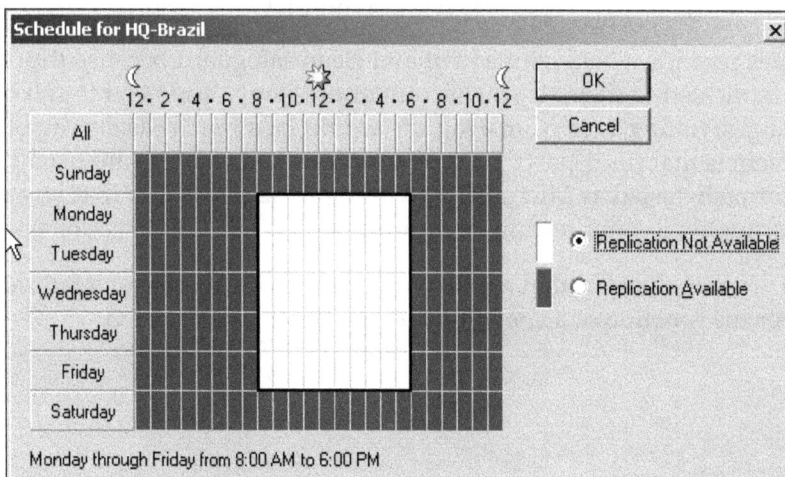

You then click on **OK** and you are returned to the Link properties. Here, you need to adjust your replication occurrence in minutes. Be careful to go in full hour increments in order to make your replications more successful. In our case, we will change the settings to 120 minutes, every 2 hours.

After clicking **OK,** we now have a replication schedule to our Brazil offices that looks something like this:

Every day from 6pm until 8am, every 2 hours replications will be initiated twice per hour from and to the headquarter. This Replication, when initiated, is of course, both ways.

This schedule leaves our AD in Brazil outdated for 10 hours every day. Considering the fact that dramatic changes can be force replicated if there is a need, this is a permissible outdating window and generally the replications that occur after 6pm should not be that large data chunks on a regular basis. In this case, it is definitely recommended to have a Global Catalog server in the Brazil site to cut down the AD traffic even more and allow most of the bandwidth for business usage.

# Lag Sites and Warm Sites

As mentioned in Chapter 2, lag sites are valuable tools for specific tasks within the Disaster Recovery process. Although you should not rely entirely on lag sites to keep your infrastructure stable, they do help in strengthening the AD for smaller mistakes, and they are very valuable, say, when the schema is upgraded, which will be necessary following the launch of Windows Server 2008. Another thing to remember is that many AD-aware or AD-based third-party applications add their own schema changes. Even Microsoft's own applications, such as Exchange, add schema additions. If these types of changes are not properly tested, they can cause major problems especially as schema changes cannot easily be rolled back.

Here, lag sites provide a very convenient and clean safeguard because the changes will not be replicated to them. If you encounter problems, and need to roll back the schema changes, rolling back from a lag site would be a much easier way of doing it. The problem is that third-party schema additions and changes are usually not quite as rigorously tested as Microsoft's own, so please make sure that you test these changes thoroughly in your testing environment.

Warm sites are actually sites that are on constant standby in case of a failure. They can take over the function of a site within a very short notice period.

# Configuring a Lag Site

When we are talking about Lags sites, several things are crucial about them and the most important thing, which makes it an actual "Lagsite", is the fact that the replication cannot occur on a regular schedule. In this section, we will look at how to configure the lag site properly so that it can actually fulfill its purpose.

What we want to essentially achieve is to have a regular site within our AD that has no logon clients. It has, however, a fully functioning replica of the forest data that simply "lags" behind in the replications. This data is the full AD database and all root configuration data as well. This site should then only replicate once a week with the rest of the forest. The catch in this is that we do not want the data from the site to go out, only from the forest into the site. We also want to achieve full replication, which means across your entire forest.

This means that you will have to create a site in your forest that contains a DC from every domain you have. For organizations that still have the empty root design, this means you have to create a root DC and a child DC in your lag site.

In order to create a lag site, you want to use the Active Directory Sites and Services MMC and simply create a new site and assign it a subnet that is reachable at least from its replication partner site.

Due to the low resource usage of the lag site, many organizations choose to build a Lag site in a virtual environment. This also allows for easy backup and moving the site if needed.

The configuration of a lag site is not really that difficult and involves only few steps more than creating a normal site. These few steps, however trivial and logical they may seem, are what differentiates this site from a normal site.

First, you will need to make sure that the subnet of the lag site is really reserved for only the lag site and no machine will ever connect to it.

Second, you will need to configure the replication schedule for the site to only be allowed once a week, preferably out of office hours. This way, you get a good copy of the AD database replicated and not much will change immediately afterwards, or has been changed, while replicating in another site. Sunday evenings would be a good time, be sure, however, to consider your other regions. The lag site design should be a very important point in conjunction with your change management. Changes cannot be implemented close to the lag site replication cycle; it would completely defeat its purpose so when implementing a change into AD, it has to be done just after the replication completes.

Third, you will need to disable outgoing replication on the DCs. This goes for all DCs within your lag site. Simply open a command prompt and type:

```
>repadmin /options DC30 +DISABLE_OUTBOUND_REPL
```

This will simply disable all outgoing replications on the DC. And as you can see in teh following screenshot, this is what the output should be. This change will stay until you manually re-enable replication.

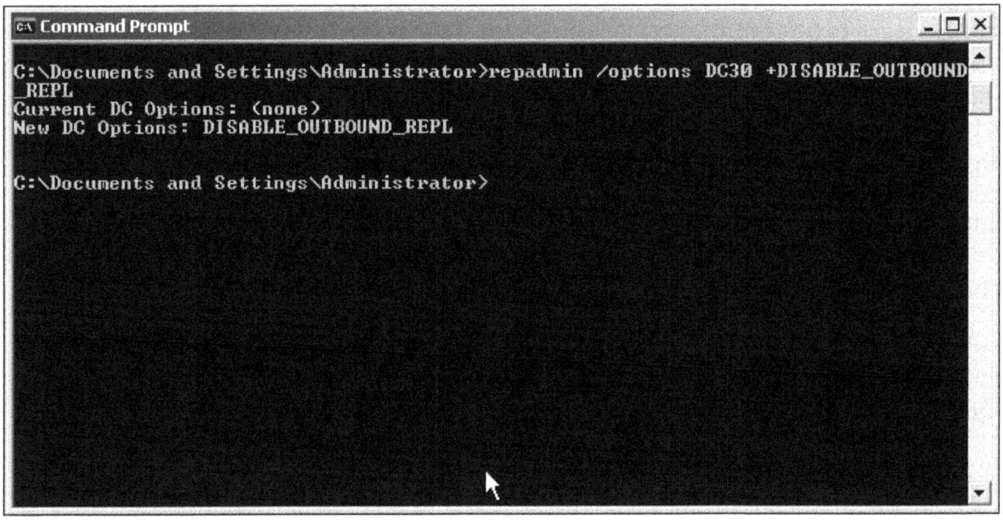

Fourth, you will need to verify that the data is replicated and it is "old" by checking in the middle of the week for example. This can simply be done by deleting a test account in the production AD and waiting until all DCs have replicated, then check on the lag site DCs and see if it's still present.

Once these four points are accomplished, you have a working lag site. Should you do a schema update or anything else crucial in your infrastructure, simply force replicate the site and if your update fails, you can quite easily and fairly quickly roll back the schema or anything else by simply setting the Sysvol primary on the lag site DC and enable outbound replication. Force sync and you should have your working Schema back.

To re-enable the outbound replication, type:

```
>repadmin /options DC 30-DISABLE_OUTBOUND_REPL
```

You can then, either with ReplMon or with the AD Sites and Services, force a replication out.

Having a lag site can be very beneficial especially during upgrade time and other modifications to the AD schema and configuration. Creating a lag site is not difficult and with the price of commodity hardware, the cost of virtualization products, and the huge possible benefit, there is really no excuse not to establish a lag site. The DCs in that site will never really have to do any processing except during replication, so generally speaking performance of the host machine is not really that important.

# Creating, Configuring and Using a Warm Site

The warm site is a concept that is still not widely adopted in regards of AD. This concept builds on running an entire site in a virtual environment just like the lag site. The warm site, however, will be a full replication partner and will always be up-to-date.

The difference is that each DC for each domain in this warm site will also contain one or more virtual network adapter run a local DNS server and an unused DHCP server. The reasons for this kind of combination is as follows:

The second network card will provide the means to join any subnet, which is meant to be the failed one. The thing to remember here is to disable the DNS registration for this network card in the TCP/IP Properties. Once added to the virtual network card, a simple reboot will make the DC register itself in it's own DNS server as a DC also for subnet or site in question. You have to wait until these DNS settings replicate out, however, before proceeding to move the Virtual DC.

The DNS server is there so that the DNS registration works smoother and easier. It will also function as a DNS server in a site recovery. If the entire site is down, then it is most likely that the local DNS server has failed as well and having a complete replica of the DNS server is a very good thing to have at a site when this do not look that good.

The DHCP server is present so that in case it is needed, you can configure a DHCP server very quickly, deploy it in the new site, and already point the clients DNS settings to the Virtual DC, making the client use the new DC immediately.

Once the Virtual DC is ready and prepped for the failed site, all you need to do is ZIP it all up and get it transferred to a PC that has the same virtualization product installed as your warm site was on. Unzip the file and start up the DC. Reconfigure the local DHCP server, if present to point the DNS server to the Virtual DC and reboot all the clients, you should have authentication working in much shorter time then your average bare metal rebuild.

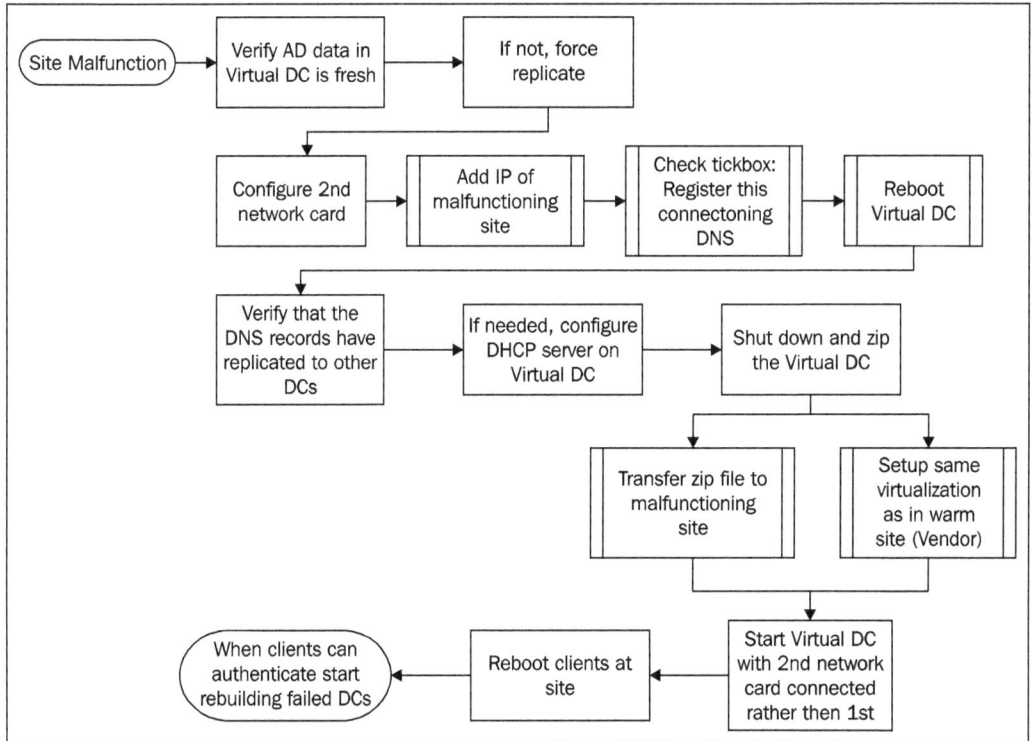

```
┌─────────────────────────────────────────────────────────────────────────────────┐
│  ╭──────────────╮    ┌──────────────┐      ┌──────────────┐                        │
│  │Site Malfunction│──▶│Verify AD data in│──▶│ If not, force │                       │
│  ╰──────────────╯    │Virtual DC is fresh│   │   replicate  │                       │
│                       └──────────────┘      └──────────────┘                        │
│                                                                                     │
│          ┌──────────────┐  ┌──────────────┐  ┌──────────────┐  ┌──────────────┐    │
│          │Configure 2nd │─▶│  Add IP of   │─▶│Check tickbox:│─▶│   Reboot     │    │
│          │network card  │  │malfunctioning│  │Register this │  │  Virtual DC  │    │
│          └──────────────┘  │    site      │  │connectoning  │  └──────────────┘    │
│                            └──────────────┘  │     DNS      │                       │
│                                              └──────────────┘                       │
│          ┌──────────────┐  ┌──────────────┐  ┌──────────────┐                      │
│          │Verify that the│─▶│If needed, configure│─▶│Shut down and zip│             │
│          │DNS records have│  │DHCP server on │  │ the Virtual DC  │                 │
│          │replicated to other│ │  Virtual DC  │  └──────────────┘                  │
│          │     DCs       │  └──────────────┘                                        │
│          └──────────────┘                                                           │
│                                   ┌──────────────┐  ┌──────────────┐                │
│                                   │Transfer zip file to│ │Setup same  │             │
│                                   │malfunctioning│  │virtualization│                 │
│                                   │    site      │  │ as in warm   │                │
│                                   └──────────────┘  │site (Vendor) │                │
│                                                     └──────────────┘                │
│  ╭──────────────╮   ┌──────────────┐  ┌──────────────┐                             │
│  │When clients can│◀─│Reboot clients at│◀─│Start Virtual DC│                        │
│  │authenticate start│ │    site      │  │with 2nd network│                          │
│  │rebuilding failed DCs│└──────────────┘ │card connected│                           │
│  ╰──────────────╯                        │rather then 1st│                          │
│                                          └──────────────┘                           │
└─────────────────────────────────────────────────────────────────────────────────┘
```

In terms of transferring, some people might add that most likely the WAN connection is down at this point. If that is the case, there is bound to be somewhere an Internet connection and if the ZIP file is password-protected, this can be used as an alternative medium. If you need to pay to use the full capacity of a local Internet café, that will still be cheaper then the time lost. If a DC is up and running, and your users can authenticate you can concentrate on bringing other essential servers back online.

# Summary

Most of the issues discussed in this chapter are explained in greater detail on Microsoft's website, or on other web resources. This chapter mainly served to list things that are helpful in strengthening your AD. Even for small and medium-sized organizations, or organizations that already have AD, these points might give new ideas of what can be done to make sure that the infrastructure, which is running the IT backbone, is available, and is stable. Implementing proper Change Management, or administrative delegation, requires some discipline. But once this process is accepted and used, things become much smoother and clearer for the management and the IT leadership. Some companies have made it a requirement to have at least one lag site within their AD and some even have a warm site with a working process in place to move it somewhere if needed. With the cost of hardware dropping continuously and free virtualization tools, the cost of having these sites shrink constantly and clearly outweigh the cost of not having them.

Creating replication schedules in AD and the documentation that shows the exact configurations is very important and crucial work and can easily lead to network performance problems in any of the sites. The proper design and understanding and updated documentation of these schedules is vital for disaster recovery since they can either help you stop the replication cycle at the right point so that bad data does not get replicated, or allow you to time exactly the replication when recovering so you know when the site or DCs in a site are operational again..

When you consider that your organization might have different time zones, a replication window that does not take that into consideration might just not replicate to the out-of-time site and that will cause your data to become outdated very quickly.

In order to see the relationship between Disaster recovery and Reliability and Security, we have to look at the different aspects of what can go wrong. Proper delegation, for example, will mitigate the risk of human error due to elevated privileges. In contrast, having a properly-secured DNS infrastructure that replicates securely and is well distributed will mean that risks of, Man in the Middle, attacks are reduced, and your DNS records will perform failover to ensure seamless connectivity to the client.

# 5

# Active Directory Failure On a Single Domain Controller

Active Directory (AD) failure, which includes corruption, is something that is dreaded by any administrator. Simply put, it means that the directory service can no longer read the Active Directory database that it has locally. This will prevent logon and authentication as well as any directory-dependent services. Essentially, it renders the domain controller useless. What's worse, though, is that several times, the replication keeps going so that the corrupted database spreads out to the other DCs.

In this chapter we will look at the different options and approaches available to recover a DC that has a database corruption. In addition, this chapter outlines, symptoms, causes, and solutions for this scenario.

## Problems and Symptoms

Let's take a look at the symptoms and then the causes.

## Symptoms

The database gets corrupted and the DC is no longer able to process and authenticate or perform directory lookups. This becomes apparent when replication fails for some reason, or a large amount of specific event log errors appear. Another symptom could be that the AD services don't start on the DC.

# Causes

This scenario can be caused by:

- A software glitch, which can due to upgrading the schema, but having customized schema entries

- An unclean AD write

- A replication that has been interrupted

- An accidental or malicious change in the AD schema with low level tools such as ADSIedit or something similar.

# Solution Process

The recovery process is as follows:

- You will have to verify that it is, in fact, a failure or corruption within the AD database, and not a network-related problem or other problem.

- You will then have to perform a specific directory restore mode recovery, where you have to decide between an authoritative and a non-authoritative mode.

- Once the recovery is complete, you will need to verify whether the DC is replicating and functioning properly.

# Solution Details

What follows is a complete outline of what to do during each part of the solution process.

# Verification of Corruption

If the AD on a domain controller becomes corrupted, or stops replicating to other DC's, or both, find out the root cause for this. A good starting point is to check again that the DNS is in order, and revert any manual changes that may have been made recently. Also, ensure that it is not a network-related problem — this means that no routers and routes have been changed, or firewalls re-configured, and the connection is not down. These are more often than not the main causes, and not an actual corruption.

If you can safely rule out those causes, you can use utilities such as ReplMon and DCDiag, which are included in the Windows 2003 support tools, available free from Microsoft's website or on your install CD. Although ReplMon is a graphical utility, it is pretty small, and one of the best tool for checking whether or not there are replication errors within an entire domain. It shows which DCs are not replicating and why. The other utility, DCDiag, scans every DC, and determines if and why they have replication and other errors.

When you have checked that all other DCs replicate just fine, you should check the Event log for specific event IDs (467 and 1018), that only occur when you have a real database corruption, and the AD jet database, which AD uses, is unreadable.

# Tools for Verification

The Windows 2003 support tools (found on your installation CD under the SUPPORT folder) and the Windows 2003 resource kit tools (found at http://www.microsoft. com/downloads/details.aspx?FamilyID=9d467a69-57ff-4ae7-96ee-b18c 4790cffd&displaylang=en) provide a variety of tools to verify if the DC is still operational, if there is actually a problem, and where the problem lies. Although the usage of these programs can also be described as part of an AD health check, in this case, we will focus on a single DC. The output from some of these tools is fairly long, and for brevity's sake, we will focus on only the relevant parts.

## ReplMon

ReplMon, short for Replication Monitor, is essential in your arsenal of tools for detecting replication errors within a domain. It can also provide you with a good view of replication partners for each DC, and allows you to run a check against an entire domain for replication errors. The following screenshot shows the default ReplMon window, while the next screenshot shows the right-click action menu for a monitored DC. To run ReplMon, simply type replmon from the command line.

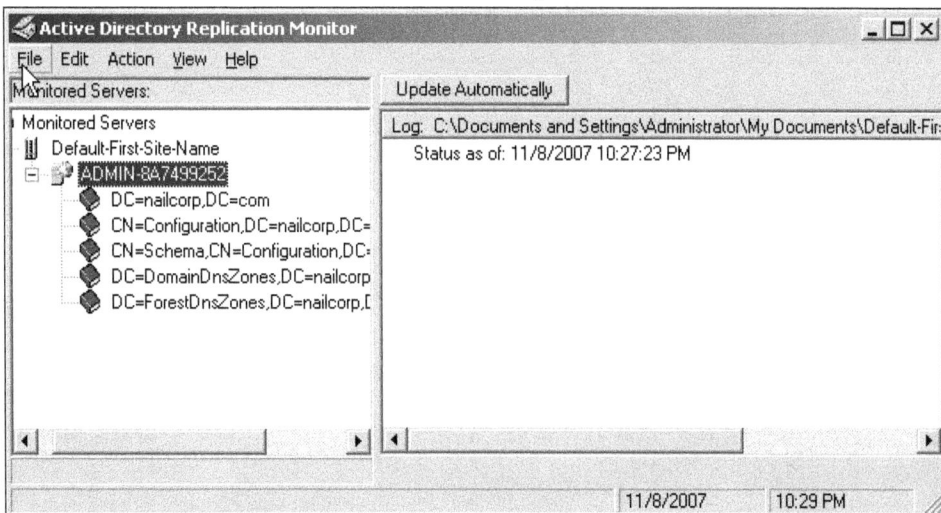

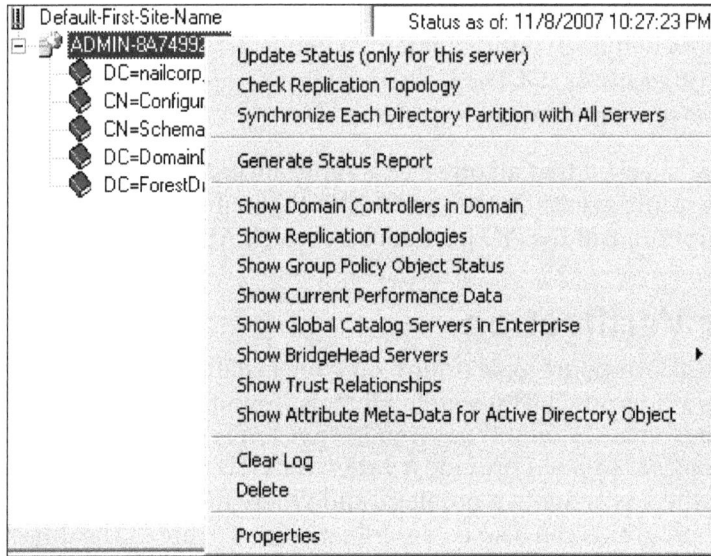

An example of where ReplMon becomes very useful is to detect errors while trying to replicate to other DCs. There are different errors for different scenarios. but, for example, a server that cannot be reached, or is offline, would show the following error in the domain-wide search for errors:

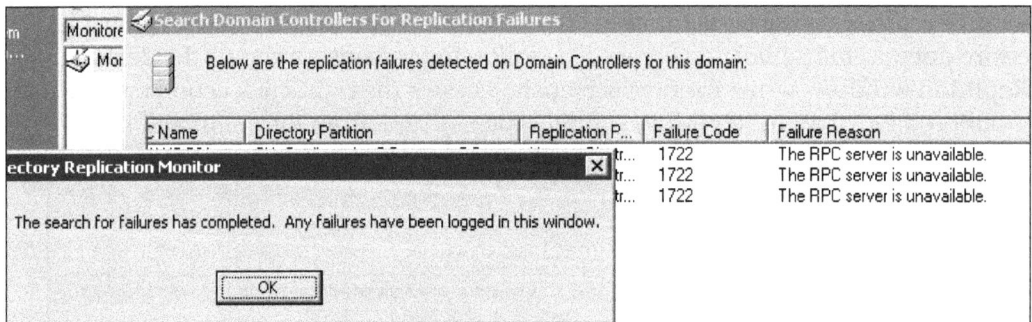

# DCDiag

DCDiag is a command line utility that performs a full check of the DC as regards AD. These tests include forest DNS tests, to check that the DNS is okay at the forest level, domain DNS tests, to do the same on a domain level, configuration test, schema test, and the FSMO test to check that all FSMO servers are available. Running it is as simple as typing `dcdiag` at the command line, and watching the output. You might want to add an output file such as `dcdiag > c:\dcdiag_output.txt` at the end, to save everything to a text file that you can read easily.

A successful DCDiag test would have the following results:

## NetDiag and DNSDiag

Both of these utilities check the network connectivity of the DC on which they are installed. DNSDiag is more geared towards Exchange, and checks that all of the essential DNS records are valid and are working, by pretending to follow the MX records. It also gives us a lot of output with regard to the domain DNS structure, and identifies if there are any problems. NetDiag checks the local networking stack. It tests all the installed protocols and services, including WINS, NetBT, and TCP/IP.

# Sonar

The Sonar.exe utility provides a GUI, which shows exactly where a replication failed, and what the state of the File Replication Service (FRS) is on each of the DCs. This is particularly useful for large environments. It also has different views that allow you to troubleshoot your FRS on a DC.

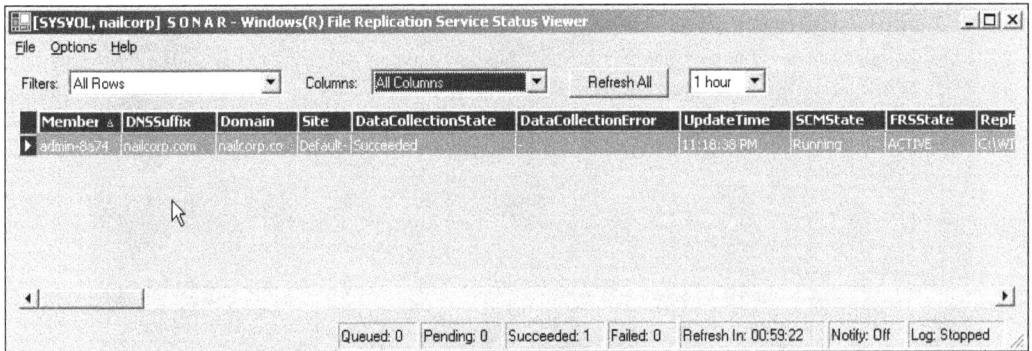

# Options to Recover and Stop the Spread of Corruption

If, in effect, you have a corrupted or failed AD database, and it hasn't spread yet, meaning it is only on one DC, you should remove that DC from the replication chain as quickly as possible. A good way is, of course, to disconnect the network connection, though this will have an impact if you are working remotely on the machine. The other option is to isolate the DC with firewall rules. This is also the safest way that still gives you access to the machine remotely. If neither option is available to you, you can use the Repadmin utility to stop outbound and inbound replication. The two options are **repadmin /options DCNAME +DISABLE_ INBOUND_REPL** and **repadmin /options DCNAME +DISABLE_OUTBOUND_ REPL,** where **DCNAME** is the name of the DC that should be disabled. If you want to enable the replication, simply retype the command with a - instead of a + so as **repadmin /options DCNAME -DISABLE_INBOUND_REPL.**

The following screenshot shows the command line for disabling outbound replication with Repadmin.

Please note that when you disable outbound replication, errors with Event ID 1115 will appear in the event log, just as errors with event ID 1113 will show when inbound replication is disabled. When either one is re-enabled, informative Event IDs 1116 (outbound) and 1114 (inbound) will appear in the event log.

The fastest way to recover from a corrupted AD database is to forcefully demote the DC to become a member server, and to promote it again to replicate off of another DC, if there is one in the same network. You should take this step only if you are sure, and have verified that the AD is actually working on the other DC. You can use DCDiag to easily verify whether everything is correctly order. You should not replicate from another DC within the same site if you cannot verify whether the DC is actually operational. Make sure that the event log does not contain any Jet database, or FRS errors such as 1173, which would indicate an internal error in the Jet Database.

You will have to perform a metadata cleanup if you force-demote the DC because a clean demotion is not an option. If you use Dcpromo normally, it will replicate its "change" out to another DC. In other words, you are spreading the corrupted or non-functioning database this way. You can easily force-demote it by running **dcpromo/ forceremoval**, and then follow the steps outlined in Chapter 4 for a metadata cleanup.

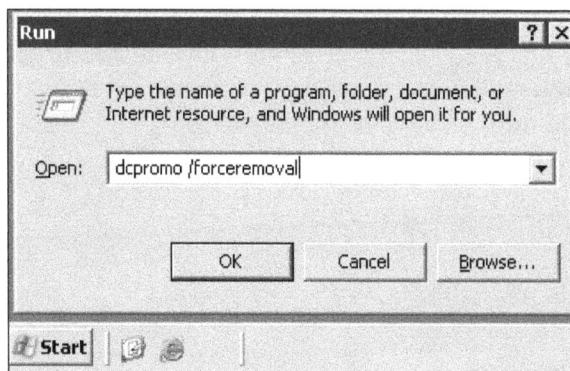

# Non-Authoritative and Authoritative Restore

To speed up the data replication of the AD, for example, for sites that have a slow or saturated network connection, or to make the whole restore process much quicker, you should perform a non-authoritative restore of the AD database. Non-authoritative restore means that you are restoring a database, but that database will not assert authority in the AD. This means that it will take all changes that the replication partners send it, where an authoritative restore is set to be the master replication in your domain. It will restore itself, and give itself such high update sequence numbers to objects that every other DC in the domain replicates from it because it is assumed it has the newest copy.

Effectively, you are restoring a backup of the AD database to its original location, overwriting the current database. This can only be done when you are in Directory Restore mode. After the database is restored, reboot your DC normally. If you have changed the boot order, reverse the order again.

> Please make sure your backups are run regularly, whether it is on tape or on disk, according to your organization's backup policy.

After the restore is complete, and you reboot the DC, the next replication will be much faster because only changed objects will be replicated to the server. This is because it has most of the AD database already, depending on how much the AD has changed, and how recent the backup was.

In a non-authoritative restore, data that is restored includes AD objects with original update sequence numbers. This requires a lot of caution, as any data that is restored with a non-authoritative restore will appear to be outdated to the AD replication system. Hence, the data will not get replicated to other domain controllers. You therefore run the risk of having the data overwritten from DCs that have not yet been restored to, and contain somewhat newer data, including other corruptions.

Since this chapter is meant for a corruption or AD failure on a single DC only, with a replication partner relatively close by, we will skip the authoritative restore. This will be addressed in the following chapters. The following figure illustrates how authoritative and non-authoritative restores work.

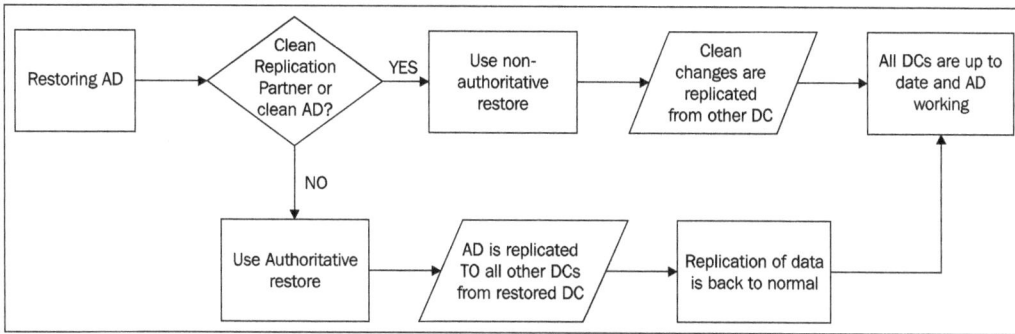

# Option One: Restoring AD from a Backup

In order to restore an AD database on a Domain Controller, you have to go into the "Directory Services Restore" mode.

To do this, reboot the DC, and at the boot prompt, which is where the boot process waits for a second before the splash screen of Windows 2003 comes up, press the *F8* key, after which you will be presented with a menu similar to the following:

**Windows 2003 Advanced Options Menu**
**Please select an option:**

**Safe Mode**
**Safe Mode with Networking**
**Safe Mode with Command Prompt**

**Enable Boot Logging**
**Enable VGA Mode**
**Last Known Good Configuration**
**Directory Services Restore Mode (Windows NT domain controllers only)**
**Debugging Mode**

**Use | and | to move the highlight to your choice.**
**Press Enter to choose.**

At the menu, select the **Directory Services Restore Mode**, by moving up and down with the arrow keys on your keyboard, and then press *ENTER*. You will then be in the same menu again. Press *ENTER* again, after which, your display will show **Directory Restore Mode** at the bottom of the screen. Your DC will now boot, but no AD-related services will be started. Once booted, restore the AD/system state from a trusted and recent backup, and reboot the machine. After the machine is rebooted, you should have working AD services with a slightly outdated AD database. Wait for the replication to take effect, and your AD will be updated.

# No Physical Access to the Machine

If you do not have physical access to the machine in question, you can achieve the same effect by editing the `boot.ini` file, which is located in c:\. This file, by default, is hidden and may be write-protected. To see the hidden files and system files, you will need to change your Windows Explorer settings, as shown in the following screenshot.

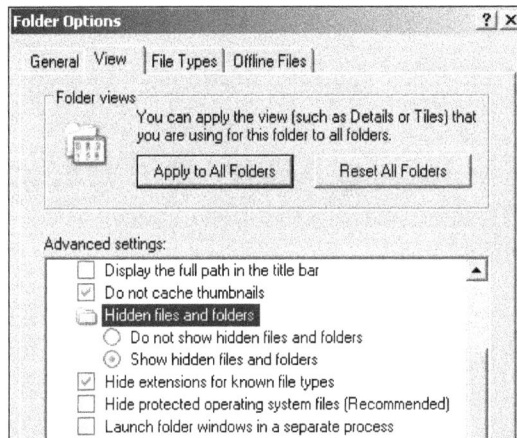

When you can see the file, check its properties, that is, whether it is read-only or not, by right-clicking on it and selecting **Properties**. However, instead of changing file permissions of system files, you can edit this quite easily with the Graphical User Interface. Some people are not comfortable editing protected files, and then you can also run into problems if you forget to un-mark or re-mark the read-only flag.

To get to the GUI editor, right-click on **My Computer** in your **Start** menu, or click the icon with the server name in the right hand upper-right, and then select **Properties**. Once you have done this, the following screen will appear:

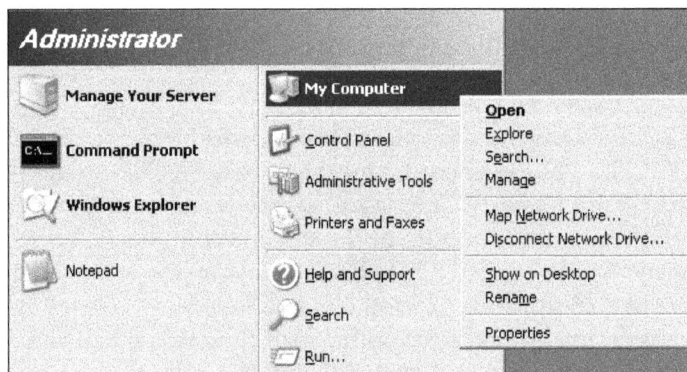

On the properties window, go to the **Advanced** tab, as shown in the
following screenshot:

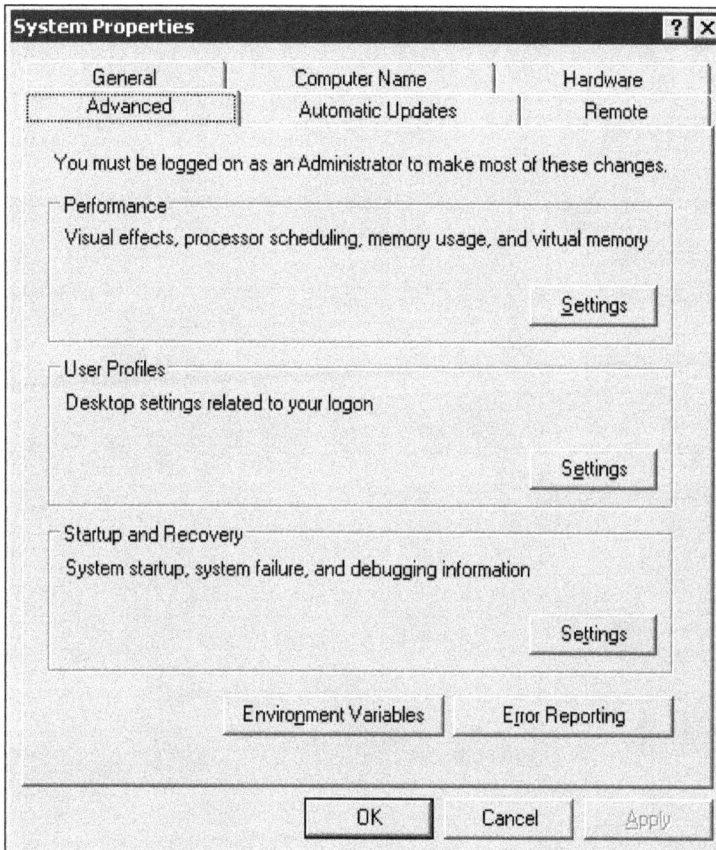

And then Click on **Settings** in the **Startup and Recovery** section of the **Advanced** tab, as shown in the screenshot below:

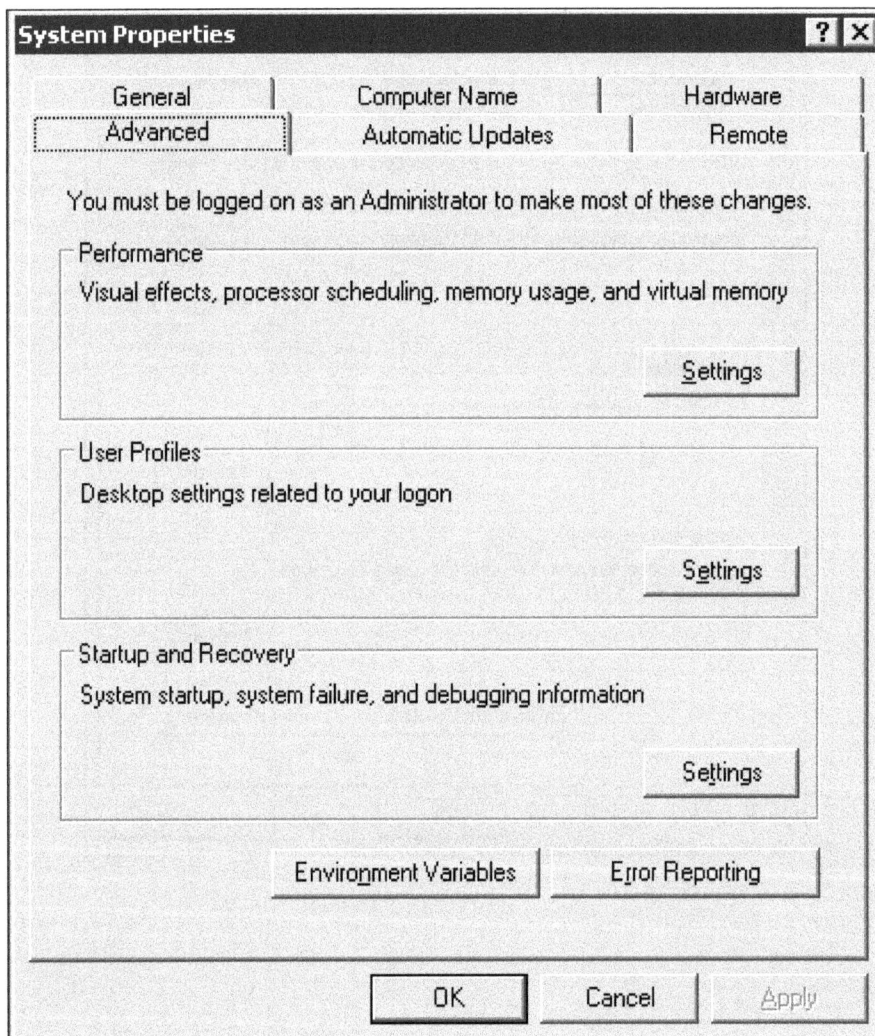

```
┌─────────────────────────────────────────────────────────────────┐
│ System Properties                                        [?] [X]  │
├─────────────────────────────────────────────────────────────────┤
│                                                                   │
│   ┌─ General ──┐   ┌─ Computer Name ─┐   ┌─ Hardware ──┐         │
│   ┌─ Advanced ─┐   ┌─ Automatic Updates ─┐   ┌─ Remote ─┐       │
│                                                                   │
│   You must be logged on as an Administrator to make most of       │
│   these changes.                                                  │
│                                                                   │
│  ┌─ Performance ─────────────────────────────────────────────┐   │
│  │ Visual effects, processor scheduling, memory usage, and    │   │
│  │ virtual memory                                             │   │
│  │                                            [ Settings ]     │   │
│  └────────────────────────────────────────────────────────────┘   │
│                                                                   │
│  ┌─ User Profiles ───────────────────────────────────────────┐   │
│  │ Desktop settings related to your logon                     │   │
│  │                                            [ Settings ]     │   │
│  └────────────────────────────────────────────────────────────┘   │
│                                                                   │
│  ┌─ Startup and Recovery ────────────────────────────────────┐   │
│  │ System startup, system failure, and debugging information  │   │
│  │                                            [ Settings ]     │   │
│  └────────────────────────────────────────────────────────────┘   │
│                                                                   │
│              [ Environment Variables ]   [ Error Reporting ]      │
│                                                                   │
│                  [ OK ]      [ Cancel ]     [ Apply ]             │
└─────────────────────────────────────────────────────────────────┘
```

In the resulting window, which contains quite a few options and sections, you can click on the **Edit** button and the `boot.ini` file will be opened in Notepad. Once editing is completed-, and the file has been saved and closed, all permissions will be reset to their original settings.

The editing of this file is pretty straightforward, yet not easily understandable for someone who has never done this. In the following screenshot, you can see the actual file displayed:

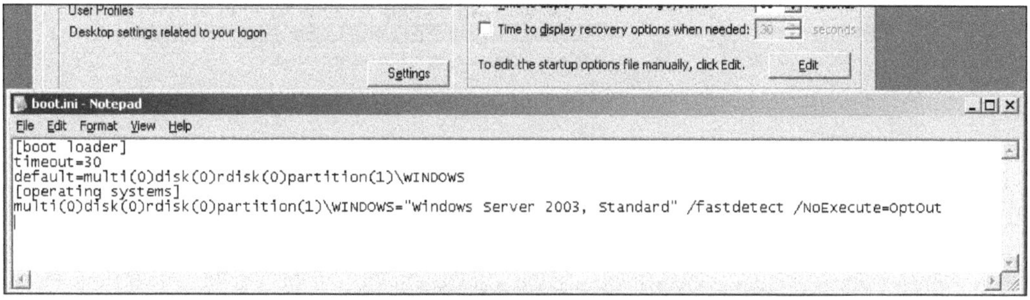

To edit the file in order to reboot in Directory Restore Mode, it is recommended to just copy and paste the last line again, and perform two changes:

1. Change the display name by adding something like Recovery.

2. Add the `/safeboot:dsrepair` at the end of the line, as shown in the following screenshot:

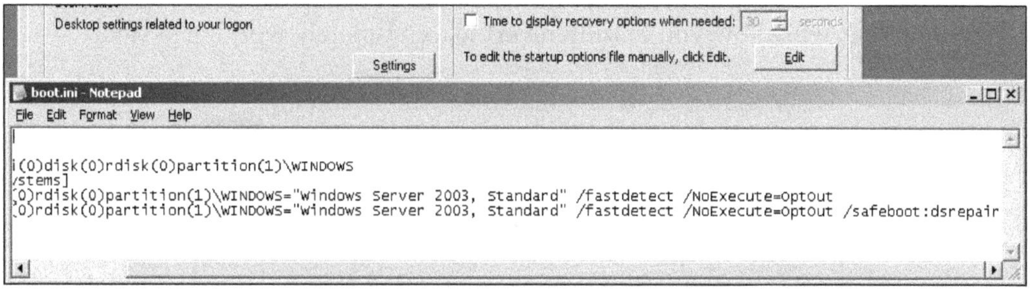

When editing is done, save and close the file as you would with any other text file, and click **OK** in the **Startup and Recovery** window so that it closes.

To select the option on which you want to boot, click **SETTINGS** in the **Startup and recovery** section again. And As you can see in the following screenshot, you can now select the boot default from the drop-down menu in the opening window:

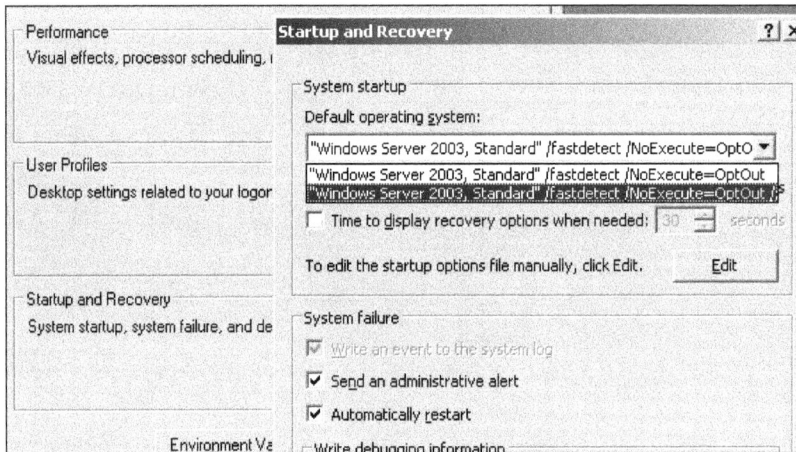

Select the Recovery line and click **OK.** Then click **OK** again to reboot the server. It will now boot automatically into the Directory Restore Mode.

## Restoring from a Backup

Once you are in Directory Restore Mode (DRM), you can use your company's backup software to recover the AD database. If you use Windows backup, you can safely backup and restore the system state of the server, as you can see in the following screenshot. This will allow you to fully revert to a completely working system.

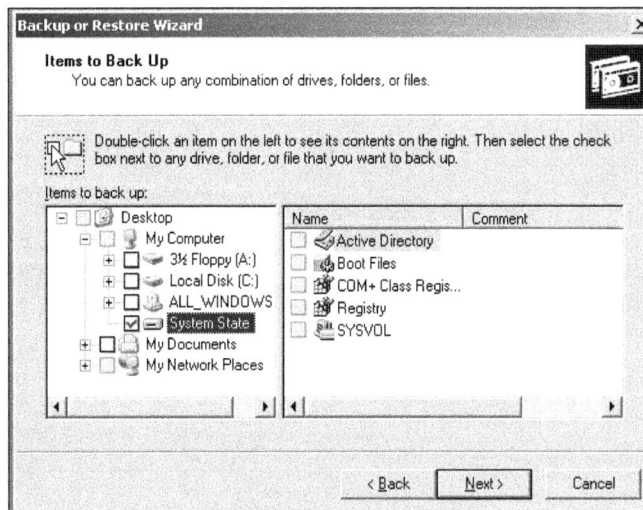

However, if you do not need to, or do not want to, recover the whole system state, you can easily choose to restore only AD from the list, as shown in the following screenshot. We assume that we have a complete backup of the server, and that we need to restore the AD database.

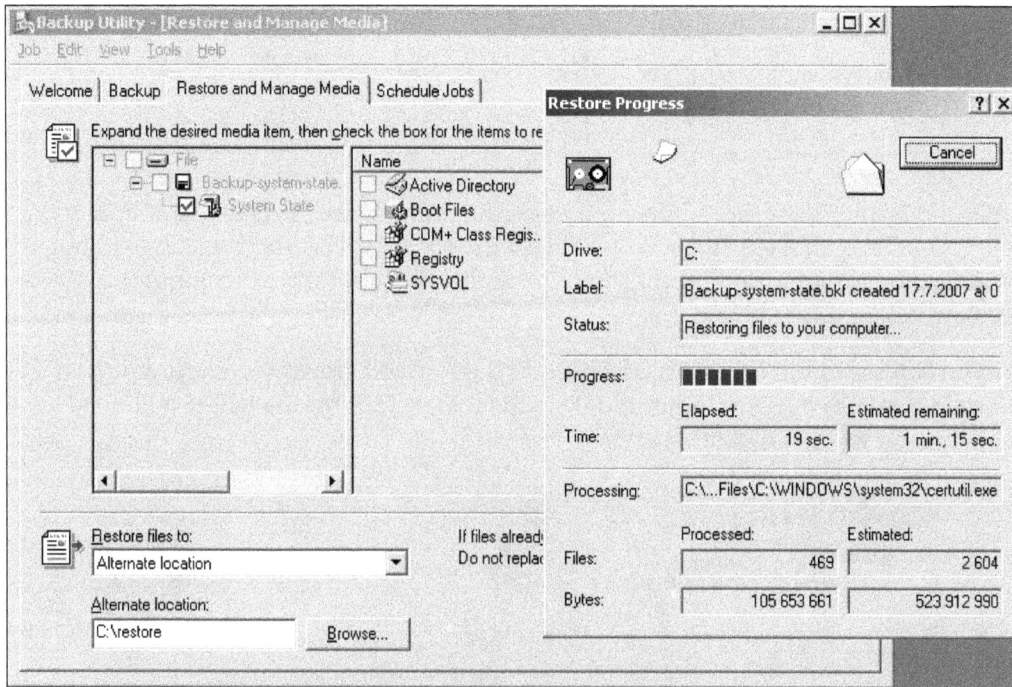

You can restore the AD or system state to a different location, or overwrite the original files, depending on whether you want to perform an authoritative or a non-authoritative restore, or even an install from media.

# Option Two: Replication

In case you have no valid recent backup media from which to restore the AD, or you need to act very fast, you can restore the AD by first force-demoting the DC in question with **dcpromo /forceremoval**.

This way, demoting will prevent replication to any replication partners, but will successfully demote the DC from the domain. If you have any important Flexible Server Master Operations (FSMO) roles running on the DC that you are removing by force, you will be presented with the following warning:

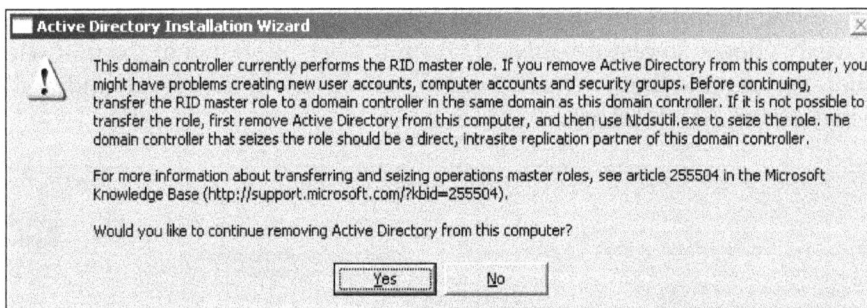

Refer to Chapter 3 for more information on the importance of FSMO, and how to seize FSMO roles. Make sure that you seize the FSMO roles after you have demoted the DC, or after you disconnect its network cable. Do not forget this though, as the FSMO roles are quite important.

As you can see in the following screenshot, the Active Directory wizard will now proceed to remove AD without updating the forest. This means that it will not replicate out its own data or changes.

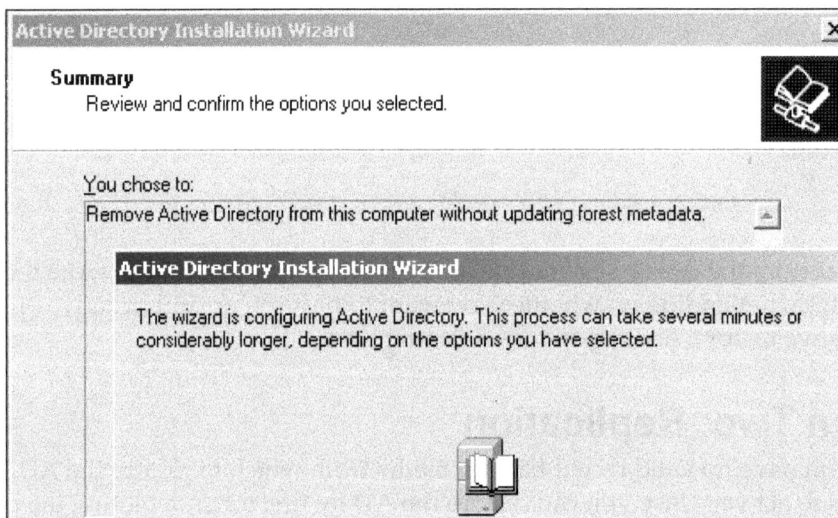

Once demoted, reboot the server, and follow the steps to remove its leftover information from AD as a DC, as described in Chapter 4. Then, verify whether the network connection is fully functional, and promote the DC again with the same name.

You should encounter no problems in completing the promotion. The AD will replicate to it during the next scheduled replication.

> If your AD is very large and contains many records or files, such as pictures in the user information, the replication to a "blank" DC will take a long time and stress your network quite heavily.

The replication option in a larger environment with a large dataset can take a long time if the other DC is either busy, or the replication link is not a very high-speed connection. The size of the AD databases can start from 1 GB and may run up to several gigabytes. If your DC has to replicate from a DC over a leased line, or an average consumer Internet class connection (2 to 8mbit), you may have to consider the other option of restoreing from a backup, or performing a non-authoritative restore.

# Option Three: Rebuild DC with Install from Media

Starting from Windows 2000 SP3, there is a **dcpromo** option available called "IFM" (install from media). This option adds a step to the DC promotion that will pre-populate the AD database on the promoted DC from a recent system state backup of a working DC, which is restored to a disk, CD or DVD.

IFM is the fastest option if you have to install, recover, or re-install a DC that is connected by only a slow link to its closest replication partner. As you are pre-populating the local AD, the replication changes it will get from its partner are much smaller, and therefore will replicate much faster.

To use IFM, restore the backup to the server BEFORE you make it a DC, and before you run **dcpromo**. A good way to do this, if you want to, or need to, restore several DCs with IFM, is to restore it to a network drive.. To prepare a backup and restore for IFM, please see Microsoft's Knowledge base article `http://support.microsoft.com/kb/311078`.

> IFM can only be used for additional DCs within a domain, not for the first DC. You can also only pre-populate, or restore a DC with a backup of the domain that you are building in.

A good option for this is to force-demote the DC, reboot it, and start it as a normal member server. You then need to clean up all of the records from the AD regarding the DC, and then perform an install from Media.

Restore the most recent backup to a separate directory, for example, `c:\restore`. This restore should be a restore of the System State of a DC, and the directory will contain sub-directories such as AD, Boot Files, Registry and so on.

Once the restore has succeeded, click on Start, Run, and enter **dcpromo /adv** as shown:

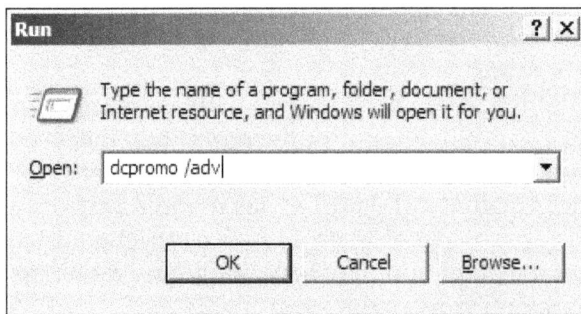

The **/adv** flag in the Dcpromo command gives you advanced options within Dcpromo, such as the install from media options.

Follow the dialog as you would normally do for a **dcpromo.** However, when you see the screen regarding Copying Domain Information, select the option: **From these restored backup files**, and navigate to and select the directory to which you restored the system state.

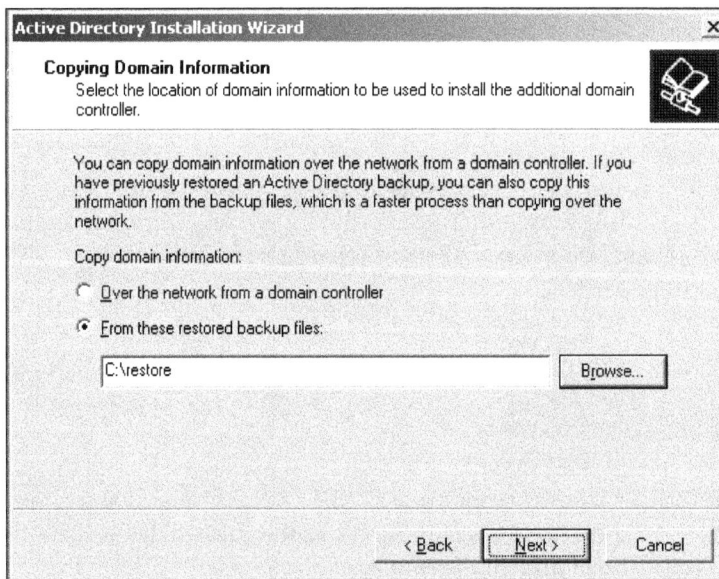

As you can see in this screenshot, you also have the option to pre-populate immediately from an existing DC. This is, of course, an option, but if your link is slow, or if your replication partner is busy serving other partners, it will be much slower than from media.

> **Not just for disaster recovery!**
>
> If you have to install several DCs for any reason, the **/adv** switch can save you the time spent waiting for the first replication, if you have a fast link, or a backup, that you can use to pre-populate.

When following the wizard, you will be asked if you want to make this DC a Global Catalog, and then you may be required to use an account with Administrator privileges in order to proceed with the **dcpromo**.

Once the **Dcpromo** wizard completes its task, and the AD records are copied from a previous backup, at the next replication only the changes since the last backup will be replicated. This saves a lot of bandwidth and time. This is especially useful for sites with a slow or saturated network connection, where replication would take far too long, so if you need to recover or install fast, this is probably your best bet.

# Summary

In this chapter, we looked at the recovery procedure in the event of a corruption or failure of the AD database on a single domain controller. This is a scenario that happens more frequently than one might expect. So, instead of "just re-installing", these options and procedures will help you get a healthy DC back in no time while limiting the amount of errors in the event log.

We also looked at some tools that will help you not only diagnose AD problems, but also allow you to perform, when used regularly, AD health tests to make sure your AD is always in perfect working order. This way, you might prevent failures because you might find the symptoms earlier.

# 6

# Recovery of a Single Failed Domain Controller

## Problems and Symptoms

In this chapter we will take a look at the steps necessary to completely recover from a failed domain controller. This could be either a hardware or a software failure. This scenario applies to a domain controller in your AD structure that is not bootable into a functioning state with a working Active Directory.

## Causes

This scenario can be caused by:

- A software problem in the form of a complete failure of the file system. One possibility could be a faulty driver.
- A complete hardware failure of the machine.
- Any other cause that even physically damages the machine to cause a non-functioning state.

## Solution Process

This process includes the following steps:

- You will need to clean the AD of all old objects that refer to the failed DC.
- You will need to clean all DNS records from the failed DC.

- You will also need to choose between different install or recovery options.

- Once the recovery is complete, you will need to verify that the DC is replicating and functioning properly.

# Solution Details

The process, aside from the restoration of Active Directory on your DC, also involves the deletion of the records in the AD of the previous domain controller. If the DNS records and objects related to the failed DC stay within AD, a lot of errors regarding replication may show up in the event logs. Sometimes, applications may fail if they have either cached or a specific domain controller information. The cleaning process should always be done. Generally, you should do this before starting the recovery in order to avoid the above-mentioned errors. However, in case of urgency, you can perform this step after you have a functioning system.

Please make sure that you write down the name of the old server, and do not give the new domain controller the same name unless it is necessary, for example, if you have an application that are that specific DC, and then only after the complete removal of all objects and records referencing that DC, and once the removal has replicated throughout your infrastructure. Because every object within the AD has its own security identifier (SID), this identifier is used as a reference many times in different areas, especially when it is a DC. If you reset the computer account and give the DC the same name, then the failed DC, all the replication links, and the AD references will still point to that account. Yet the new DC itself is using another SID and will not communicate, while other servers will also refuse to communicate with it. Dcpromo will exit with an error when trying to promote a server that has the same name if the AD has not been cleaned beforehand.

Please note that any of the steps related to the deletion of old records must be done from another functioning Domain Controller within the AD tree.

# Cleaning of Active Directory before Recovery Starts

Cleaning the AD is always needed if there was an unclean removal of a server. Unclean means that the normal Dcpromo way failed, or hasn't been run for reasons that cannot be fixed. The majority of this chapter will deal with this removal, simply because it is very important and necessary to understand.

To illustrate the steps necessary to recover a single DC failure, you can check this flowchart for guidance and visualization. It shows all the steps involved in recovering a single DC, and how to determine your course of action.

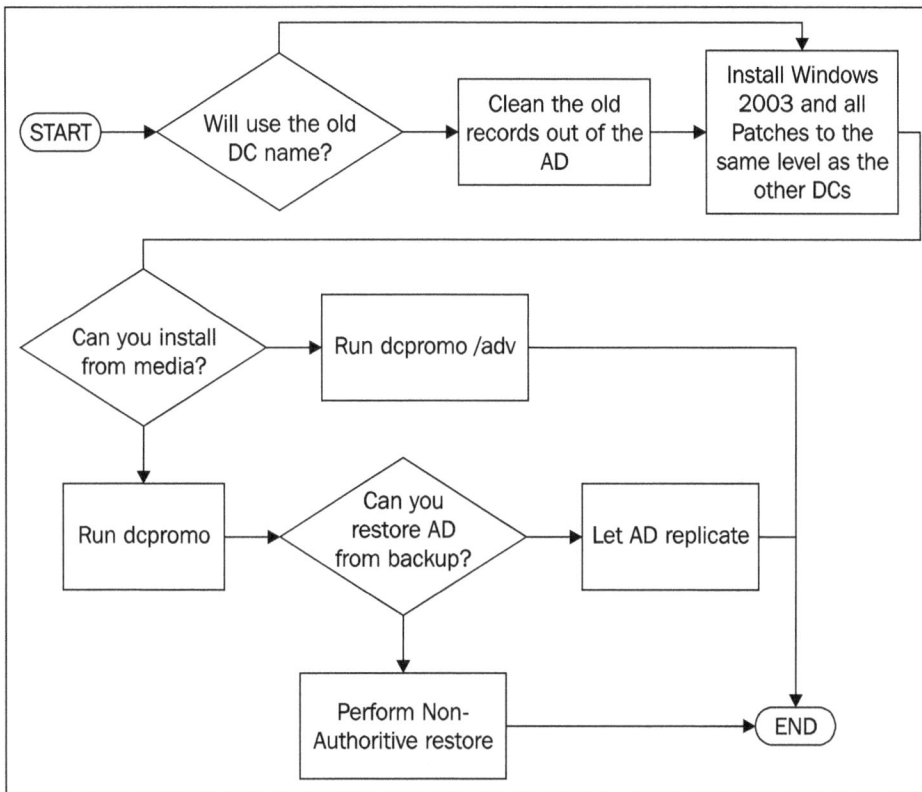

By referring to the flowchart, you can speed up the recovery, as you can see the course of action that you need to take. In case of a recovery where the DC will not have the same name as the failed machine, you can, for example, delay the deletion of the old records until you have completed the recovery. This buys you some time in situations where you might not have a failover DC in place.

## Active Directory Deletion of Old Domain Controller Records

Microsoft Knowledgebase articles outline the deletion of old AD records. However, these articles are sometimes unclear and not in-depth or well explained. The following description outlines the necessary steps clearly and includes information about what each step does.

Windows 2003 R2 makes the procedure a little shorter and easier than Windows 2003 RTM and Windows 2000. You can go through this procedure from any fully-functioning and normally-replicating DC within your domain. The procedure will accomplish the following things: XE "solution, failed domain controller recovery: old AD records, deletion steps"

- Removal of the NTDSA or NTDS setting subjects
- Removal of any incoming AD connection objects that are used by other DCs to replicate from the DC that is being removed
- Removal of the computer account of the failed DC
- Removal of the FRS (File Replication Services) Member object and the FRS Subscriber object, so that replication to and from the DC will no longer take place
- Trying to seize flexible single operations master roles (FSMO) that are held by the DC that is being removed

> Make sure you are at the console of a DC other than the one you are deleting.

The following steps are all done from the Windows command prompt (cmd.exe), and very little is done with any graphical tools. Please make sure you type the commands correctly because typographic errors can have severe consequences.

## Introducing ntdsutil.exe

This utility is one of the most valuable tools for low-level AD tasks, especially in disaster recovery.

Ntdsutil.exe is basically a maintenance utility for the AD database. Using a menu-driven interface, which is all command line-based and not exactly intuitive or user friendly, it allows you to perform very complex tasks within the AD structure. These tasks include managing the FSMO roles and being able to seize or transfer them, creating application partitions, and, of course, removing metadata within the AD that is still left from a DC that either did not get demoted properly, or has failed.

Ntdsutil.exe has undergone many feature enhancements since its introduction in Windows 2000. The latest version ships with Windows 2003 Service Pack 1 (for more information on the older version of ntdsutil.exe, see http://www.microsoft.com/technet/prodtechnol/windows2000serv/reskit/distrib/dsfl_utl_nzzw.mspx?mfr=true, and for some of the changes present in the enhanced version of ntdsutil.exe please see http://technet2.microsoft.com/windowsserver/en/library/819bea8b-3889-4479-850f-1f031087693d1033.mspx?mfr=true).

> 📝 When you use ntdsutil.exe, be aware that incorrect usage can result in a non-functioning AD. So please make sure you understand and follow each step correctly.

## Removal Procedure

In our NailCorp environment, which is illustrated in the following figure, assume that DC1 in the headquarters has failed and needs to be recovered.

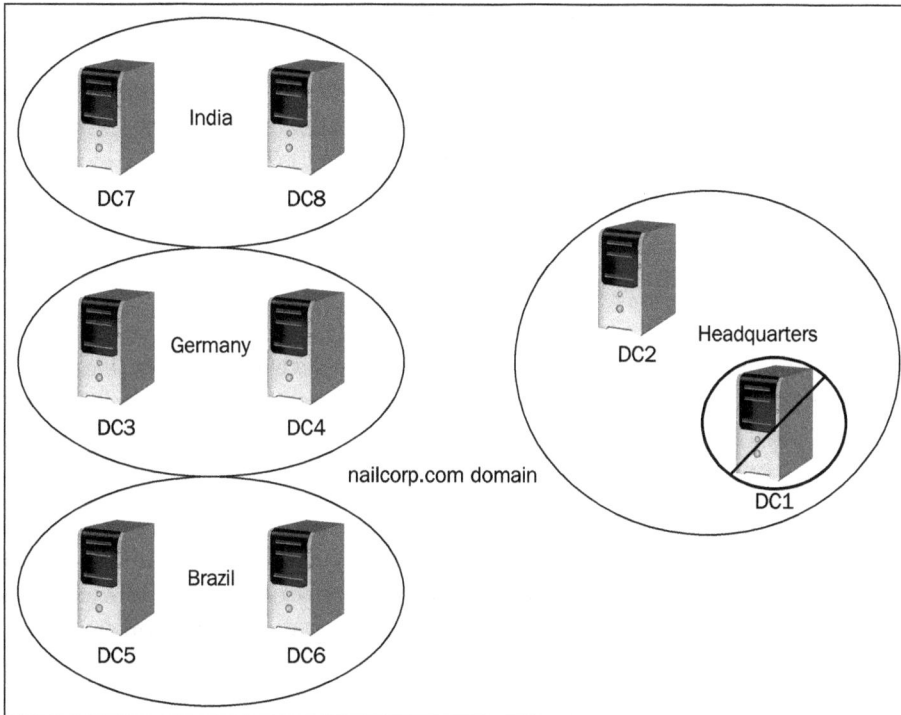

To begin with, you need to open a command prompt by going to Start | Run and typing **cmd** , and then pressing *Enter*.

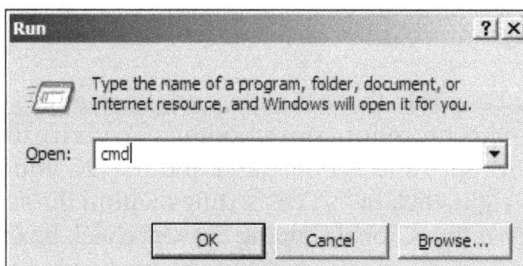

At the command prompt, type `ntdsutil`, and then press *Enter*. At the following prompt, type `metadata cleanup`, which will present you with the following screen:

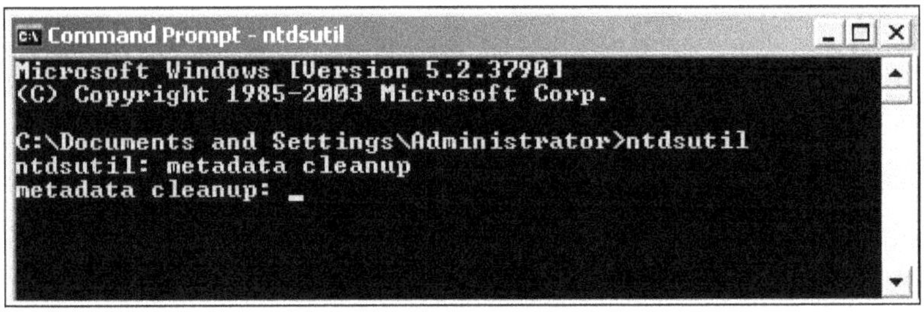

```
Command Prompt - ntdsutil                        _ □ ×

Microsoft Windows [Version 5.2.3790]
(C) Copyright 1985-2003 Microsoft Corp.

C:\Documents and Settings\Administrator>ntdsutil
ntdsutil: metadata cleanup
metadata cleanup: _
```

The metadata cleanup basically puts you in a really low-level maintenance mode within AD. Unless you understand what to do, your can cause a lot of damage with a few keystrokes, and could end up with a completely non-functioning AD.

At the metadata cleanup prompt, type `connections`, and press *Enter*. This option is used to connect to the specific server where the changes occur — which could be either the local server that you are working on, or another fully functional AD Domain Controller.

If you are logged in as a user who does not have administrative rights (Domain Admin), then you can change to a privileged user before going to connections by typing `set creds` *Domain\Username Password*, and then pressing *Enter*. If you have a null password, you can type *null* as a password.

Next, you need to connect to the server that you want to use. This server should be a Global Catalog server (GC), because it holds all of the information about all of the objects locally, and does not reference out to any other servers if needed. Although the recommendation is to have one GC per domain, because of replication overhead, many organizations make every DC a GC.

> If you try to connect to the same server that you want to delete, when you are actually deleting the record, later on in the process, you might get an error like this:
>
> Error 2094. The DSA Object cannot be deleted0x2094
>
> Therefore, it is necessary that these actions are carried out from another DC.

The DC should ideally be within the same site, and if not, at least within the same domain, to make this procedure run smoothly. To verify that you are on a GC, simply open the AD Sites and Services and find the DC you are working on within the sites. Then, right-click on NTDS Settings within the server, and choose **Properties**. You can see if the "Global Catalog Server" check box is selected as seen in the following screenshot:

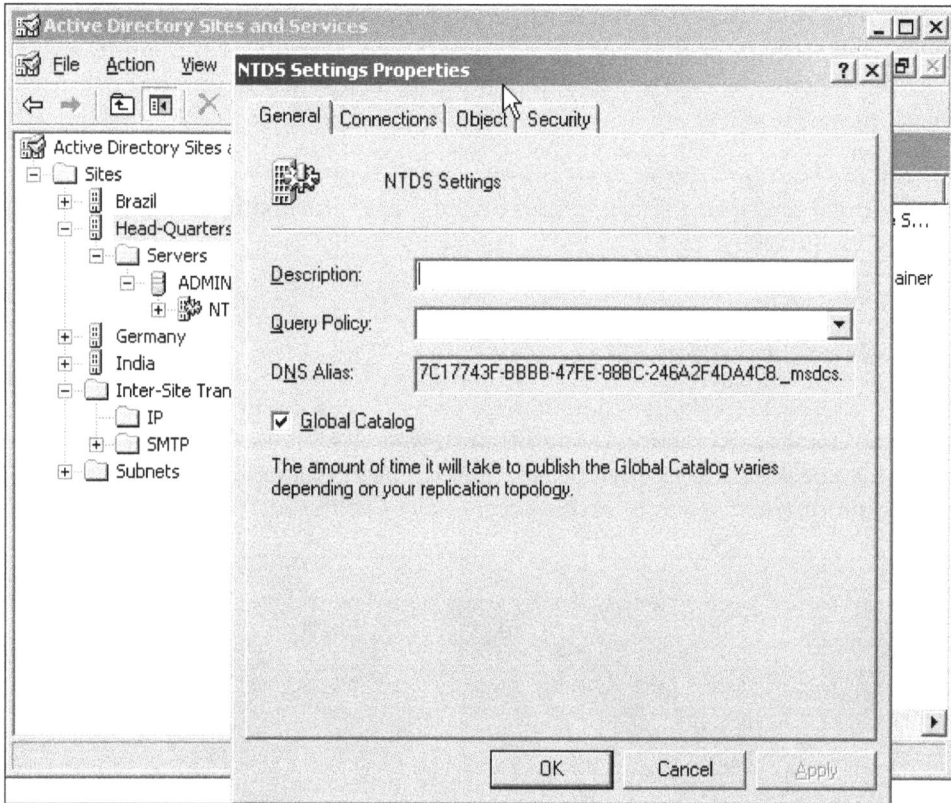

You can then proceed to connect to the DC by typing, `connect to server` *servername* (where *servername* refers to the GC you are connecting to) and then pressing *Enter*. In our example of nailcorp.com, this would be dc2. You can perform this from the actual DC you are connecting to, such as dc2. Also worth noting here is that even though you are running ntdsutil locally on a machine, you can execute and run commands and actions on a different machine.

You should then receive confirmation that the connection has been successfully established. If an error occurs, verify that the domain controller being used in the connection is available, and that the credentials you supplied have administrative permissions on the server.

When you are bound to the server, once you get the command prompt without errors, type *quit* and then press *Enter*, so that you are returned to the metadata cleanup menu interface.

At the prompt, type:

```
>select operation target
```

This will pass you to the state where you can select the domain to which you want to make the changes. At the following prompt, type `list domains` and press *Enter*. You will then be presented with a list of domains in the forest. Each domain has an associated number by which it can be selected and identified.

```
Command Prompt - ntdsutil                                          _ □ ×
Microsoft Windows [Version 5.2.3790]
(C) Copyright 1985-2003 Microsoft Corp.

C:\Documents and Settings\Administrator.NAILCORP>ntdsutil
ntdsutil: metadata cleanup
metadata cleanup: connections
server connections: connect to server dc2
Binding to dc2 ...
Connected to dc2 using credentials of locally logged on user.
server connections: quit
metadata cleanup: select operation target
select operation target: list domains
Found 1 domain(s)
0 - DC=nailcorp,DC=com
select operation target:
```

Now, type `select domain` *number* at the prompt, and press *Enter*. In this case, *number* is the number associated with the domain of which the server you are removing is a member. This means that if the failed server is, in our case, nailcorp. com, then that is the domain to which you need to connect. So the number would be the number associated with nailcorp.com. The domain you select is used to determine whether the server being removed is the last domain controller of that domain. If it is, then ntdsutil will perform additional cleanups such as the deletion of records and trusts pointing to other domains, such as the one from which you are now connecting. If the failed server is the last one in the domain, it is obvious that you are in a domain that has a trust relationship. However, this is a very dangerous step as it results in the complete deletion of your domain. So unless you are absolutely sure you want to delete all references to it, don't do this!

You are now connected to the domain that you want to work with. You now need to select the site where your failed DC is located. As you will notice, the whole process is fairly logical, and follows the same hierarchy that you have in your AD:

- Connect to the domain (or root domain).
- Connect to the domain that the failed DC is a member of.
- Connect to the site where the DC is located.

This is just as hierarchical as it is in the Sites and Services tool, but you can perform more low level operations using this utility than you can with the GUI.

At your current prompt, type `list sites` and press *Enter*. A list of sites, each with an associated number, appears. The same principle with the numbers is in effect as with the domain selection.

Now, type `select site` *number* and press *Enter*, where *number* is the number associated with the of which that the server you are removing is a member. You should receive a confirmation, listing the site and the domain that you chose.

```
Command Prompt - ntdsutil                                                    _ □ ×

(C) Copyright 1985-2003 Microsoft Corp.

C:\Documents and Settings\Administrator.NAILCORP>ntdsutil
ntdsutil: metadata cleanup
metadata cleanup: connections
server connections: connect to server dc2
Binding to dc2 ...
Connected to dc2 using credentials of locally logged on user.
server connections: quit
metadata cleanup: select operation target
select operation target: list domains
Found 1 domain(s)
0 - DC=nailcorp,DC=com
select operation target: select domain 0
No current site
Domain - DC=nailcorp,DC=com
No current server
No current Naming Context
select operation target: list sites
Found 4 site(s)
0 - CN=Head-Quarters,CN=Sites,CN=Configuration,DC=nailcorp,DC=com
1 - CN=India,CN=Sites,CN=Configuration,DC=nailcorp,DC=com
2 - CN=Germany,CN=Sites,CN=Configuration,DC=nailcorp,DC=com
3 - CN=Brazil,CN=Sites,CN=Configuration,DC=nailcorp,DC=com
select operation target:
```

At the prompt, you need to perform the next logical step, which is listing the servers in the site, just to verify that you are actually in the site that you want to be in, and that the server in question is listed. To do this, type `list servers in site` and press *Enter*. A list of servers in the site, each with an associated number, is displayed.

Type `select server` *number*, where *number* is the number associated with the server that you want to remove. You will receive a confirmation listing the selected server, its Domain Name System (DNS) host name, and the location of the server's computer account that you want to remove.

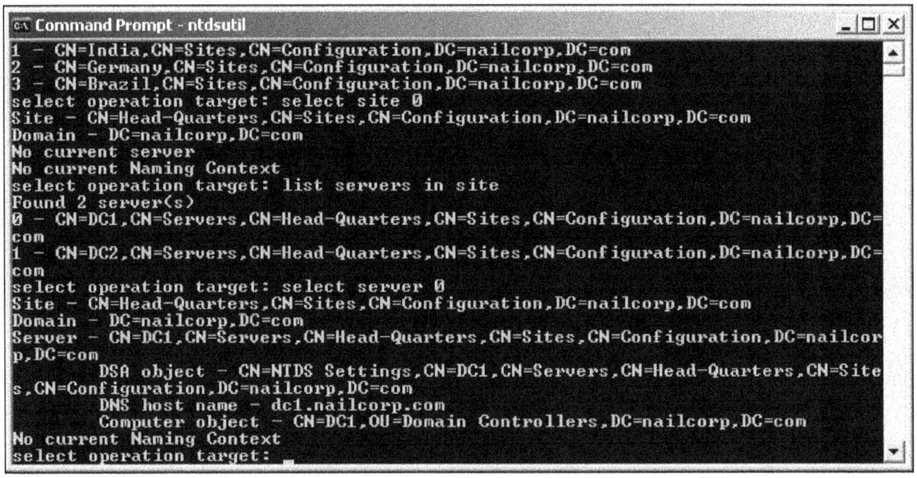

You have now selected the server that you want to delete, and that server listing is now saved in ntdsutil's memory. You now need to type `quit`, and press *Enter* to return to the metadata cleanup interface.

Finally, you are at the step where you can remove the selected server. Type `remove selected server`, and press *Enter*. This action will prompt you with a pop up, to confirm that you are aware of what you are about to do, as shown in the following screenshot:

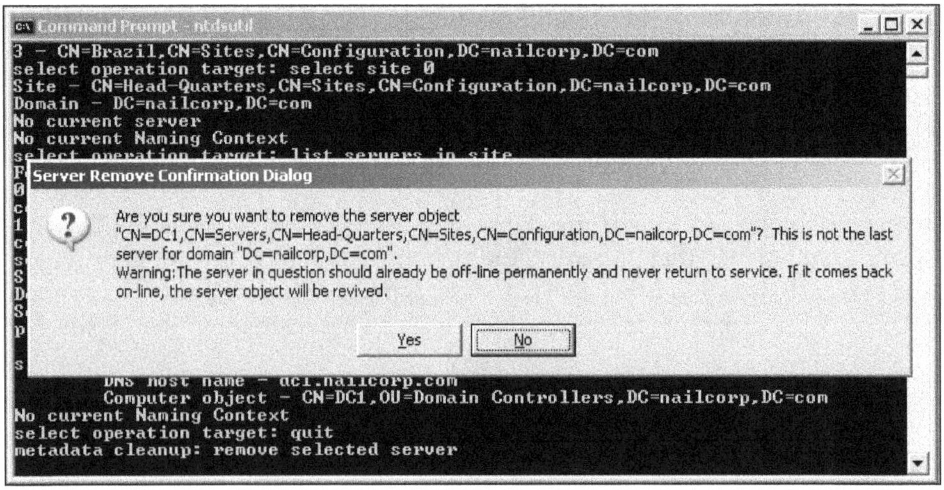

Confirm the action, and ntdsutil will try to seize the FSMO roles hosted by the failed DC. Should there be such roles, ntdsutil will prompt you again to make sure you want to seize the roles to the current DC, as shown in the following screenshot. You will be prompted for confirmation for each role that it tries to seize, and this could take a few minutes.

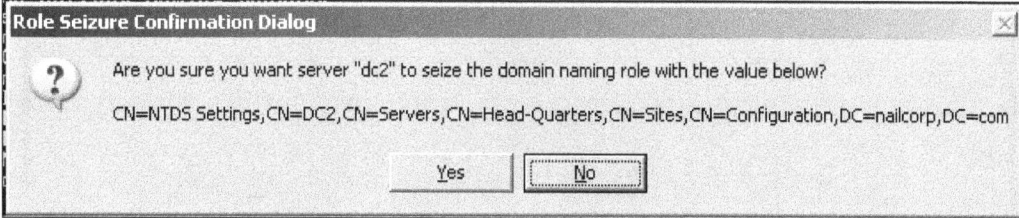

You should now receive confirmation that the removal was completed successfully with output similar to the example shown here:

Type `quit` at each interface to quit the ntdsutil utility. You should receive a final confirmation that the connection was successfully disconnected. You will now be returned to the normal Windows command prompt.

You can now close the command prompt, either by typing `exit` or by clicking on the X in the upper-right corner of the window.

### Windows 2000 Server and Windows Server 2003 RTM (pre-Service Pack 1) Additional Steps

In order to perform the following steps, you need to have the ADSIedit utility installed. This can be installed via the support tools package on the Install ation media. Once you have installed the support tools, you can run ADSIedit by typing in `adsiedit.msc` at the Start | Run prompt and clicking **OK**.

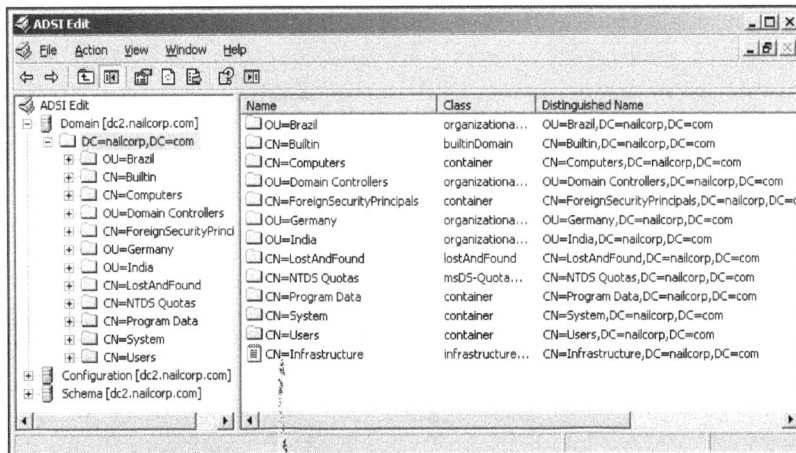

### First Part: Remove the Computer Account

Open **ADSI Edit** and expand the **Domain** section; then select your domain name (in our example, **DC=nailcorp, DC=com**) and expand that. Next, open **OU=Domain Controllers** and right-click on the DC that you want to **Delete**. Select delete from the menu, and then navigate back to your domain name.

### Second Part: Remove the File Replication Subscriber (FRS) Object

Navigate to your domain again, and expand **CN=System**; then expand **CN= File Replication Service** and finally, within that, expand **CN=Domain System Volume** (SYSVOL Share). Right-click on the DC that you want to delete and click **Delete**. Navigate back to your domain name (in our example, **DC=nailcorp,DC=com**) and close **ADSI Edit**.

# DNS and Graphical Actions Needed to Complete the Process

We have now successfully removed the metadata information from the AD database.

Use AD Sites and Services to remove the domain controller. To do this, follow these steps:

1. Start **Active Directory Sites and Services** from Administrative tools.

2. Expand **Sites**.

3. Expand the server's site. The default site is Default-First-Site-Name.

4. Expand **Server**.

5. Right-click on the domain controller, and then click **Delete**.

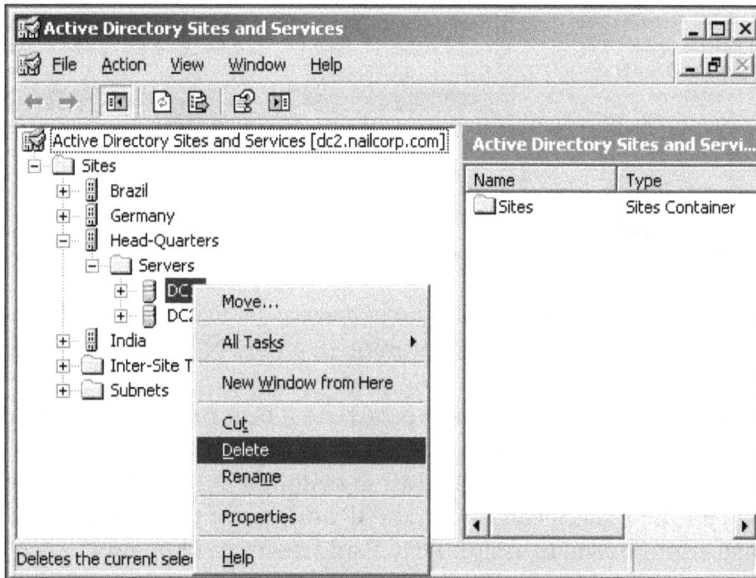

Next, use the DNS MMC (Administrative Tools—DNS) to delete the A record in the DNS. The A record is also known as the Host record. To delete this record, right-click on it, and then click **Delete**.

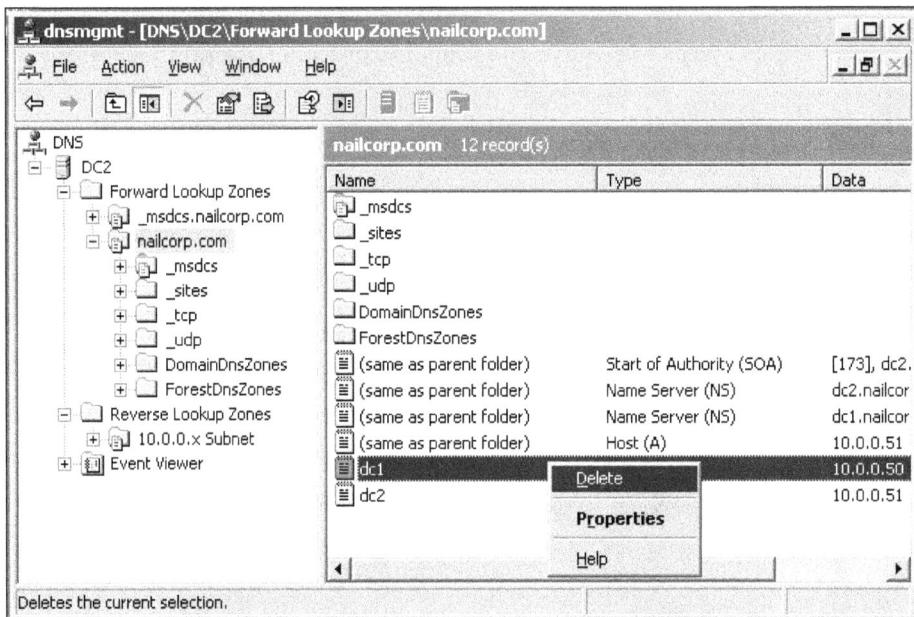

Remove the cname record in the _msdcs.*root domain of forest* zone in DNS. Assuming that the DC will be re-installed and re-promoted, a new NTDS Settings object is created with a new GUID and a matching cname record in the DNS. You do not want the DCs that exist to use the old cname record. As a best practice, you should delete the host name and all other DNS records. If the lease time that remains on Dynamic Host Configuration Protocol (DHCP) address assigned to the offline server is exceeded, then another client can obtain the IP address of the problem DC. Although some administrators choose to assign DHCP addresses to Domain Controllers, this is a very bad idea and should never be done. Every DC should always have a fixed and permanent IP address.

To do this, expand the **_msdcs** container, right-click on **cname**, and then click on **Delete**.

> If this is a DNS server, remove the reference to this DC under the **Name Servers** tab. To do this, in the DNS console, click on the domain name under **Forward Lookup Zones**, and then remove this server from the **Name Servers** tab.

Please make sure that you also remove the server from your reverse lookup zones. Reverse lookup zones are often omitted by administrators, because the administrators do not see the necessity in having them do not understand the need to have them. Although it might appear that they are not necessary, a lot of management features and under-the-hood operations within AD make use of them. Even though your AD can function without them, operations will function more smoothly and as per standards, when they are present. Reverse lookup zones are also necessary for sites to function properly within AD.

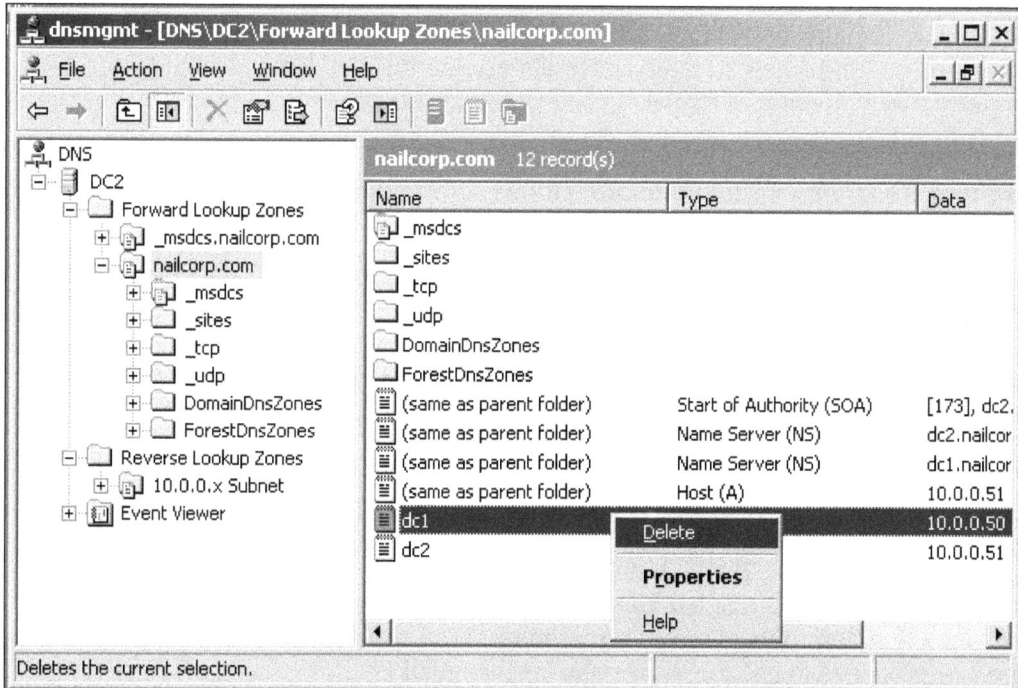

After the completion of these steps, all records of the old DC should have disappeared from the AD, and the new DC should be fully working.

This procedure might look rather daunting and long. In reality, however, this can be carried out in a matter of minutes, and the changes force-replicated throughout your infrastructure. To force-replicate easily, use Microsoft Support tools such as ReplMon, from the Windows 2003 Support tools, which allows you to not only force-replicate your AD to all of the DCs, but also to troubleshoot. By the time the new DC is installed and recovered, the replication of the old record removal should be far ahead of your installation, so you should not encounter any major issues.

To be sure, however, remove the records, and then on each major hub site, force a replication out to the child sites.

## Recovery of the Failed DC

The recovery at this point, that is after the removal of the reference objects and metadata, is a pretty standard Dcpromo, regardless of whether you choose to retain the old name. But please bear in mind that the computer account did get deleted from the AD. If you have a second DC in the same data center, the transfer of the database won't take that long. However, should you have a restoration from backup, or an install from media, your steps will vary. These steps will be addressed in subsequent chapters of this book.

Setting up domain controllers is out of the scope of this chapter, but the steps required to set up a new domain controller are identical to those normally required to setup a new domain controller in an existing domain.

This scenario applied to a DC that completely fails in an environment having at least one more DC from which to replicate. In this case, you need to clean the AD of the old DC, and then install a new one.

# Summary

In this chapter, we have elaborated on the steps to recover a completely failed DC. We have discussed the removal of the DC objects and the DNS records of the failed DC, and elaborated on why this is necessary.

Even though the removal of the old records may not appear to be very important, a part of this chapter explained in detail why the removal of old records is such an important step, and how it is done correctly. The recovery of a completely failed or broken DC is, as mentioned, a matter of installing a new one. The situation becomes trickier when, for political or other reasons such as applications that use specific servers, you need to use the same name as the failed DC.

By following the steps outlined in this chapter, you will end up with an AD that is clean, as though the old DC had never existed.

# 7
# Recovery of Lost or Deleted Users and Objects

One very common issue that occurs time and again is the accidental deletion of User or Computer accounts or any other object within Active Directory. The overwhelming majority of these occurrences are caused by human error as in either writing a wrong script or clicking the wrong button too fast.

In this chapter, we will go through the different methods of restoring these deleted objects, and will also look at how to minimize the impact that such a deletion can have on your business.

## Problems and Symptoms

Due to erroneous actions, one or more objects within the AD have been deleted. This can include User and Computer Accounts, OUs, printers, and so on.

A really big headache can happen If you have a lot of sub-OUs (OUs that are part of a parent OU) and the parent gets deleted by accident, this can cause a big headache.

## Causes

This scenario is usually caused by one of the following:

- User error, accidental deletion
- Software that deletes objects, and deletes more than it should
- Scripting mistakes

# Solution Process

The process of recovering deleted objects, including their group memberships, is very complex, and differs between operating systems. There are several methods available to do this, but in order to fully understand why these methods are so complex, we need to understand a little more about AD and its way of storing and deleting data and objects.

## Phantom Objects

Phantom objects are objects within your AD that you cannot view through any AD viewer or LDAP query. They are created more as low-level tracking objects than anything else, within the AD database.

Phantoms are created when, for example, you add a user from another domain to a group within nailcorp.com. Because since the AD needs to know to where it should reference the object, a phantom object is automatically created, which serves as kind of a forward link towards the object in the other domain. Put simply, they are object reference objects that are automatically created by AD. For more in-depth information regarding Phantom Objects, please see Microsoft's knowledgebase article 248047 at: `http://support.microsoft.com/kb/248047` and Microsoft's Technet article here: `http://www.microsoft.com/technet/prodtechnol/ windows2000serv/reskit/distrib/dsbg_dat_dstm.mspx?mfr=true`.

## Tombstones

When an object is deleted, it does not actually get deleted immediately. Instead, most of its attributes are cleared out, "(esc)DEL:GUID" gets added to its Distinguished Name (DN), and it is moved into a hidden area called DeletedObjects for a specific amount of time before it is completely deleted out from the AD.

This is called making the object a tombstone, which is a good analogy as it relates very closely to real life. Having a tombstone in a cemetery tells us that a certain person of a certain name is buried there; it does not, however, tell us about their other attributes such as the person's hair color or which clubs the person was a member of during their life. The process that takes place when you delete an object in AD is exactly the same.

You might wonder why we can't have an immediate deletion instead. This is because of the de-centralized, or multi-master, design of AD. If an object is deleted on a DC (say, DC1), then that object and all its references would be completely wiped out of the database. On the next replication, another DC, say DC2, will still have the object that has already been fully deleted, and will not know what to do with it because there are no longer any references to it in your AD database. But on DC2, the references still exist locally — they are called lingering objects. However, if the object is moved to the DeletedObjects and cleared of all attributes, every DC will understand the action and follow suit. Then, the process of clearing the object out later on is automated again, and every DC knows the time limit.

This limit is called a tombstone lifetime (TSL), which is 60 days, by default, in Windows 2000 and 2003 pre Service Pack 1. In Windows 2003 post Service Pack1 and R2, the tombstone lifetime is 180 days.

One word of caution here — if you have upgraded your AD infrastructure from Windows 2000 or Windows 2003 RTM to post-SP1 or R2, then the tombstone lifetime will not automatically increase. You will have to do this manually.

There are different aspects to be considered before deciding whether the tombstone lifetime should be increased or not. A good reason to increase it would be to provide greater flexibility to remote offices that have disconnects for longer time periods, where backup replication over slower lines is not possible. Another good reason to do so would be if you had a de-centralized AD infrastructure, or only allowed DCs to be pre-installed at a certain location, in which case the shipment of that DC to its destination can under some circumstances, exceed the TSL.

On the other hand, to increase the TSL might not be a good idea in an environment with a lot of -user account turnover-. This, for example, includes test environments and short-term contractor authentication. Having tombstone objects a TSL of 180 days can increase the size of your AD database, because the tombstone objects are still kept. In high-volume AD environments, the defaults should be enough, provided that all DCs are connected by quite stable and reliable WAN connections.

To read more about tombstones and the tombstone lifetime, you can check Ulf Simon Weidner's site at `http://msmvps.com/blogs/ulfbsimonweidner/archive/2005/10/29/73552.aspx` and this Windows IT article: `http://windowsitpro.com/article/articleid/41576/ad-tombstone-objects.html`.

# Increase the Tombstone Lifetime

To manually increase the tombstone lifetime, use the ADSI Edit tool. This is installed when you install the Support tools, located on your install media in the folder called **SUPPORT**. To start ADSI Edit, run `adsiedit.msc` from the **Run** command in the **Start** menu.

Once loaded, you will need to expand the configuration section, and within it, the **CN=Configuration** of your Root Domain. There, expand the **CN=Services**, and then **CN=Windows NT**. You will see a **CN=Directory Service**, and on that folder, you need to right click and select **Properties**. You will be see a dialog box containing a long list of attributes. Scroll down to **tombstoneLifetime**, select it and then click on **Edit**. Change this to **180** and click on **OK** and then **OK** again. That's it! The tombstone lifetime is now set to 180 days. The following screenshot shows the expansion and the properties window:

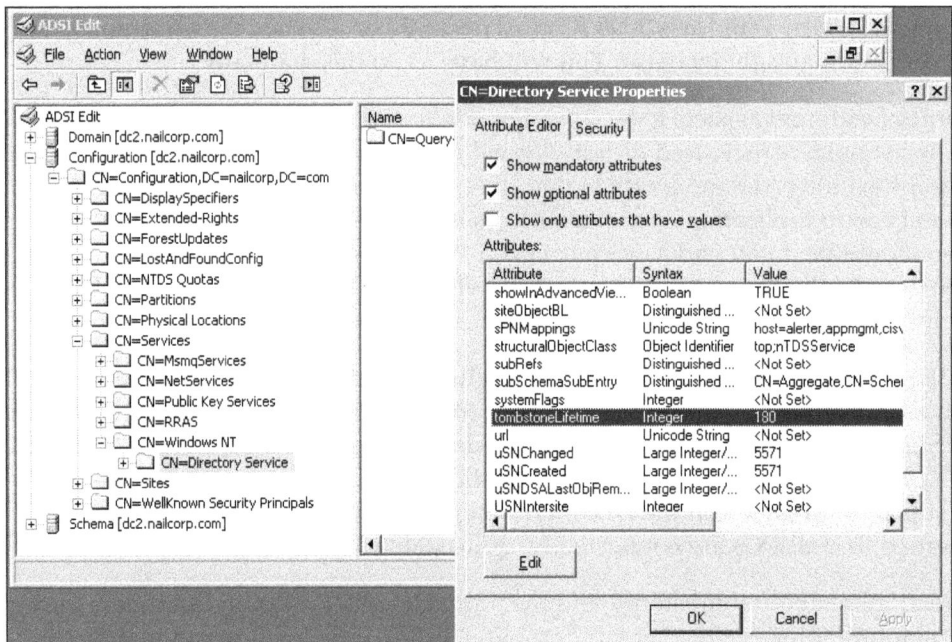

For Windows 2000 Servers, the ADSI Edit tool is slightly different.

You need to expand the same folders and also right click on the **CN=Directory Service** to get to the properties. Once there, you will find different tabs, from which you need to select the **Attribute** tab. In the view that comes next, you need to select **Optional** and in the following window, click on **tombstoneLifetime**. Type **180** at the prompt and click on **Set**. Then click on **OK,** and you are done.

# Lingering Objects

If your AD is based purely on Windows Server 2003 R2, or the tombstone lifetime has already been increased to 180 days, the chance of lingering objects appearing in your AD is not high. If you have still on a tombstone lifetime of 60 days, then the chances of them occurring in your AD is higher.

There are many ways for lingering objects to occur, which range from clock shifting caused by a system battery failure to a prolonged downtime of a network link, and many others.

The reason why lingering objects appear is actually quite simple, but can be difficult complex to understand. To make this as simple as possible, we will look at two DCs, DC1 and DC2, that are replicating once a month. This is to make our example simpler. Now, these DCs replicate every 30 days and the tombstone lifetime is set for 60 days. Consider that on day 2, just a day after the replication, an object is deleted from DC1. The next replication is in 29 days, and for some reason, the link between the two DCs fails a day before the replication, and starts functioning again the day after. Now you have another 30 days, which, by the time the DCs replicate the next time, will be 59 days since the object was deleted. Should the next replication fail for whatever reason, the object will be permanently deleted from DC1. This means that all record of its existence is gone.

Now, the next time DC1 replicates with DC2, the object does not exist within the AD replication from DC1; but it does from DC2. DC2 will not know what to do with the object and neither does DC1. While neither can forcefully delete it, it will just be left as it is, without any references or pointers to it.

In other words, lingering objects are objects that have not only been deleted and moved to the Deleted Items container, but also deleted permanently from the AD. Neither of these changes has been replicated to a certain DC. If the DC has been offline for a longer period than the tombstone lifetime, then the situation we touched upon earlier actually occurs. An object exists that the AD does not know what to do with. Although it is quite unlikely that a DC is offline for 180 days (half of one year), it is not unheard of either, especially in smaller organizations where local IT staff are not always present, or in the event that the second DC in a site was turned off, or it failed for some reason, and when the replacement part arrived, it was turned back on. If this took more then two months and several employees were let go during that time, or a part of the organization was sold, then there will be a lot of lingering objects the next time that DC is booted.

Even though lingering objects can occur in an AD, they can be prevented. Even if you do have them, there are step-by-step guides available from Microsoft to how to remove them in Windows 2000 (`http://support.microsoft.com/kb/314282/`) and Windows 2003 post SP1 (`http://technet2.microsoft.com/windowsserver/en/library/77dbd146-f265-4d64-bdac-605ecbf1035f1033.mspx?mfr=true`).

In order to see if you have lingering objects, you can check the Event log for certain Event IDs. Although having lingering objects might not have any noticeable effects, they can cause problems for Exchange, or any application that might just try to access the object. If you want to check for Event IDs in your AD that show the presence of lingering objects, you should check for IDs 1084 (no such object on the server), 1388 (received an update for an object that should have been present, but was not), and 1311 (a domain controller replicated, and an expected object was not present). These indicate that there are lingering objects present in your forest.

To check if there are lingering objects, check for Event IDs 1862, 1863, 1864 (DC has not recently received replication information), 1311 (Knowledge Consistency Checker was not able to build a tree topology), and 2042 (too long since last replication with source server).

Other indications could be a user or group in the Global Address List in Exchange that causes errors in sending email. For a more technical description of phantoms, deleted objects, and lingering objects, please refer to the Microsoft article `http://support.microsoft.com/kb/248047`.

# Prerequisites

The process of restoring deleted users and objects in AD requires a recent and trusted backup. Effectively, a System State backup is needed for the processes outlined here. Almost all third-party backup applications can, and will, take System State backups. However, you can also use this with the backup application NTBackup, shipped with Windows Server 2003 and Windows 2000 Server. It can be found in the Program Menu, Accessories, and System Tools folder. Once Backup is started, you can easily select the System State for backup to either media, or even just a file, as shown in the following screenshot:

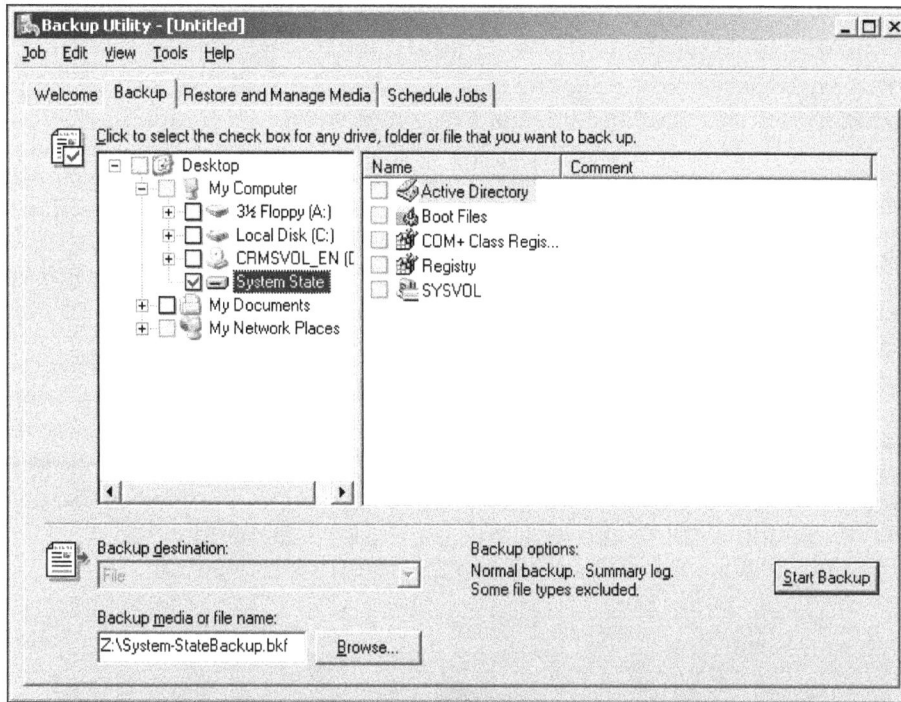

Whichever application you use, please make sure that you take regular System State backups that includes AD backups of DCs, especially Global Catalogs.

## Scenario

In nailcorp.com, the entire OU Brazil has been deleted by accident. In this case, we have a valid System State backup of DC1, and the Support tools have been installed. We will, however, go through all three methods of restoring the OU, including its objects and sub-OUs. Within that OU, there were several users including one Domain Admin account.

# Method One: Recovery of Deleted or Lost Objects with Enhanced NTDSutil

This method only works with DCs that are post-Windows 2003 Server Service Pack 1. As most of this book directed at post-SP1 releases of Windows 2003 Server, we will start with this.

In the previous versions, it was necessary, to restore the objects twice to restore their Group Memberships. We will see more of this later. With the enhanced ntdsutil, this is no longer necessary, and during the restore process, several files are generated that are used with various command line tools to complete the restoration.

For the first step, you need to either have a proper replication cycle in place so that there is a replication delay, or at least make sure that you know where the Global Catalogs are. Many companies choose to make all of their DCs Global Catalogs (GC), but the number that you have does not matter. The first thing to check for is if you can find a GC that has not replicated the deletion yet. A good approach is to check GCs that you know have a lower replication frequency than others.

The reason why we need a GC to do this is because only GCs house Group Memberships that are external to your domain. When you find a GC without the changes replicated yet, open a command prompt and disable inbound replication to prevent those changes from taking effect. In nailcorp.com, we want to disable inbound replication on DC2, and to do this we run the command `repadmin/options DC2 +DISABLE_INBOUND_REPL` as shown in the following screenshot:

The Repadmin switch is rather confusing because the + and – in front of the `DISABLE_` designate the flags to add or to remove. In this case, we are adding the flag of inbound replication that is disabled. With a – we would remove it again.

If you cannot find a GC that has not been replicated, from example because some time has already passed since the deletion, then you need to find a GC that will act as your recovery DC and proceed to execute the following steps from that machine. You need to find a System State backup of the GC that is just before the deletion, so that it still contains all of the deleted objects.

Next, you need to boot the DC into Directory Services Restore (DSR) mode. If you are unsure of how to do this, please check Chapter 5 for detailed instructions. When the DC is in DSR mode, perform a restore of the System State backup. Please make sure that you use the Advanced section to restore the junction point in the System State. This is necessary, as without it the restore is likely to fail. When running the

Restore Wizard, you will be asked some basic questions, and on the final screen you will see a button, **Advanced**. Click this, and then select **Overwrite the files on disk,** and click **Next**. There, you will find the junction point question as seen in the following screenshot:

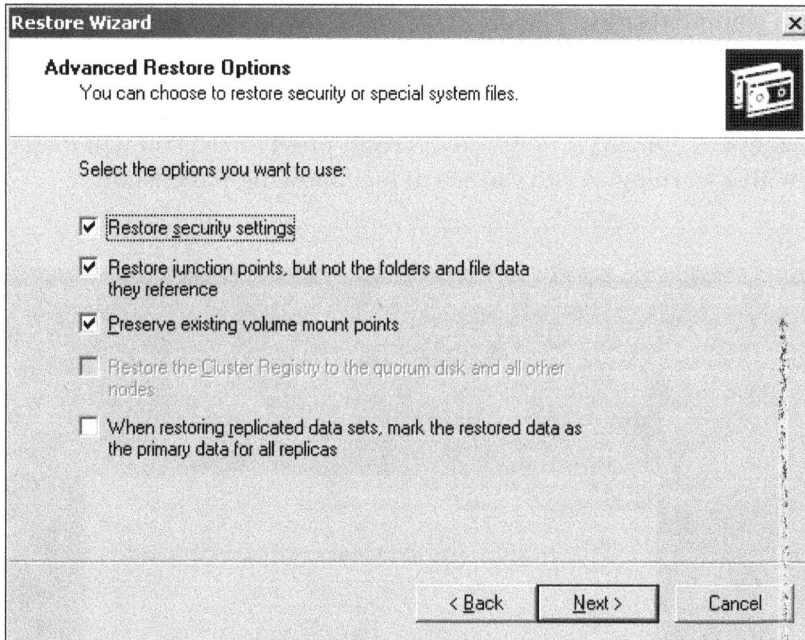

When you click on restore, a large amount of data, especially if you have a large organization, will be restored to its original location. When the restore is complete, do not reboot, but instead launch NTDSutil from the Start | Run menu. At this point, you have a non-authoritative restore, and if you reboot now your DC will be completely out of sync, especially as you have disabled inbound replication.

In NTDSutil, type `authoritative restore`, and press *Enter*. If you want to restore the whole database authoritatively, then you would just type `restore database` and press *Enter* again. This would make the AD database on this DC the highest-ranking one in the domain, and all other DCs would replicate the whole database from this machine. Of course, this could also cause a lot of issues, especially if this function is misused by someone who has domain administrator rights. This essentially marks the restored database as the primary source of replication. Any changes in this copy will be replicated to all the other DCs. So, if the person has a database version that he or she would like to restore, this would cause that database to be copied everywhere. If this is a malicious user, this can potentially wipe your AD database, or remove or introduce a lot of objects. This step is something that should be planned and supervised carefully.

The way NTDSutil works that will increase the version number of every single object in the database by 100,000. As everything has a version number that is much higher than all of the other AD databases, every DC will replicate the entire database. This is very bandwidth-consuming, and may not be something you would want to do simply because there might already have been bigger changes in other OUs than just the ones you want to restore.

To restore an entire subtree authoritatively, you need to be in the authoritative retore menu in NTDSutil. Once there, in the case of nailcorp.com, simply type `restore subtree ou=Brazil,dc=nailcorp,dc=com` and press *Enter*. You will then be prompted with a warning as you can see in the following screenshot:

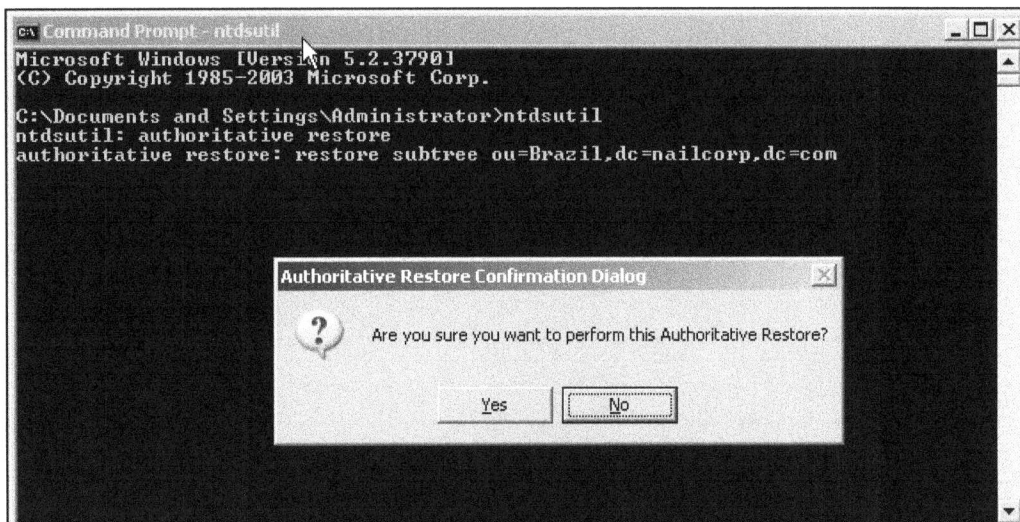

Click on **Yes** and you will be given information about text files that have been created, regarding backlinks and objects that have been authoritatively restored. The files are logs and the `.ldf` file can be used in other domains, where the user had access and was a member in local groups, to re-add them. This also has to be done from a DC in DSR mode in that domain. Now type quit and then quit again to exit NTDSutil. You now need to reboot the server without an active network connection, because the `+DISABLE_INBOUND_REPL` flag is cleared on reboot.

Once the DC has been booted in normal AD mode, type the Repadmin command to disable inbound replication and then connect the DC to the network again. At this point, you want to force the authoritatively restored objects to the rest of the forest. This can be accomplished with the Repadmin command followed by the `/syncall` flag, like this:

```
Repadmin /syncall DC1 /e /A /P
```

The flags here mean that you are replicating to the entire enterprise (/e); you are replicating all Directory Partitions (/A); and you are pushing the updates from your DC (/P).

After this has completed you need to verify whether the users have been restored everywhere, and whether they belong to their respective security groups.

The .ldf file that is generated by the authoritative restore is also used to recover security group memberships via backlinks. However, if your forest is at a Windows 2003 functional level, and only users and computers were deleted and not security groups or interim, then the restore rebuilds all of the users group memberships automatically, as you can see in the following screenshot.

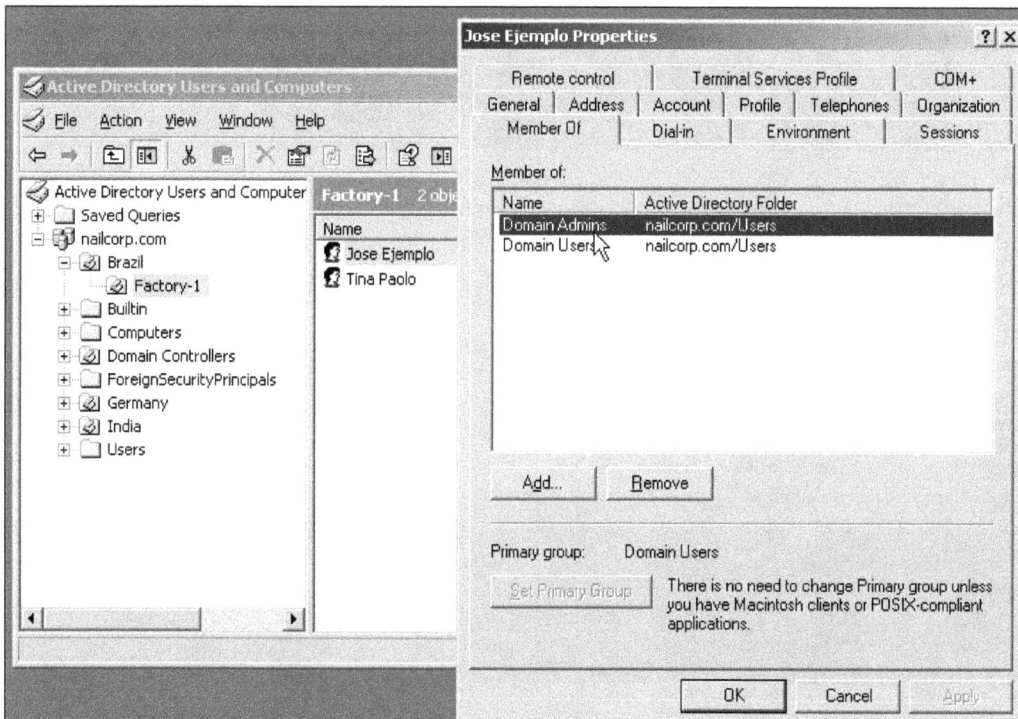

If you did not have any of these options, you will need to add these backlinks as well. This can be done from within the normal AD mode of a DC.

The .ldf files that were generated are in the same as the one that you used when you ran NTDSutil, most likely c:\Documents and Settings\USERNAME. They are named according to the date and time of the restore, so they are fairly unique, as a single restore takes more than a second.

To recover the security group memberships, of one or more restored users, simply open the command promt, and use the Ldifde utility, with the following command:

```
ldifde -I -f ar_XXXXXXXXXXX_links_nailcorp.com.ldf
```

This opens the LDAP directory editor (ldifde), and inserts (-i) data from a file (-f). In the nailcorp.com, example, two records were modified because these were within the restored OU, as you can see in the following screenshot.

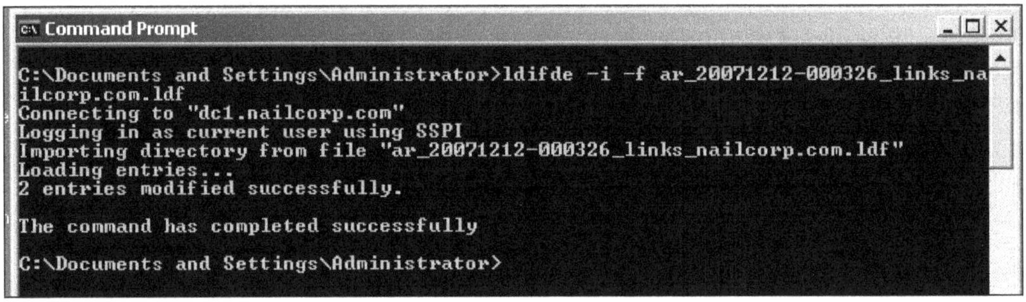

The last thing to do is to remove the restrictions on the inbound replication, so that the only flags left on the DC are is_GC. From the command prompt, type repadmin /options DC1 -DISABLE_INBOUND_REPL and press *Enter*.

Your replication will now work just as before, and will you have your security groups restored as well as all of your user accounts. The following screenshot shows the removal of the restriction.

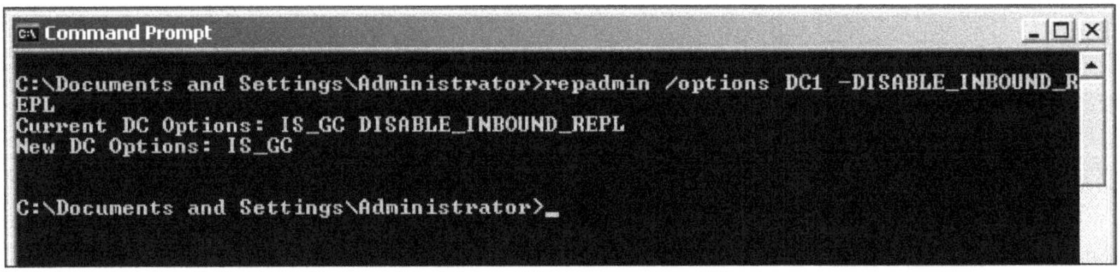

# Method Two: Recovery of Deleted or Lost Objects with Double Restore

Sometimes, the brute-force way of restoring is just as effective as using finesse and taking your time. If you are pushed for time and do not have many changed objects within an OU that you need to restore, or your forest is not on the Windows 2003 Server or interim functional level, then this way might be your best bet.

The problem with this method is that any change made to any security group memberships that were done to any of the users within that OU between the system state backup and the restore will be lost. This is because instead of modifying the security groups, you just go back in time to the previous state. In organizations that do not have much fluctuation in their security groups, this might not be a big issue. But in some large organizations, this can actually be a showstopper.

This method will work on any Windows Server version from 2000 onwards.

To start with, you need the System State backup. Next, you need to authoritatively restore the OU, as you did in the previous method, and then reboot the DC to replicate the authoritative restore outbound.

Next, repeat these steps. Reboot the DC into DSR mode, and again perform an authoritative restore but DO NOT restore the System State from backup. Just run the same NTDSutil commands again, exactly as you did after the restore of the System State had completed.

The reason you do this is because on the first authoritative restore, security memberships are not restored. However, on the second time, restore and take precedence over the already-replicated objects.

Once you reboot, force the replication out again and remove the inbound replication restriction. You have completed the restore! Although this is not suitable in many situations and for many organizations, for some, it is a viable and fairly quick recovery.

# Method Three: Recovery of Deleted or Lost Objects Done Manually

This is one of the procedures that you need to, or can do, if you do not have a valid System State backup at hand, or when a full restore is not really a valid option.

As we mentioned earlier, when an object is deleted, it is not permanently wiped but is instead moved to a hidden folder called `DeletedItems`. Because the folder cannot be seen through the usual tools to manage AD, it is rather difficult and complex to go into this folder and restore anything from it. There are third-party tools available, such as AdRestore, which is a free command-line tool by Mark Russinovich and was originally developed by Sysinternals (`http://www.microsoft.com/technet/sysinternals/utilities/AdRestore.mspx`). AdRestore, however, works only on Windows 2003 DCs and uses a Windows 2003 Server feature called undelete primitives. It uses these primitives to re-animate deleted objects without going through this whole process.

It is also worth noting that this procedure is only supported on a cleanly installed Windows 2003 DC, and not a DC upgraded from Windows 2000 Server. Windows 2003 Server post-SP1 includes the population of the sidHistory attribute. This attribute allows the re-animation, as the object's original SID can be read and restored from the sidHistory.

In order to complete this procedure, we will be using tools that come from the Microsoft Support tools, located on the install media.

To start the procedure, launch the utility `ldp.exe` by typing `ldp` in your Run option in your Start menu and clicking **OK**. This is a graphical utility and should look as shown in the following screenshot:

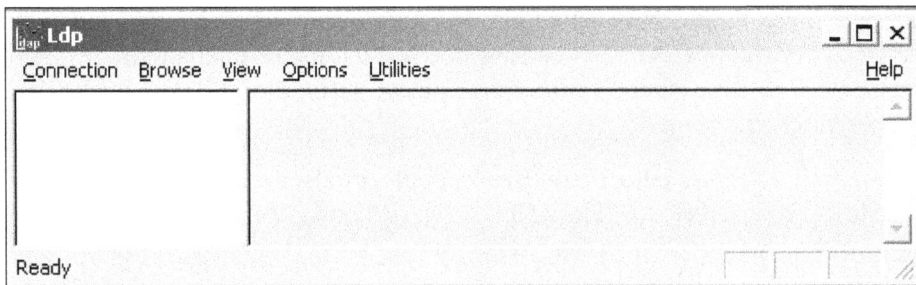

When the application is loaded, choose **Bind...** from the **Connections** menu, and enter the credentials of a domain administrator and click **OK**. You should see a lot of text regarding the LDAP authentication and then, in the end, a message indicating you have been authenticated as administrator, as shown in the following screenshot.

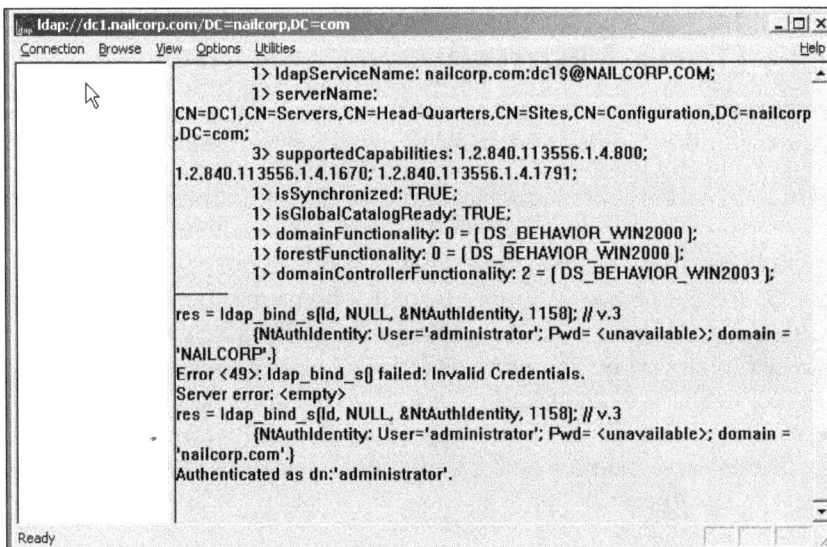

Once you are bound to the DC, go into the **Options** menu, and select **Controls**. In the **Load Predefined** drop-down box, you need to select **Return Deleted Objects.** Once you do so, a long number will be displayed in the Active Controls, which is **1.2.840.113556.1.4.417**. Also, make sure that the radio button in **Control Type** is selected for the **Server**. All these options can be seen in the following screenshot.

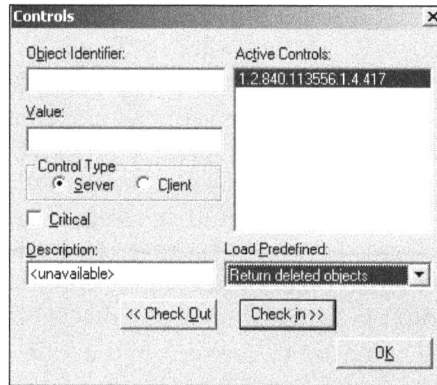

Now you can select the **View** menu and then click on **Tree**. You will be asked for a BaseDN, which is selectable from a drop-down box. Select the place where the deletion occurred. In our case, it happened in the nailcorp.com domain. So we need to add **cn=deleted Objects** to the **DC=nailcorp,DC=com** drop-down, and then click **OK**. You do not need to specify the OU in this because all objects move into a single deletedObjects folder within a domain.

Now, on the left hand most of the application, you will see a new item called **cn=deleted Objects,DC=nailcorp,DC=com,** as shown in the following screenshot.

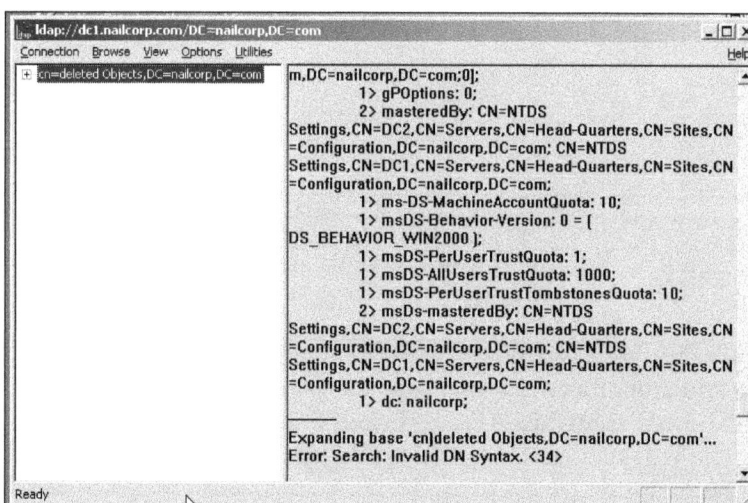

Expand the **deletedObjects** line and browse to the object you want to undelete. Right-click on the CN of the object, and select **Modify**. In our case, we will re-animate the Jose Ejemplo user. The **Modify** screen can be daunting at first, because you need to know the attributes to modify. However, it is fairly simple to use, as there are very few clicks to be made.

First, in the **Edit Entry** section, we type the attribute `isDeleted`, we leave the **Values**, we leave field empty. Next, we select the **Delete** option button in the **Operation** section. , and then click on **Enter**. Do not click on **Run** yet. Next, in the **Attribute** field, enter **distinguishedName**, and in the **Values** field, enter the full path of the location to where you want to restore the object. In our case, we want to restore the object into an OU called Factory-1 within the OU Brazil, both of which we specify. So, to restore the object, the **Value** field would be **cn=Jose Ejemplo,ou=Factory-1,ou=Brazil,dc=nailcorp,dc-com** where the **cn** specifies the name of the user. Before you click on **Enter**, make sure the **Operations** radio option is set to **Replace**. Next, you need to ensure that both the **Synchronous** and **check-boxes** are checked, before clicking on **Run**. The whole window can be seen in the following screenshot:

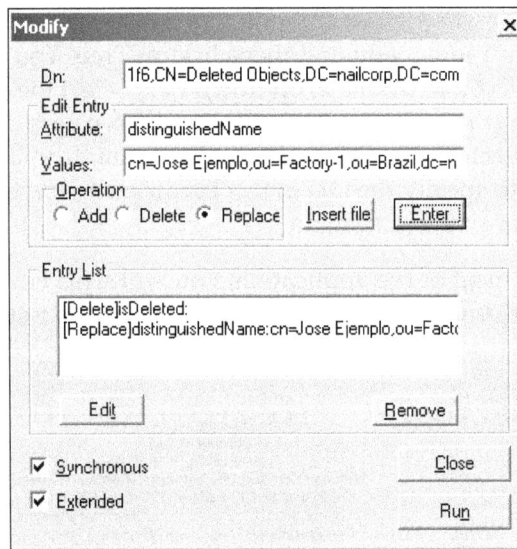

Once you click on **Run**, and the process is completed, click on the **Options** menu and then **Controls** again. In the resulting window, click on **Check out** and then **OK**.

Note that while the object is restored with the same SID as before, all group memberships and any other values besides the login account name, ObjectGUID, SID, and LastKnownParent, are gone and need to be re-added. If you run Exchange 2000 or later, you will also have to remove all Exchange attributes and reconnect the user to his or her mailbox.

This method is useful if only a couple of objects were deleted and you do not want to go through the whole restore process, especially if you have a large organization. However, re-animating many objects this way is very tedious.

# GPO Recovery

The last thing you need to do is, of course, restore the Group Policy Objects (GPO) that were applied to the OU that you just recovered. This is not covered by an authoritative restore. While GPOs are objects, they are not objects in the same way as other objects in the AD. To back up and recover GPOs, you will have to use the Group Policy Management Console (GPMC), which is a free download from Microsoft (`http://www.microsoft.com/downloads/details.aspx?FamilyID=0A6D4C24-8CBD-4B35-9272-DD3CBFC81887&displaylang=en`) and while writing this, was at Service Pack level 1. Essentially, the GPMC is just a MMC snap-in. In the following section, we will go through the essentials of how to back up and restore using GPMC.

## Backing Up Using the GPMC

Launch the GPMC, which can be found in the Administrative tools. Once launched, expand the forest and then the domains. Then, expand the domain in question (nailcorp.com, in our example), and then expand **Group Policy Objects,** as shown in the following screenshot.

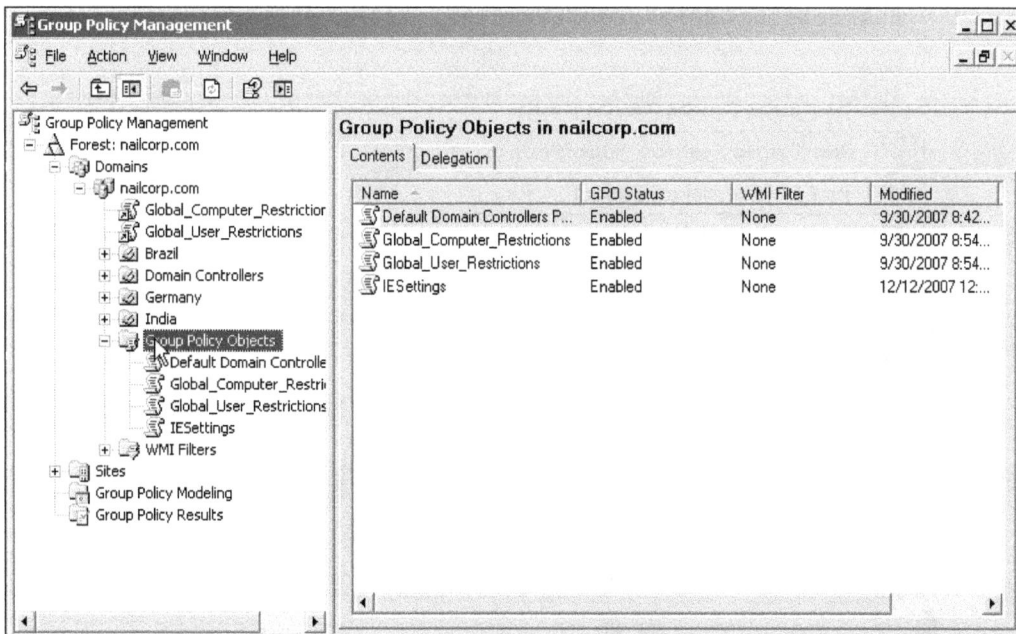

You will see all of the GPOs within the domain listed in that container. NailCorp only has the IESettings that is non-standard and should be backed up. To do this, right-click on the GPO in question and select **Backup**. Or, to back them all up, right-click on the **Group Policy Objects** container and select **Back up all**. Both options can be seen in the following screenshots:

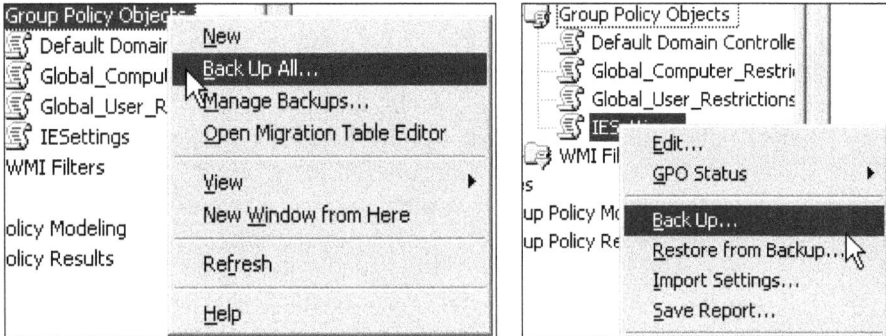

You will also need to provide a location on the file system, or networked drive, and a description for the backup. Then click on **Backup**. This might take a few minutes but a progress bar and a small report will be shown during execution, as shown in the following screenshot:

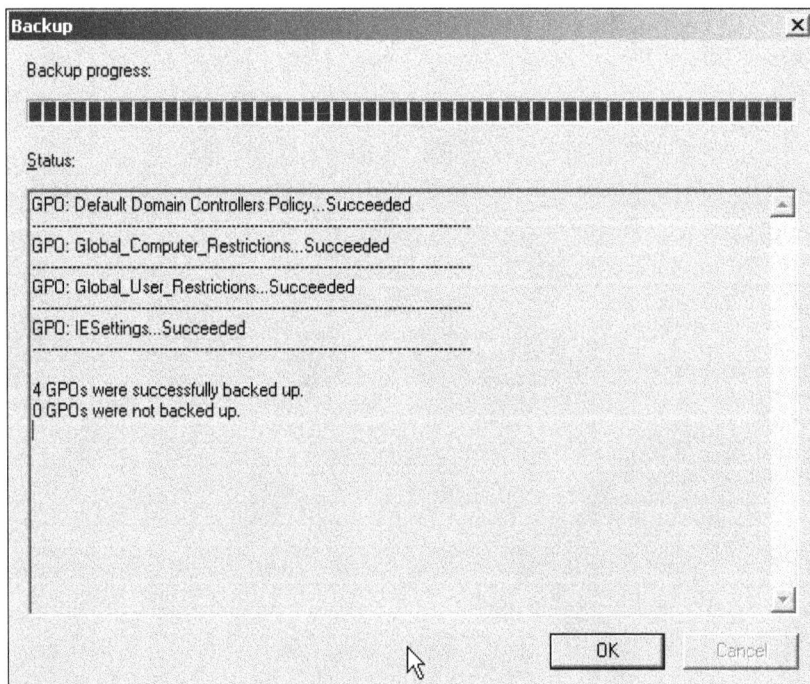

The backup, however, is just a folder for each GPO named after the GPO ID, containing several XML files. So if you have a lot of GPOs, these folders by themselves are pretty meaningless. However, they can be zipped up and backed up to tape, which is our primary objective.

# Restore Using the GPMC

To restore, or even just to move the GPOs between domains, you need to launch the GPMC again, and navigate to the same container, **Group Policy Objects**. Then, right-click on the container and select **Manage Backups.** In the resulting window, navigate to the folder where you restored your backed up policies. As soon as the GPMC notices that there are backed-up GPOs in the folder, it will display them in a much friendlier manner, though you can still see the cryptic GPO ID in the column on the right, as seen in the following screenshot:

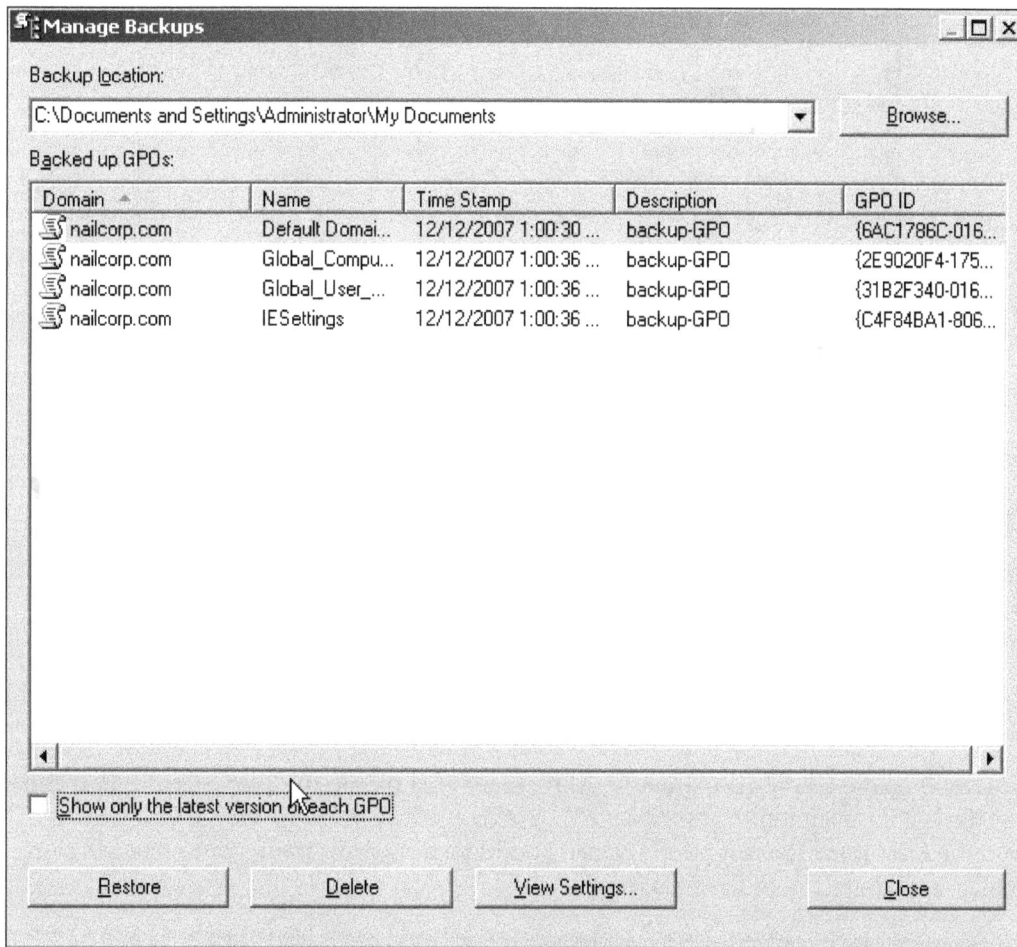

To restore the GPO that you want, simply click on it once, and then click on **Restore**. A pop-up will prompt you for your confirmation, and you have to select **OK**. The restore will progress, and then you will be passed back to the **Manage Backups** window, which you can then close. You will now have the restored GPO in the **Group Policy Objects.** However, it is not linked to where it was before. This has to be done manually. Simply right-click on the OU to which you want the GPO to be linked, and select **Link GPO**. All GPOs will listed, presented and you simply select the one you want to apply and click on **OK**. You can then close the GPMC, as your GPOs are also restored.

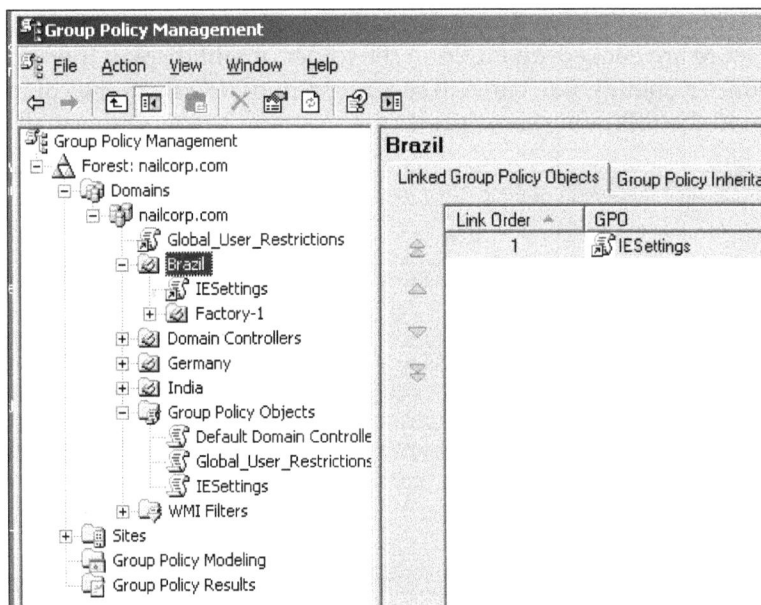

# If You do not have the GPMC...

Although the GPMC is a great tool, it is not installed everywhere. If you do not have it installed, you can still recover the old, deleted GPOs, by carrying out a quick, though not-so-simple a, procedure.

First, you need to restore the most recent backup of your AD to an alternate location. You also have to know the GUID number of the policy that you want to restore.

You then create a new GPO in your AD and leave it blank. In its properties, you can see the GUID assigned to this new GPO. Next, you will need to reboot your server into the **Directory Restore** mode. Once you have done this, navigate to the following folder, and delete all of the files in it:

```
%SystemRoot%\Sysvol\Sysvol\DomainDirectory\Policies\{GUID}
```

where GUID is the number from the newly-created policy. Once the folder is empty, navigate to the folder to which you restored your backup of the AD, to locate this folder:

```
SysVol\C:\Windows\Sysvol\Domain\Policies
```

> This path will vary if you have don't have your system drive on C:.

Then locate the GUID of the policy you want to restore. Now, simply copy all of the files into the folder:

`%SystemRoot%\Sysvol\Sysvol\DomainDirectory\Policies\{GUID}`, where GUID is your GPO created earlier.

Restart your server and the GOP will now have all of the policy settings that you had lost. You can now apply it again to wherever it was applied before.

As this step is rather time consuming, consider using the GPMC instead.

# Summary

We went through an important process in this chapter, and one that is likely to come in handy for an Administrator. Understanding the way this process works is very important. By making regular System State backups, the battle is already half won. Although restoring deleted objects and users is possible, and not all that difficult once you know the right steps, it is important to be aware of one's actions within the AD. As mentioned at the beginning of this chapter, most user and object deletions are human errors, and we should look at mitigating this possibility, by providing better training, documentation, or access controls.

For further reading, Microsoft's Best Practises for managing Windows networks (`http://technet.microsoft.com/en-us/library/Bb727085.aspx`) is highly-recommended. It describes, in great detail, ways to prevent mass deletions from happening, and describes the tools or processes to be implemented in order to do this.

# 8

# Complete Active Directory Failure

## Scenario

Throughout your Active Directory (AD) forest, all DCs fail, giving error messages regarding the AD database failure or the inability of the DCs to load the AD database. As every DC is non-functional, though bootable, you cannot recover a single DC or a single site. You will have to rebuild your complete forest, and without much time-delay. This scenario has a major impact on the user and all other applications that rely on AD for authentication or service. For example, this includes HR and payroll applications.

## Causes

This scenario can be caused by the same reasons as those discussed in Chapter 7, such as a software problem, or human error. However, in this scenario, the replication has not been caught, and all the DCs are located at a single location. This is particularly possible in smaller organizations.

## Recovery Process

Recovering the entire AD forest involves restoring every DC in the forest. You will have to recover them either from a trusted backup, or by reinstalling AD using the Active Directory Installation Wizard. When you recover the forest, you effectively recover each and every domain in the forest back to the time at which the last trusted backup was performed. By doing this, you will lose any additions to the AD since that backup was taken, such as:

- All objects (users, computers, and so on) that were added since the last trusted backup.
- All updates made to existing objects since the last trusted backup.

Additionally, if we assume that all of the DCs in the forest no longer function correctly, any software applications that were running on the DCs will need to be reinstalled and configured, once the forest is recovered.

If there has been a corruption in the AD database and it was replicated out to the entire AD infrastructure, you cannot use any of the previously-described ation methods, because of the massive scale of the restoration effort.

> Forest recovery should always be the last resort, and should be approved by the Managers and Directors in charge, such as the CIO and CEO. Please be aware that this step will mean the loss of AD data that was created since the last known good backup, and that this procedure cannot be undone.

# Part One: Restore the First DC of Your Root or Primary Domain

The following steps need to be performed while the "recovery" machine is physically isolated (that is, its network cable is not attached, and therefore, it is not connected to the network, or it is located on a completely-isolated subnet). You could keep it connected to the network, but you need to be absolutely sure that all other DCs are offline. This is to ensure that there are no replications coming in or going out during this process. For an overview of the procedures that we will follow, please see the following flowchart. It might seem daunting at first, but when done correctly, it is the fastest way of recovery.

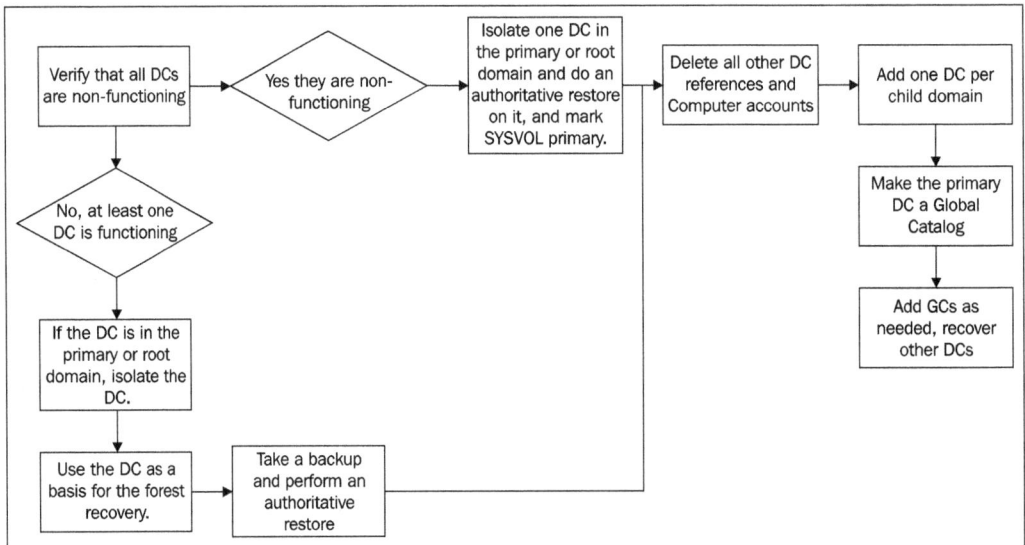

# Step One: Restoring the AD Data

While restoring AD, you first need to mark the SYSVOL, the primary dataset of the AD, because this is the first DC in the domain. There are different ways to do this. However this, but the quickest way is to do an authoritative restore on the DC and, if you are using NTBackup, go to the Advanced section, and select the option. When restoring replicated data sets, mark the restored data as primary for all replicas, as you can see in the following screenshot.

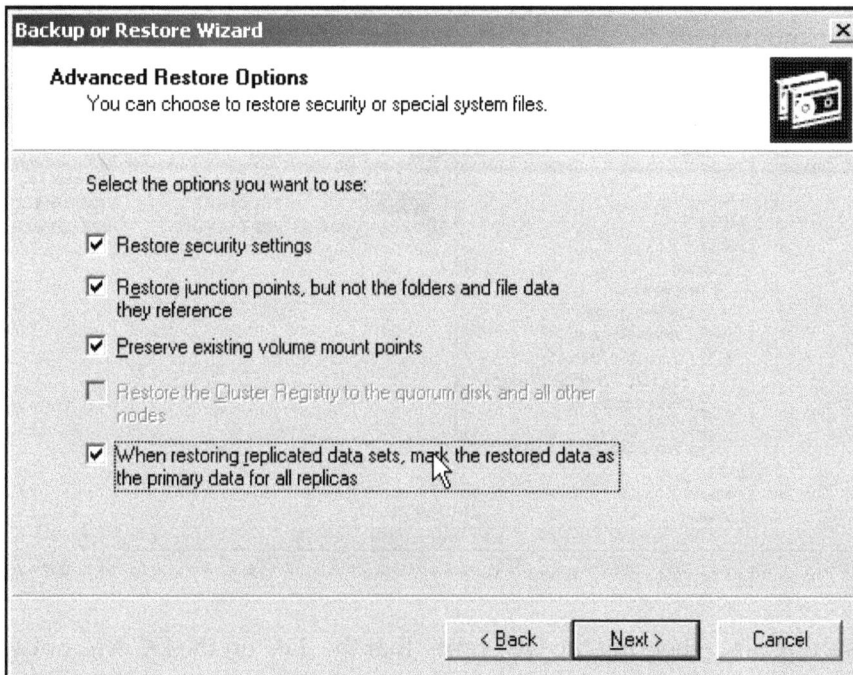

The other way is to change the BurFlags registry key located in `HKEY_LOCAL_`
`MACHINE\SYSTEM\CurrentControlSet\Services\NtFrs\Parameters\Cumulative`
`Replica Sets\[GUID]` to `D4`, as shown in the following screenshot. If you have
more then one GUID listed under the **Replica Sets** key, click on the GUID of each
domain, and look in the pane on the right to see where the **Replica Set** root points
to. This should then tell you which domain you are replicating. If you only have one
GUID, then it is very likely that your Replica Set root is in `C:\Windows\sysvol\`
`domain`, or wherever your Sysvol share is located. You can check and accomplish this
setting, and change it if necessary, by running regedit from the Run... command in
your command prompt.

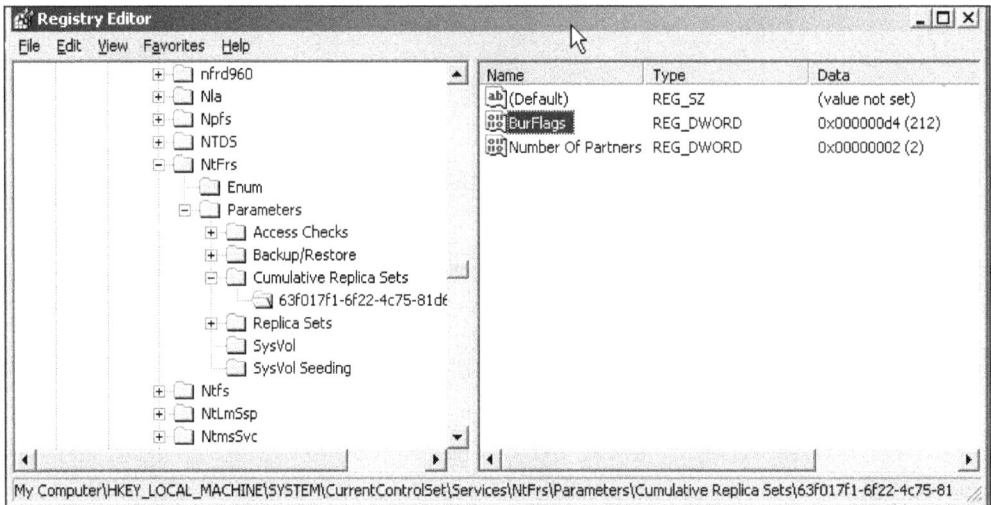

After restoring and rebooting the DC, verify that the data on the DC was not affected
by the failure, by performing AD users and computers lookup tests. Alternatively,
check that all the information is in AD and the JetDatabase works, which means that
there should be no error messages in the Event Log. If the data you are recovering
is damaged, or the DC shows errors in the Event Log and the AD cannot start, then
repeat the restore step using a different backup.

Continue to the next step only after restoring and verifying the data, and before
connecting this computer to the production network, where other malfunctioning
DCs might still be online. If you are sure that there aren't any other malfunctioning
DCs online, you can connect the recovered DC to the production network.

## Step Two: Recovering DNS Services

If you have DNS zones stored in AD, you need to ensure that the local DNS Server
service is installed and running on the DC that you have restored. If you have
dedicated DNS servers, you can skip this section.

The recovery DC should be configured with its own IP address as its preferred DNS server. This is configured in its TCP/IP properties as is visible in the following screenshot. This is necessary so that you can access and work with the DNS zone locally. It will then replicate, together with the rest of the AD data, out to the next recovered DCs. This DC is now the first DNS server in the forest.

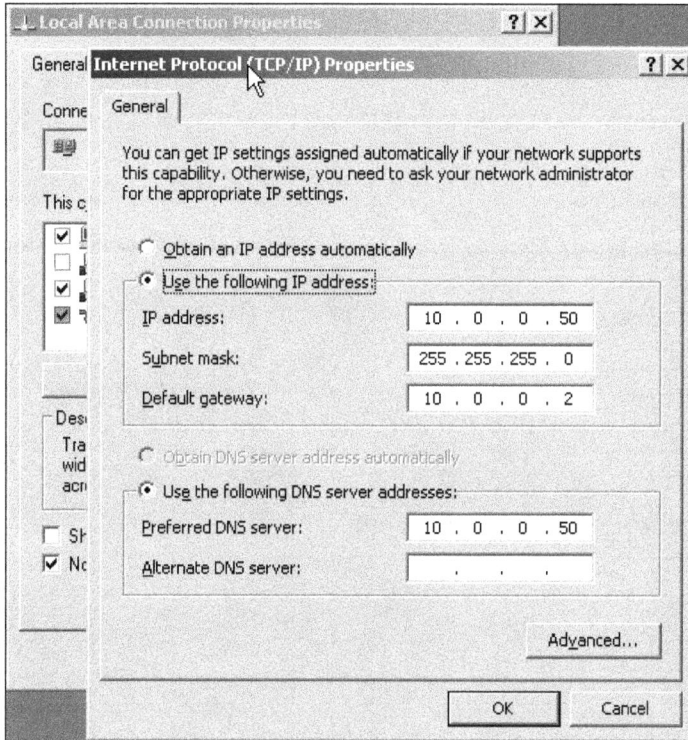

If this DC was not a DNS server prior to forest failure, you need to install the service. To do this, install it from the Control Panel's Add and Remove Program section, where it is located under Windows Components.

Once you have a DNS service running, you need to configure it as it was before. Create a new forward-lookup zone with the correct domain name, and then configure the settings for the zone. The recommended settings are that you allow secure updates only and that the zone is AD-integrated. Once the zone is configured as it was before, stop and start the Netlogon service from the command prompt, by executing the commands `net stop netlogon` and `net start netlogon`. This will register the required domain controller locator records for the DC with the DNS server, hence making it a working AD zone.

# Step Three: Changing Global Catalog Flags

If the restored DC is enabled as a global catalog, you need to disable this by un-checking the checkbox in AD's Sites and Services, as shown in the following screenshot:

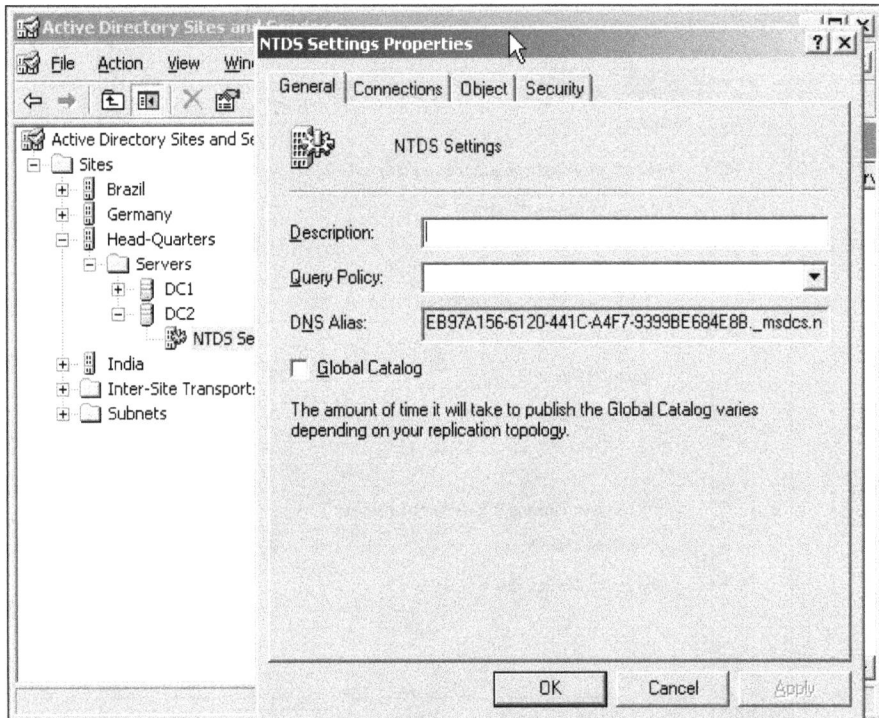

The reason why you need to uncheck **Global Catalog** (GC) is that if you are restoring a GC from a backup, this may result in the GC holding newer data for one of its partial replicas than the actual corresponding domain. This means that the GC may contain some newer data for a domain than the actual authoritative domain partition. In this case, the newer data would not be removed from the GC, and it could end up replicating to other GCs. For this reason, you should disable the GC flag immediately after you have restored the DC. When you remove the GC flag, the DC will remove, or delete, all of its partition replicas, and the DC will become just a regular DC. Once you have the GC flag removed, you should reboot the DC to ensure that the DC GC Store gets emptied, and then re-enable the GC flag to make it a GC once again.

# Step Four: Raise the RID Pool Value by 100,000

This step is necessary because, after the backup, new objects might have been created in the AD and these new objects will have been assigned new security principals. The problem comes when you restore the data but access to resources on servers has been granted to new security principals. Later on, you can create new users, or recreate the ones that were lost due to the failure, and these objects are assigned the same SIDs that were in use before. As a consequence, you can end up in situations where users have access to resources but shouldn't. When we raise the RID pool values by 100,000, the chances of the new objects obtaining the same SIDs as those previously in use becomes very slim because that would mean your backup would not be very recent at all, if there have been that many new objects.

To raise the RID pool value, you need to have the ldp utility introduced in Chapter 6, and therefore the Windows Support tools, installed. Launch `ldp.exe` and on the **Connection** menu, click on **Connect,** and type the name of the recovery DC. Then on the **Connection** menu, click on **Bind** and enter your Administrator username and password. Next, click on **View** and then **Tree**, and then type the distinguished name (DN) path for the RID Manager which, in the case of nailcorp.com, would be: `CN=RID Manager$,CN=System,DC=nailcorp,DC=com`. Once you have entered this, all of the attributes of this object are displayed on the right. The value that we need is **rIDAvailablePool**, as you can see in the following screenshot.

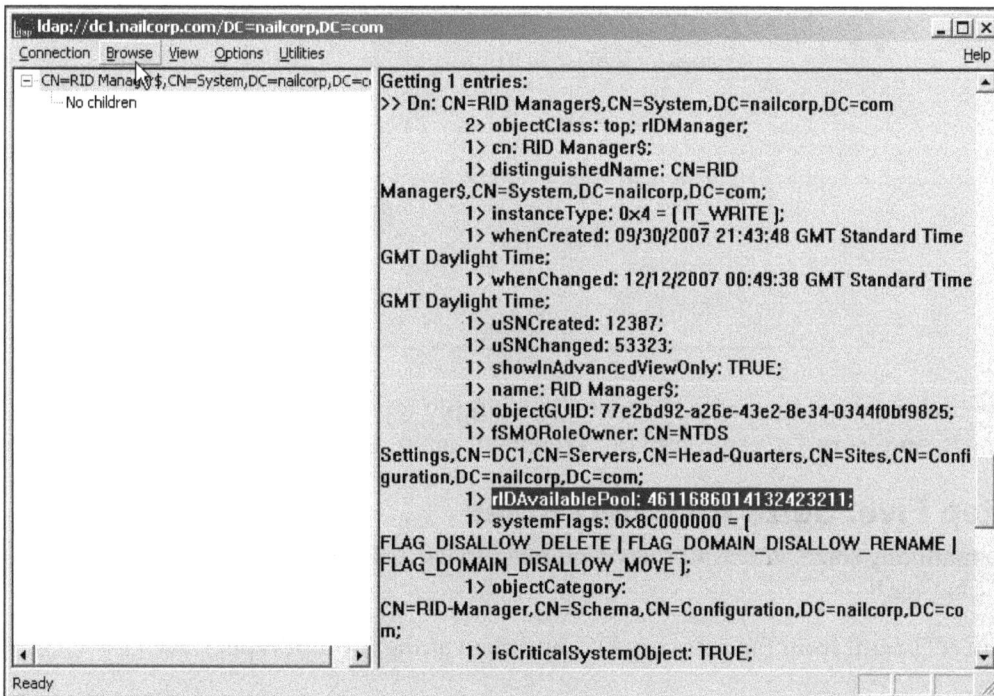

Copy the value of this setting and insert it into the Large Integer Converter from the **Utilities** menu. You will be given a Low Part and a High Part number. These represent the beginning of the RID pool (Low Part) and the total amount of RIDs that can be created in the domain (High Part). For nailcorp.com these are 2603 and 1073741823, respectively. Once we increase the amount by 100,000, the next RID pool that will be allocated will start with 102603 instead of 2603.

In order to change the value, click on **Browse** in ldp, and then click on **Modify**. Now, Add 100,000 to the **rIDAvailablePool** value and type the resulting number into the **Values** field. For nailcorp.com, the number 4611686014132423211 changes to 4611686014132523211. In the DN field, type **CN=RID Manager$,CN=System,D C=nailcorp,DC=com** and in the **Edit Entry Attribute** field, type **rIDAvailablePool**. Then, Select the **Replace** operation and click **Enter**, and then click on **Run** to run the operation. You can used in this example, filled in the following screenshot:

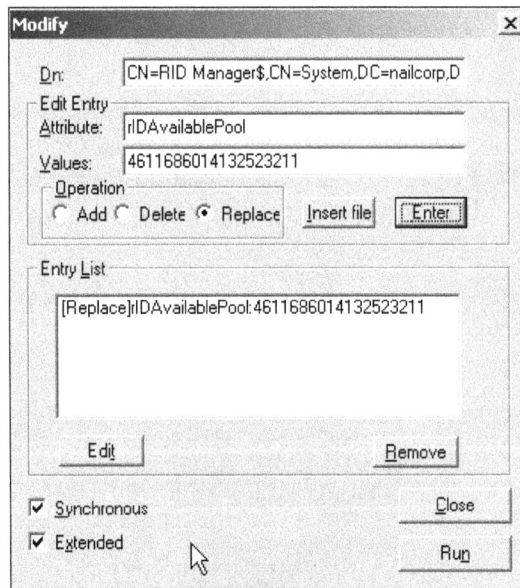

To check whether the value has increased, simply type **CN=RID Manager$,CN=Syst em,DC=nailcorp,DC=com** into the **Tree** view again, and check the resulting number.

## Step Five: Seize All FSMO Roles

To manually seize all FSMO roles, you need to use NTDSutil introduced in Chapter 6.

Run NTDSutil from the recovery DC, and then at the prompt type:

```
>roles
```

You will be moved into the FSMO Maintenance prompt where you need to type:

```
>connections
```

Next comes the Server Connections prompt where you need to enter the name of the server to which you want to connect. In this case, you want to connect to the recovery DC, which for nailcorp.com is DC1. You would therefore type:

```
>connect to server DC1.nailcorp.com
```

You can now quit this prompt by typing:

```
>quit
```

You are now back at the FSMO maintenance prompt, where you can now seize the roles by typing the following commands:

```
>seize domain naming master
```

```
>seize schema master
```

```
>seize infrastructure master
```

```
>seize pdc
```

```
>seize rid master
```

For the first two, you will need to be an Enterprise Admin. For the latter two, Domain Admin will suffice. Once you start seizing a role, AD will try to transfer it. However, if it fails, AD will issue an error and then seize it. Once the seiz is done, an ldap output will be shown with a list of servers and the roles that are currently held by them, as shown in the following screenshots.

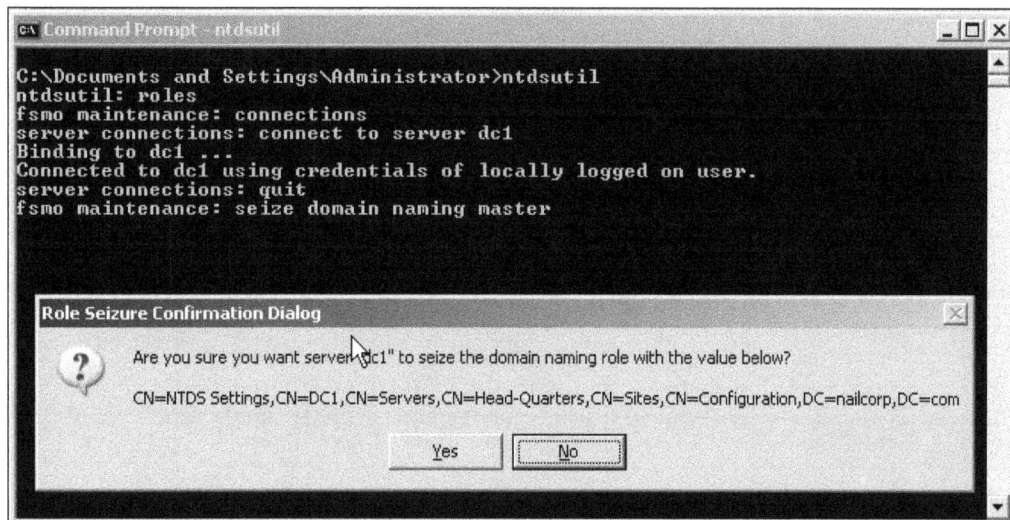

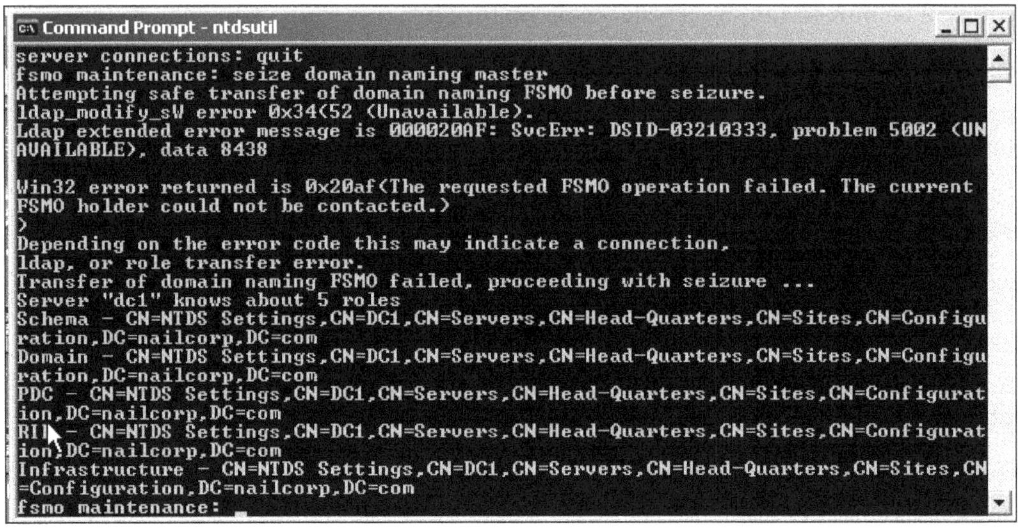

```
[cmd] Command Prompt - ntdsutil                                    _ |□| X|
server connections: quit
fsmo maintenance: seize domain naming master
Attempting safe transfer of domain naming FSMO before seizure.
ldap_modify_sW error 0x34<52 (Unavailable).
Ldap extended error message is 000020AF: SvcErr: DSID-03210333, problem 5002 (UN
AVAILABLE), data 8438

Win32 error returned is 0x20af(The requested FSMO operation failed. The current
FSMO holder could not be contacted.>
>
Depending on the error code this may indicate a connection,
ldap, or role transfer error.
Transfer of domain naming FSMO failed, proceeding with seizure ...
Server "dc1" knows about 5 roles
Schema  - CN=NTDS Settings,CN=DC1,CN=Servers,CN=Head-Quarters,CN=Sites,CN=Configu
ration,DC=nailcorp,DC=com
Domain  - CN=NTDS Settings,CN=DC1,CN=Servers,CN=Head-Quarters,CN=Sites,CN=Configu
ration,DC=nailcorp,DC=com
PDC - CN=NTDS Settings,CN=DC1,CN=Servers,CN=Head-Quarters,CN=Sites,CN=Configurat
ion,DC=nailcorp,DC=com
RID - CN=NTDS Settings,CN=DC1,CN=Servers,CN=Head-Quarters,CN=Sites,CN=Configurat
ion,DC=nailcorp,DC=com
Infrastructure  - CN=NTDS Settings,CN=DC1,CN=Servers,CN=Head-Quarters,CN=Sites,CN
=Configuration,DC=nailcorp,DC=com
fsmo maintenance: _
```

## Step Six: Clean Up the Metadata of All Old DCs

When we introduced NTDSutil in Chapter 6, we also did a metadata cleanup for an old DC. We need to carry out exactly the same procedure here. The problem is that you have a recovered forest, but the forest contains all of the old DC objects for all of the other DCs. Removing all other DC entries can be quite tedious, especially in large organizations, but is a necessary step. For clarity and brevity, the following figure shows a flowchart of the commands and actions to be run for each old DC, in order to remove them from the AD. Please be sure to delete server and computer objects for all other DCs in the forest root or primary domain, that you are restoring from a backup, except for the recovery DC.

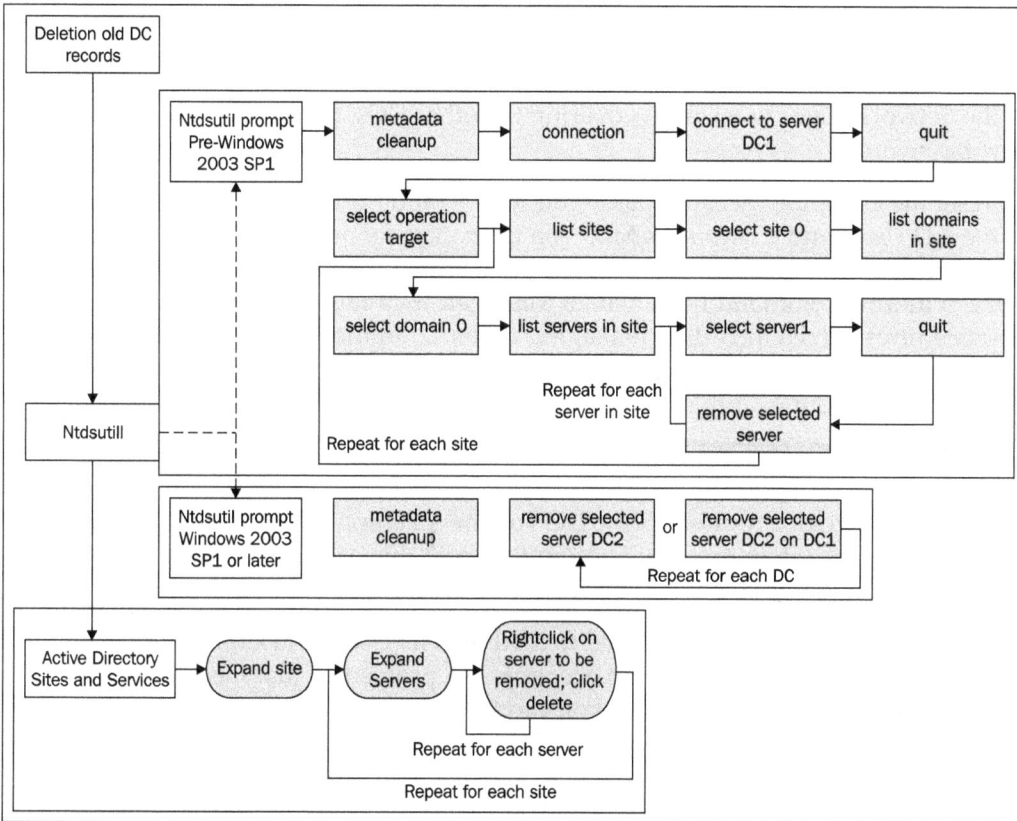

# Step Seven: Reset the Computer Account and krbtgt Password

The following steps will reset the computer account password and the krbtgt user account password.

The krbtgt account is the security principal used by the Kerberos service. It provides the security secret for two major services, the Authentication services and the Ticket-granting service. This account cannot be deleted or renamed, and in the AD Users and Computers MMC, it will always show as disabled. Its password is changed automatically on a regular basis, but it follows the same GPO as any other account in your forest. The steps to reset the krbtgt account must be done as many times as you have the allowed password history count in your domain GPO. The default is two.

The same principal applies to the Computer Account. The objective of this procedure is to clear out any old passwords from the password history of these accounts. By doing this, the recovery DC will not replicate with any potentially damaged DCs in the network. Once you start recovering the other DCs, they will replicate these new passwords.

To reset the Computer account password, you would normally need to right-click in the AD Users and Computers MMC on the computer account. For DCs, this is different. For this procedure, we will use the command line utility Netdom. Netdom is the Windows command line Domain Manager. It allows you carry out a multitude of procedures, which including managing trusts, computers, and even connecting a Windows XP-based computer to the domain. To proceed, open the command prompt and, for our example of nailcorp.com, type the following:

```
>netdom resetpwd /server:DC1 /userD:Administrator /password:<your
password>
```

In this command, `DC1` represents the DC you are resetting, (the recovery DC) and `userD` represents a domain admin account. Repeat this procedure at least twice, as it is the default, unless you have a specific password history count for this account.

To reset the krbtgt account, you need to load the AD Users and Computers MMC, and reset it as you would any other account. The problem is that this account is hidden most of the time. However, you can find it simply by choosing **Find** from the **Action** menu in the MMC and typing in krbtgt. Then, select the account in the results window, and right-click on it. Click on **Reset Password** and type a new password that conforms to your domain password policy. Re-type the password to confirm and click **OK**, as shown in the following screenshot:

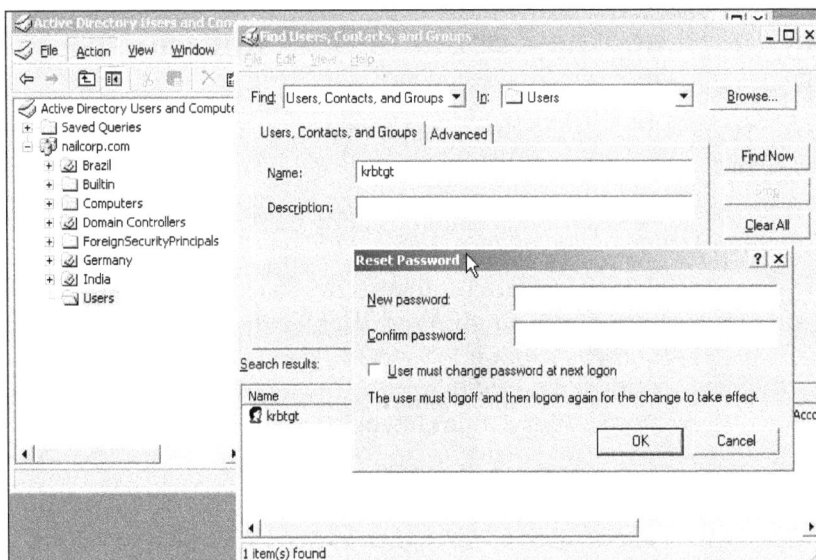

# Step 8: Reset the Trust Passwords

Reset the trust password twice (or up to your password history count) for all trusts between this domain and all other trusted domains. This must also be done for all child and parent domain trusts within this domain. To be clear about this, reset the passwords from the recovery domain first, and reset all outgoing trusts from this domain. Make a note of these passwords somewhere until later, because you will use them later, to restore the trusts when you recover the other domains within the forest.

Resetting the trust passwords ensures that the DC doesn't replicate with potentially damaged DCs outside its domain. By setting the same trust password when restoring the first DC in each of the non-root or non-primary domains, you will ensure that this DC will then replicate with each of the recovered DCs. Because the subsequent DCs in the domain are recovered using the Active Directory Installation Wizard, the new passwords will be replicated automatically during that process.

In order to complete this step on Windows 2003, make sure you have the Netdom. exe from the Windows 2003 SP1 Support tools. If you do not have this, you can download it from here: `http://go.microsoft.com/fwlink/?LinkId=70775`.

Open a command prompt and type the following, for a simple parent-child domain where you are currently recovering the parent:

```
>netdom trust nailcorp.com /domain:logistics.nailcorp.com /resetOneSide
/PasswordT:<your new trust password> /userD:administrator /pawwrod0:<your
admin password>
```

As you can see, the parent domain (nailcorp.com) is mentioned before the `/domain` flag, which contains the child domain. Unlike the previous procedure of `netdom resetpwd`, we will only perform this step once for every trust. Use the same switches if you are resetting a non-parent child trust. Always put the recovery domain first.

# Part Two: Restore the First DC in Each of the Remaining Domains

The procedure for recovering the first DCs in each of the child domains within the forest is very similar to the procedure for the root domain.The only difference is in the trust password rest procedure. However, here is brief overview what needs to be done, and in what order. Again, please make sure that this DC is isolated from the production network, or at least from the failed DCs. It should, however, be able to communicate with the recovered root DC.

> **Step 1**: Restore the AD data and make sure you mark the SYSVOL primary for this domain.

> **Step 2**: Restore/recover DNS services.

**Step 3**: Reset the Global Catalog flag for the DC.

**Step 4**: Raise the RID pool value by 100,000 to ensure that there are no SID conflicts or overlaps.

**Step 5**: Seize all Flexible Master Server Operations (FSMO) roles that belong on a domain level.

**Step 6**: Clean up the metadata of the failed DCs within the domain. Make sure you remove all server and computer objects as well.

**Step 7**: Reset the computer and krbtgt account for the DC.

**Step 8**: Reset the trust password.

In order to reset the trust password of the parent domain you will have to reverse the switches that you used earlier in the root or primary domain. This will look something similar to the following:

```
>netdom trust logistics.nailcorp.com /domain:nailcorp.com /resetOneSide
/passwordT:<password you specified before> /userO:administrator /
passwordO:<domain admin password>
```

As mentioned before, the Administrator needs to be an account that is a domain admin in the recovered domain.

At this point in time, you should have one DC in the root or primary domain, and one DC in each of the child domains. These DCs should now be joined to the production network before proceeding any further. At this point, these DCs form an AD forest that is secure, and none of them will replicate with any of the old, failed DCs. The reason we have one DC in each child domain first is so that we can establish the forest and have it replicating and functioning. Once we have the sites and services replicated, and all the old records of the old DCs have been purged are no longer listed, adding a second DC in each domain becomes easier, and there are also less error messages in the event log, regarding replication.

# Part Three: Enable the DC in the Root Domain to be a Global Catalog

Because you disabled the Global Catalog earlier, you should now need to enable it again in the root or primary domain, by selecting the checkbox in the NTDS Settings, in the AD Sites and Services MMC.

Although it is preferable to have a GC in the root or primary domain, it is also possible to select any of the restored DCs to be a GC. If you had all DCs as GCs earlier, start with the root DC, and make sure that it has replicated and is a complete GC, before adding any other GCs.

You can do this by monitoring the Directory Service Event Log for event ID 1119 to indicate that this DC is a Global Catalog server. You can also verify this by examining the registry key to see if it has a value of 1:

```
HKLM\System\CurrentControlSet\Services\NTDS\Parameters\Global Catalog
Promotion Complete
```

This is shown in the following screenshot:

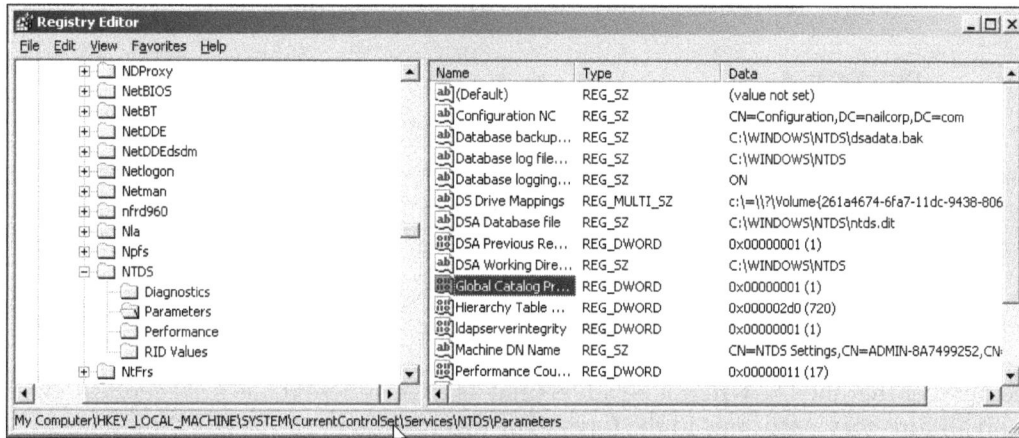

In an ideal situation, each of the restored DCs will be a replication partner of the root DC, and in order to see these, you can use the following command to see all replication partners for the root DC:

```
>repadmin /showreps /v
```

The Knowledge Consistency checker (KCC) should have created the necessary replication objects for the source DC and partition in the root DC, which you can also verify by using the above command.

You can now forcefully sync the child DCs with the root DC (now a GC) by either using ReplMon and synchronizing from each DC to the GC, or by using the Repadmin/syncall command.

You can also use:

```
>repadmin /sync logistics.nailcorp.com DC1,nailcorp.com dc1.logistics.
nailcorp.com
```

This command as it stands, will require a functioning DNS. You can, however, replace the child DC with its GUID, which you can obtain from the DNS server under the **_msdcs.nailcorp.com** zone in the domain. This is shown in the following screenshot:

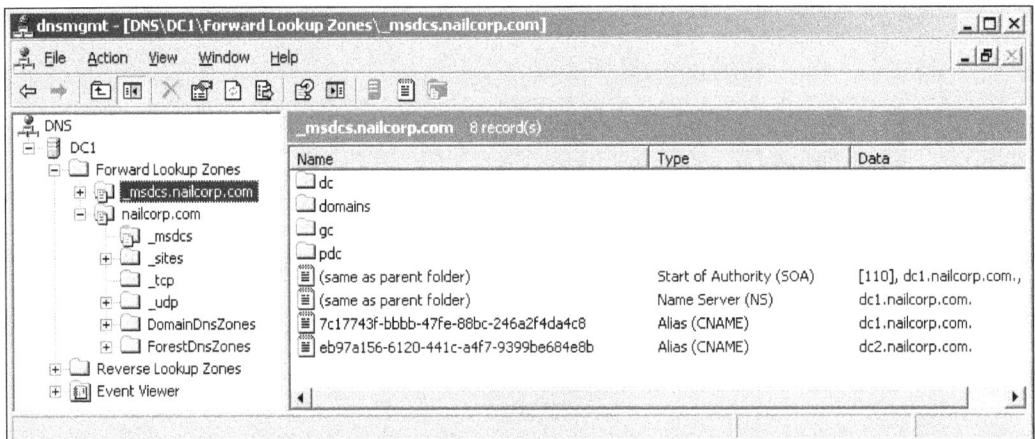

Remember that the DC will not be advertised as a GC unless it has fully replicated with all directory partitions in the forest. For this reason, the to-be GC should be forced to replicate with all of the restored DCs.

Having a GC in each domain is vital for the forest, and it should be available at all times. For example, without a GC in a Windows 2000 'native' domain, users cannot log on. Also, in the absence of a GC, the Netlogon service running on the DCs in each domain, aside from the root, won't be able to register or delete records on the root DNS servers.

At this stage, you should have a stable forest, with one DC for each domain and one GC. You should now take a fresh backup of each of the DCs that you have just restored. Next, you can begin recovering other DCs in the forest by installing AD using the Active Directory Installation Wizard (dcpromo.exe).

# Part Four: Recover Additional DCs in the Forest by Installing Active Directory

You now have a functional forest, and you can add additional DCs as you would in a normal environment. At this point, your clients should be able to authenticate in all of the domains, and resources should be granted as usual. However, the load on these DCs might actually be quite high. You should therefore add additional DCs to each domain as soon as possible.

However, please keep in mind the following points for each DC that is recovered in the AD:

- Do not use an old backup to restore additional DCs. Instead, use the backup from the DC in the domain to which you want to add another DC. Perform an Install from Media (IFM) as discussed in Chapter 6, or simply use the replication when you install the AD on the DCs.

- As this is now a clean AD forest, the re-use of DC names used prior to the loss is all acceptable, and is actually the least-disruptive method, because applications that rely on DNS names or NETBIOS names will function without any changes.

- Configure each server with the first DNS server in the forest (the first DC restored in the root domain) as the preferred DNS server in its TCP/IP properties. The secondary DNS server should be itself.

- If the DCs were running the DNS service before the forest malfunction, re-install the DNS service or configure the clients to use different DNS servers.

- Make this DC also a Global Catalog server. If you have more then 100 users in your domain, you should also make this DC a Global Catalog server, as per Microsoft's recommendation (`http://technet2.microsoft.com/windowsserver/en/library/d9a82c36-8e7f-491a-81ec-532f73ea70e71033.mspx?mfr=true`)

Please note here that the last three points in the list are required only until your forest has enough DCs running and replicating and that are sufficiently stable to be used in production. After that, you can revert to your own DNS strategy, which you used before.

## Post Recovery Steps

Once all of the DCs in the entire forest have been restored, you can revert to your old DNS configuration including the preferred and secondary servers on each DC. The only thing you have to watch and verify when check, is that each restored DC is still replicating data, and no DNS issues arise.

Once these DNS servers are configured as they were before the failure, the name resolution should be restored. Don't forget to delete any records of DCs that have not been restored, or have been renamed.

Also, remember that you should delete WINS records for all DCs that have not been recovered.

At this point, you can re-distribute the FMSO roles to other DCs in the domain or forest to enable more GCs, or to replicate your pre-failure setup.

Also you should re-install any software applications that were running on the DCs prior to the failure. By restoring AD on the first DC in the domain, the registry was also restored because they both are part of System State data. Keep this in mind if you had any applications running on these DCs, and if they had any information stored in the registry.

Please note that as you get more and more DCs restored and connected again, the network traffic will increase dramatically due to the replications. To prevent saturation of the network, make sure you don't connect too many DCs at any one time, or try Install from Media.

For further reading, the Microsoft Best Practices Documents to AD Forest Recovery is very highly recommended:

For Windows 2000 Server: `http://www.microsoft.com/downloads/details.aspx ?displaylang=en&FamilyID=3EDA5A79-C99B-4DF9-823C-933FEBA08CFE`

For Windows Server 2003:

`http://www.microsoft.com/downloads/details.aspx?FamilyID=AFE436FA-8E8A-443A-9027-C522DEE35D85&displaylang=en`

# Summary

This chapter provided a step-by-step guide to forest recovery and, as mentioned at the beginning of this chapter, this is something that should be used only as a last resort. It's a very time consuming process when you have to remove all of the old records and reset passwords. Proper AD documentation will help immensely in this scenario. Something to be understood is that in medium to large organizations or multinational organizations this scenario will not be accomplished within a day. This will be an outage for several days until you have a fully recovered a functional forest. On the other hand, large organizations should have safeguards in place, such as proper replication schedules, that will allow stopping the replications and hence, minimizing the DCs affected.

When performing a forest recovery, monitoring, checking for errors, ensuring data availability, and making sure that servers are registered in the DNS and can communicate, are standard good practices to follow. There is nothing worse than recovering a forest and then realizing after several restored DCs that they are not replicating because of either miscommunication, or mis-configuration.

# 9

# Site AD Infrastructure Failure (Hardware)

## Scenario

When we discuss Disaster Recovery, the site failure on a hardware basis means that all the DCs in a site location are physically non-functional. In this case, we assume that a complete site (Brazil) in our nailcorp.com domain is in a state where the hard drives of the servers cannot be used in another server.

## Causes

The causes for a complete site failure can be anything from a natural disaster to any other bigger accident or incident. You can, for example, have a break in the water pipe that runs through the walls of the server room. Once the water builds up enough pressure, the wall bursts, and the water leaks into the server room. This can cause short circuits and water damage.

A natural disaster linked to water would be flooding. Flash floods are not easy to predict, and can happen in regions where big rivers are located.

## Recovery Process

Having an entire site physically non-functional is rare in medium to large organizations because standard best practices would require that the server room be located at least on the second floor, and sufficient circuit breakers and other measures be in place to prevent physical damage caused by natural disaster such as flooding.

However, for any kind of business, smaller sites can really be just a sales office and contain a DC that has multiple functions, such as print and file server. Once this office and the single DC get damaged, the entire site is out. If the office was then in an area where WAN connections are already slow, and of bad quality, having the entire office use the WAN for authentication can cause serious strain on the network resources. Of course, the WAN link could also get damaged in the event of a disaster, as the networking equipment is usually kept in the same room.

Recovering an entire site is a very straightforward process in itself, and is closely related to the DC AD failure recovery discussed previously. There are however, certain steps to be followed, and certain things to be taken into consideration, such as different hardware and software on the new or old DCs.

## Considerations: Different Hardware and Bare Metal

Depending on the age of the DCs, but very likely in the event of a complete hardware failure, is the fact that you might not have the same server model at hand while restoring the DC. The problem with a bare metal recovery, that is for a machine with nothing installed, is the Hardware Abstraction Layer (HAL). The HAL is basically the hardware layout of the computer. This should match as closely as possible to one of the failed DCs. Use the same hardware type, or something as close to it as possible. Also of great importance are the processor and chipset architectures. Do not, for example, try to recover a Windows 2003 server that had an Intel Processor onto AMD CPU architecture.

There are differences in processor architectures as well, and you should always keep the same type of architecture even for restoration. If you would have a DC running on an Advanced Configuration and Power Interface (ACPI) with a single processor, you can restore it to a multi-processor machine. However, you will need to update the HAL in order to use the extra processors. Neither downscaling is possible, nor is mixing between ACPI and Multi Processor Systems (MPS). You can easily find out what the current DCs are by opening the Device Manager on the DC and expanding the Computer part. It will tell you the architecture that the machine is running, and by expanding the Processors part, you can see what kind of processors there are, and how many there are. This is, of course, if you do not have a detailed inventory list available currently, as you can see in the following screenshot. For DCs and disaster recovery, this is important information.

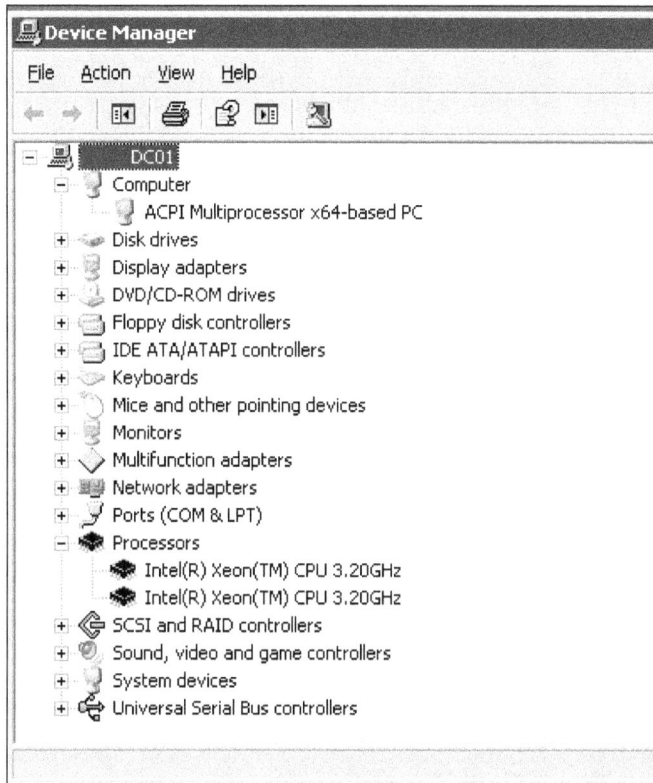

In order to increase chances of a successful restore, remove any unwanted hardware on the new DC for the recovery process, such as extra network cards (NICs) and unneeded peripherals. If your NICs are onboard, and cannot be removed, set them to disabled in the machine's BIOS.

Another point is that unless you have a standby machine somewhere that is the exact duplicate of the DCs, disk cloning a DC such as with Symantec Ghost ® is not really a viable option. Even then, it is not a good idea because you won't know the changes on the System and would have to make an image every time you update the DC.

# Considerations: Software

For a restore to go smoothly, you should ensure that all the software aspects are the same as on the failed DCs. This includes the Services Pack level and patch levels. For Windows 2003 RTM or post SP1 there is no minimal level, whereas on Windows 2000, at least Service Pack 4 should be installed. If you have a Windows 2003 SP1 or a later version installed, the new DC has to have at least SP1 installed as well. Otherwise, you will boot into the following error message:

**Windows could not start because of an error in the software. Please report this problem as: load needed DLLs for kernel. Please contact your support person to report this problem.**

In case of this error message, you will have to boot into safe mode, and copy the Hal.dll and Ntoskrnl.exe files from the Service Pack 1 CD to the DC. If you do not know where to copy these files to, check the file Setup.log in C:\windows\repair\.

# Restore Process

A prerequisite for this process is a working DNS server, unless the DCs themselves host DNS servers as well. Then, this can be restored. Just make sure you install the DNS service before restoring. This means that your DNS server needs to be fully working, and the zones and zone files for our AD domain are in order, and functional. If you have an external DNS, the easiest way to verify this is to resolve a DC name from the site. It should resolve the IP of the old DC. Another good method, is to try and resolve the domain name itself by typing: **nslookup nailcorp.com** from the command prompt. If you get a valid response, then your DNS server is functioning. If not, you will have to get the DNS server restored and functional first. If you do not have an external DNS, meaning your DCs host the DNS servers, then just make sure the service is installed before you continue.

The restore process for an entire site, as mentioned, is very similar to a single DC recovery of AD. Therefore, the following flowchart is almost the same except a few extra steps. The following figure gives you a brief overview of the process and what steps are involved.

| Does new hardware match the failed DCs? | → | Is a very recent full system state backup available | → | Install Base OS to the same SP level as the failed DC | → | Give Server same name as a failed DC |

For HAL changes, disable as many components as possible

Do not make member of the domain

| Restore the second DC in the same manner or just re-install | ← | Verify DNS, TCP/IP and AD | ← | Install missing drivers as needed | ← | Restore trusted backup with advanced options |

| Verify that the DCs are replicating | → | Reset trusts when WAN becomes available to the domain |

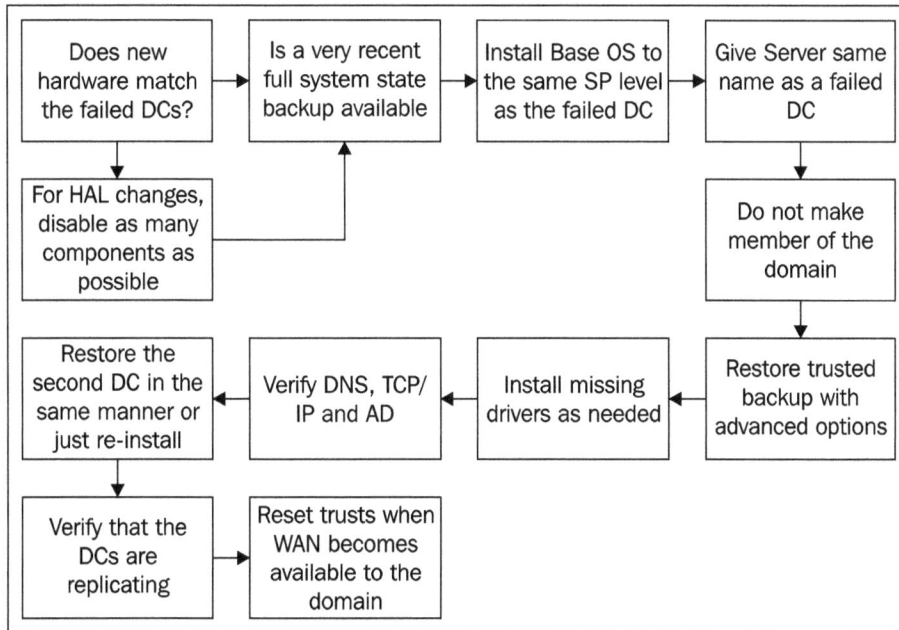

While this seems very logical, you might wonder why you would recover the second DC and any additional DCs, and not just replicate from the restored DC. Both are possible. If for some reason, you have to keep the same name of the recovered DC, recovery is your only option since, at this point, you cannot do any domain or forest-wide changes such as the removal of a DC. If the DC has any incoming replication partners, these links will not be removed from the AD until the next replication. To keep your AD as stable as possible, it is recommended that you change as little as possible such as metadata cleanup until all replication links are back online.

## Step One: System and System State

When you back up your DCs, make sure you back up the system drive (C:\). In our case, we are using Ntbackup to back up the required parts.

Make sure you install the new DC in the same manner as the old DCs were installed. This means that the windows folder, if it was on C:\winnt, needs to be on the same drive and in the same directory, just like all other aspects of the machine. From a software environment, it needs to be nearly identical to the old DC. Make sure you also have the same amount of additional drives as the old DC in case the SYSVOL was located on another disk.

[
For Windows 2000, the SYSVOL folder needs to be selected additionally when backing up, if it is located on another drive.
]

When you perform the next steps, you need to be sure that the old DCs will never be turned on again in the same network as the recovery DCs.

## Step Two: Restoring

Create a folder called `backup` on your new DC and then copy the file `boot.ini`, which can be found on the root of your boot drive, to the following folders: `C:\backup`, `%systemroot%\Repair`, which is usually in `c:\winnt` or `c:\windows`, and all subfolders of repair as shown in the following screenshot.

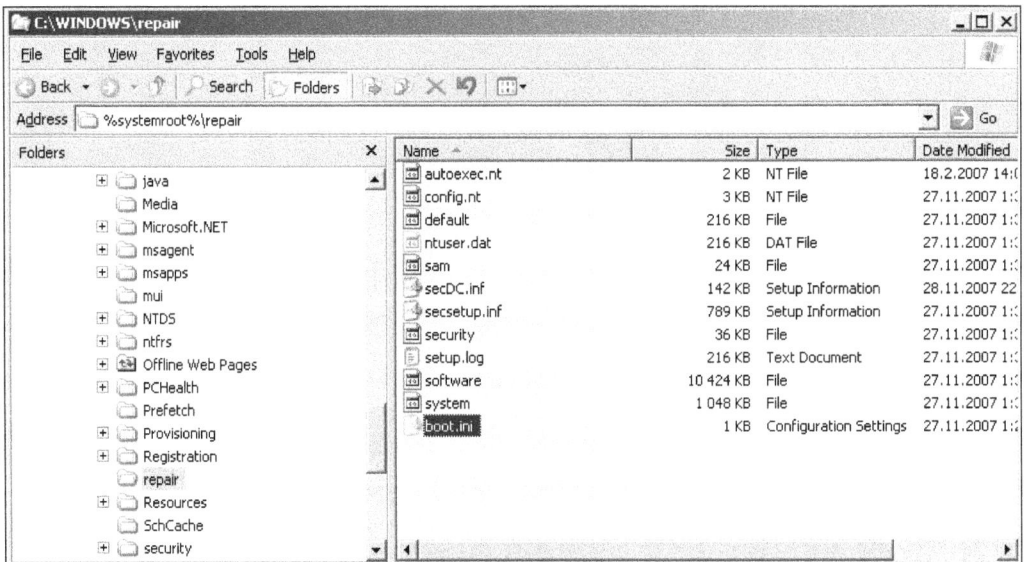

Next, launch the backup utility and make sure you have the backup accessible on the server, or via a tape drive, or on another server. In the **Tools | Options | Restore** tab, make sure you select **Always replace the files on my computer** as you can see in the following screenshot. You can then proceed to restore the system drive and the system state. Also, make sure that services that are not needed currently, such as DNS, are all turned off.

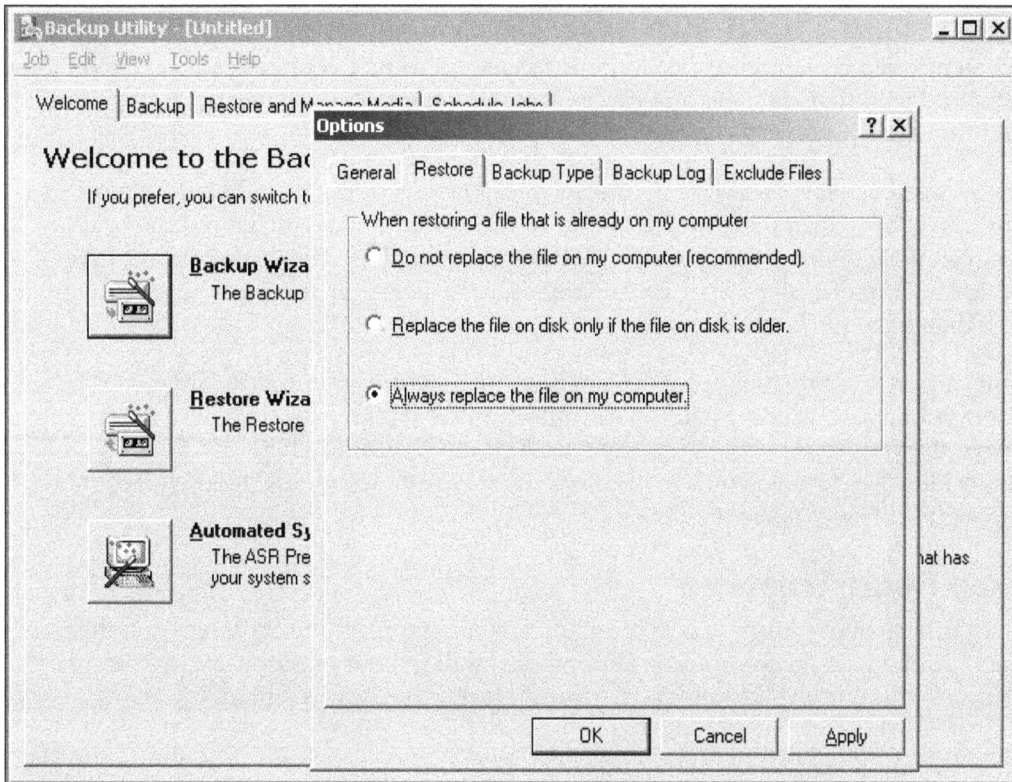

When the restore process is complete, do not reboot your DC just yet. Replace the boot.ini file in the c:\ root, now with the one in your backup folder. Also, replace all the boot.ini files in %systemroot%\repair, and all its subfolders with the backup one.

> Please make a note that if in Windows 2000, you have the SYSVOL on another drive, you need to include it separately in the restoration.

If you have DNS services running locally on the DCs, verify whether the restore actually works properly, start the service, and then add the DCs own IP to the DNS server settings in the TCP/IP properties. Then, verify whether you can actually resolve names from the DNS server that is hosted locally. If needed, re-install the hard disk controller drivers. Then, reboot the server. After boot, verify whether everything works by examining the Event log, and running DcDiag. Running NetDiag, at this point, will give you a lot of errors because you are still cut off from the rest of the domain.

## Step Three: Additional DCs

As mentioned earlier, you should perform as few drastic changes as possible on the domain level, such as metadata cleanup, until you are fully connected to the domain and the forest again.

If you want a fast solution, and your recovered DC is actually a Global Catalog, you can simply install a new DC, join it to the domain, for which you now have a recovered DC. Now, replicate the AD data from that DC. This installation can be performed according to your specifications, or as per your company's policy. You will then have two working DCs.

You can also restore the second DC in the same manner as the first. This would be especially necessary if you have applications that use the specific DC name. When the restore is done, just make sure that the replication between the two DCs is working. To do this, you can just create a new user on one DC, and wait for the replication. Then, delete it again.

## Step Four: Trusts

With this recovery, there is one problem. If your site is offline for long from the main domain, its machine account password will fall out of scope, and the security channel (trust) to the domain fails. You can test if the trust is still ok by typing:

```
>netdiag /test:trust
```

If you get a message that the trust relationship failed, you will need to manually reset the machine password.

To do this, stop the Kerberos Key Distribution Center (KDC) in your Service and set it to manual start. Then, issue the following Netdom command from a command prompt:

```
>netdom resetpwd /server:direct_Partner /userd:DOMAIN\admin_user /
password:adminpasswd
```

The `direct_Partner` in this command is the closest replication partner of the recovered DC, outside the site. You can find the replication partners, if you have the Windows Support tools installed, by typing at a command prompt:

```
>repadmin /showreps
```

Also, the `userd` and `password` in the command are not typos, and if you do not want to type your admin password in the command line, you can type * without the quotes and it will prompt you for your password silently. Once these commands are issued and completed, reboot the server and log in normally. Then, start the KDC and set it back to automatic.

# Step Five: Replicate

The last step is to verify whether you can replicate from both DCs to the rest of the domain. It has to be said that if your Active Directory Sites are set up correctly, a replication link to the new second DC is automatically created from the same main replication partner as the recovered DC, once your site comes back online.

To force replication, you have several options and the easiest one is of course to use Active Directory Site and Services. In the case of nailcorp.com, we expand Sites, Headquarters, Servers, DC1 and then click on NTDS Settings. On the right-hand pane, you will see the replication link. Right-click on it and select **Replicate Now**, as shown in the following screenshot.

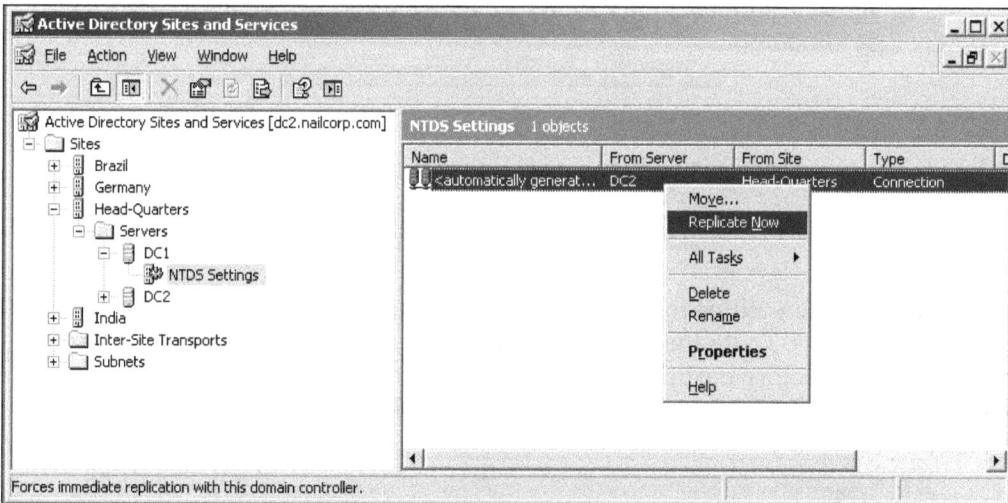

While you can also start replications with Repadmin, it is a rather complex process. More information can be found in Microsoft's Knowledge Base article 232072 at http://support.microsoft.com/kb/232072/.

Another quick way to replicate is with ReplMon, which is included in the Support Tools as well. After launching it, you can just right-click on **Monitored Servers**, and then on **Add server**, select the replication partner server and click **ADD**. Once added, you will see the directory partitions under the server. Expand the ones you need to synchronize, and you will see an icon that represents two servers with a small red cross if your replications have failed in the past.

Right-click on the partner, and select **Synchronize with this Replication Partner**.
ReplMon will then start the replication. You can see this in the following screenshot.

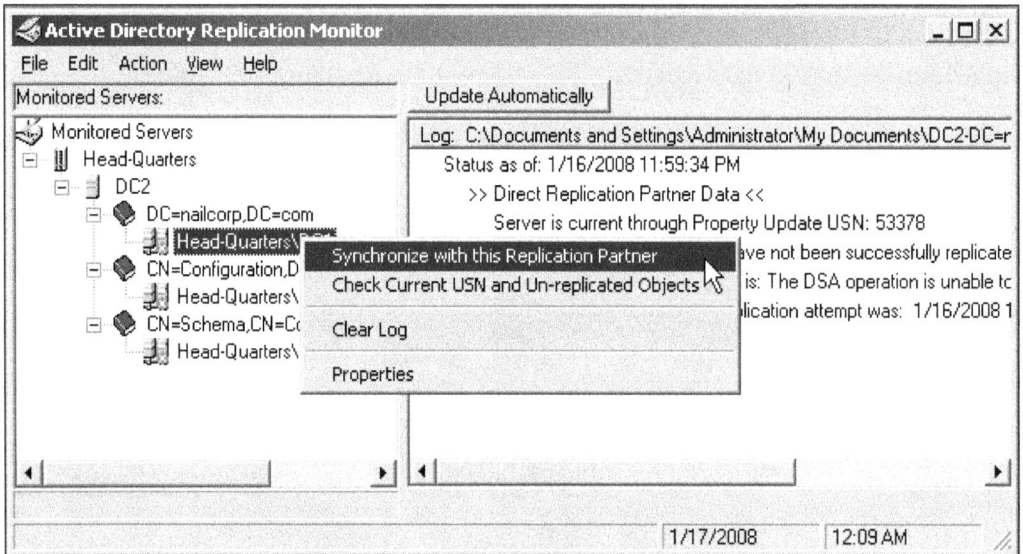

If your site had been offline for a long time, it may be a good idea to synchronize all
directory partitions. To do this, simply right-click on the Replication Partner itself,
instead of the Directory partition, and select **Synchronize Each Directory Partition
with all Partners**, as shown in the following screenshot.

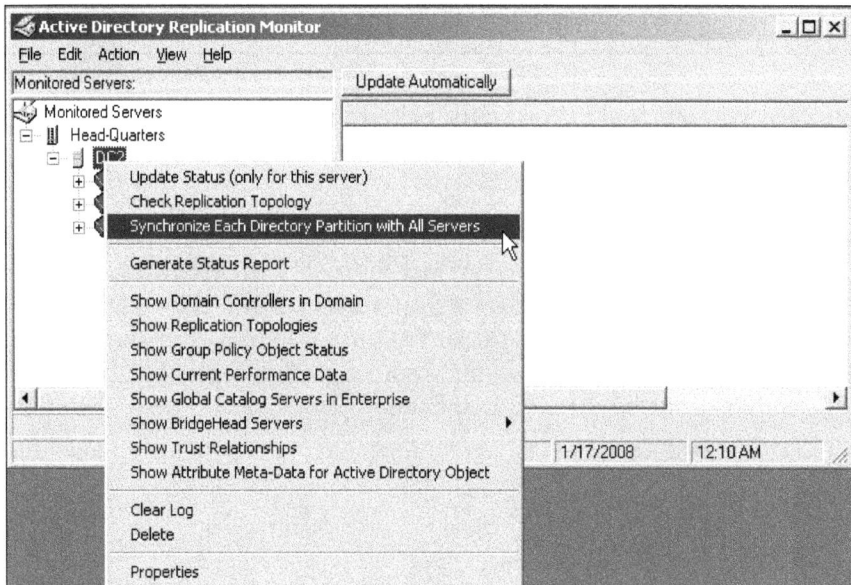

Once you've verified the replication, the disaster recovery of your site has been successfully completed. If you encounter errors regarding the target replica, such as the one shown in the following screenshot, you need to reset the trust password. Or, in the case of multiple replication partners, wait for the rest of the domain to replicate the password change. You will get this error if you try to synchronize in ReplMon with a partner that has not yet gotten your new trust password replicated. Once it is replicated, this error should not appear anymore, if you re-test the replication with that partner.

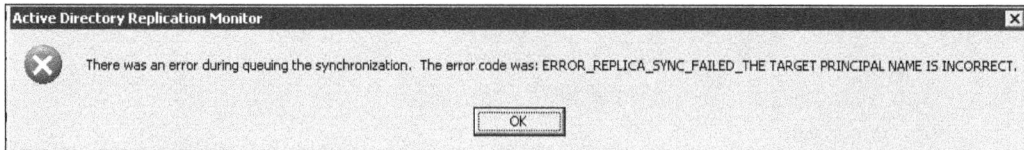

**Active Directory Replication Monitor**

There was an error during queuing the synchronization. The error code was: ERROR_REPLICA_SYNC_FAILED_THE TARGET PRINCIPAL NAME IS INCORRECT.

OK

# Virtual Environments

Virtualization has become quite synonymous with Disaster Recovery. Many companies choose to have a bigger server, and host their DCs virtually. There are actually several reasons that favor this. One such reason is the fact that you can back up the entire DC by backing up a few files. If you do this daily, or twice a week, you will have a strong base to create a very fast recovery. Another reason is that, hardware is getting cheaper and the layer between virtualization and hardware is becoming thinner. This means that you lose very little performance when you run a machine virtually nowadays.

However, if you do not have virtual DCs, a virtual site that can be shipped on a hard drive fairly quickly might just be the solution for a quick and not-so-painful recovery, or at the least, the functionality of services until the physical DCs are restored,.

You could create a virtual site in your AD, and place one or two virtual DCs in it. These DCs are in a totally separated LAN segment that is connected to only one other site for replication and replicate just like any other site within the AD. The DCs, however, have no production subnet and physical sites attached to them, and therefore, won't serve any authentication requests. They should, however, have a second NIC installed, but not activated. If there is need for a DC, simply change the IP information on the second NIC on one DC to reflect the damaged subnet and restart the Netlogon process so that it registers this IP to the DNS servers as well. Then, move it in Sites and Services to the damaged site, and wait for AD replication, to at least a few DCs. Shut the Virtual DC down, and copy it to a portable media, which can be a DVD or a portable hard drive.

Once on location, you can use any powerful PC, and the free version of VMWare Server or Microsoft Virtual Server in order to boot the Virtual DC again. As you have an IP assigned, of the failed network and Sites and Services, and configured for the DC to authenticate for this subnet, the client machines will be able to authenticate while you either replace the failed DC with completely new machines, or try to recover them over time. This setup is illustrated in the following figure:

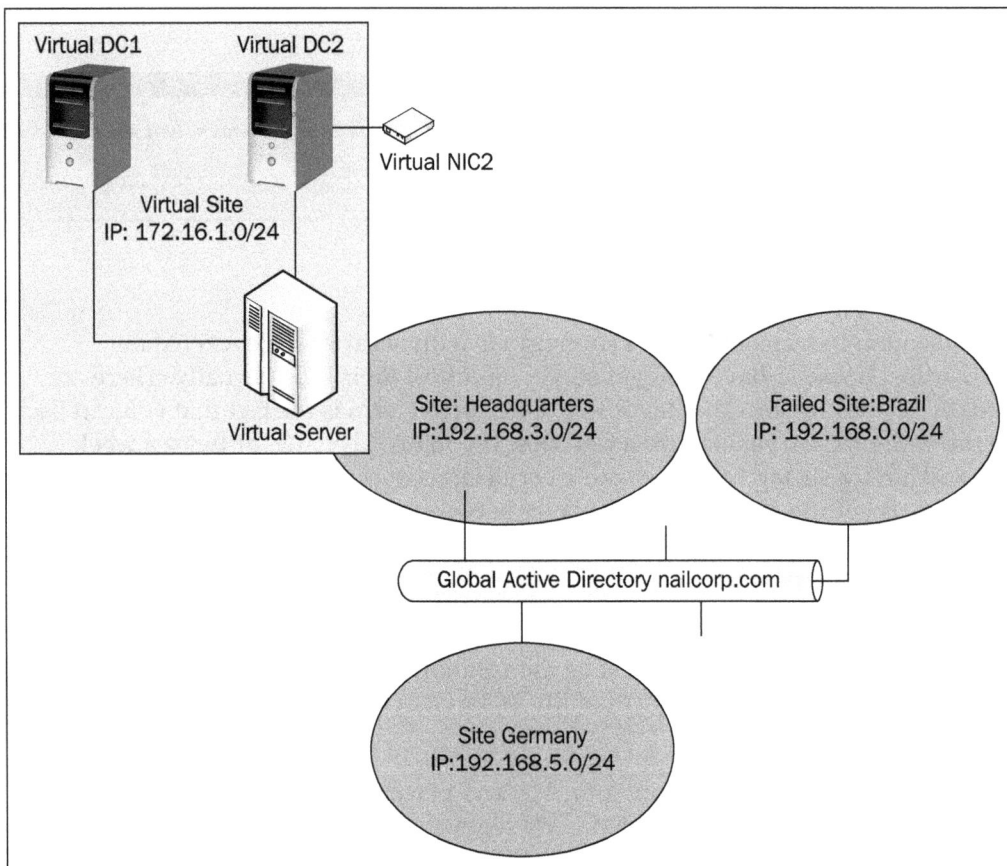

This way also, when the WAN link comes back online, you will get only the changes that have happened since you moved the Virtual DC replicated. You can, once the WAN is up again, install new DCs, and replicate off the Virtual DC.

This is a quite an inexpensive way to make sure you always have a "spare" site available, which can be transferred and installed fairly quickly.

# Summary

As with any restore process, there are many steps involved to recover an entire AD site. After a successful restore, it is a good idea to monitor the replication logs, and to verify that the domain, including the recovered site, is functioning correctly. In this chapter, we also addressed the issue of different hardware of recovery DCs. This is still an issue with Windows 2003. However, if the hardware is matched fairly closely, the recovery will work, and Windows 2003 is more forgiving, even with motherboard and some chipset changes than Windows 2000 is.

When designing a Disaster Recovery plan, the virtual option is actually quite appealing and quite a few companies are implementing Virtual DCs instead of physical ones, specifically for the purpose of recovery.

# 10
# Common Recovery Tools Explained

After describing the recovery steps needed for several different scenarios, there might still be some doubts lingering about a few steps that either overlap, or we didn't look at in depth as it was outside the scope of the chapter.

Some of the things we will go through in this chapter maybe not exactly be a requirement for the recovery process, but would still be useful to know and easier to understand when referenced.

These things include replication scheduling with AD Sites and Services; why setting up sites is so important; how to configure a replication schedule for a site properly; and what specific toolkits you should have installed, or at least have ready to be installed, on your DCs. We will also look at some tools for diagnosing problems, such as DcDiag.exe and NetDiag.exe to how you can use them to try and fix small issues.

We will first start with the software toolkits.

## Software for Your DCs and Administration

Although the software packages installed on the DCs used within this book might not be a specific recovery step in the true sense, when you are hard-pressed for time you don't want to start looking for tools and programs; you want to have them installed and ready to work on, anywhere you need.

There are many tools we use within this book. Instead of copying the specific executables to your DCs, it is much easier to install the toolkits as part of the deployment when you install a DC.

# Windows Support Tools

For both Windows 2000 and Windows 2003, the support tools package is a must-have. This is included on the installation CD under `Support/Tools`, as shown in the following screenshot, which shows the contents of a 64-bit installation CD. The location of Windows 2003 Small Business Server Support Tools is on CD 2 of the SDS CD set.

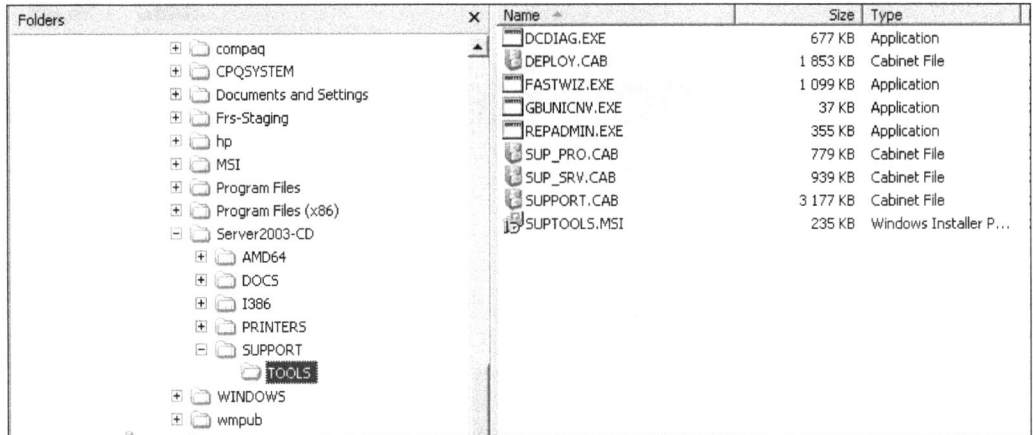

As you can see, what Microsoft considers the most essential tools, namely DcDiag. exe and Repadmin.exe, are available as standalone executables. Among many medium and large-sized organizations, it is considered a best practice to install the support tools on every DC. This is so because the support tools package provides you with essential tools that you can use for troubleshooting when errors appear in the event log, or the DC starts behaving strangely.

Once you have the Support Tools installed, you will have an additional entry in your Start menu for Windows support tools, which contains a link to the Help file and a shortcut to the command prompt.

# Windows Resource Kit Tools

The Windows Resource Kit traditionally only came as books in the NT 4.0 era. With Windows 2000, Microsoft started making the tools that are included in the Resource Kit available online for free download. You can still purchase the books as well, which are quite useful because they describe each tool and its application in great detail. However, the tools themselves can easily be downloaded. The links are listed here:

- For Windows 2000 (Server and Advanced Server):
  `http://support.microsoft.com/kb/927229.`

- For Windows Server 2003 32bit: `http://www.microsoft.com/Downloads/`
  `details.aspx?FamilyID=9d467a69-57ff-4ae7-96ee-b18c4790cffd&disp`
  `laylang=en.`

For Windows Server 2003 64bit, there is no Resource Kit because Microsoft's website clearly states that the tools are not supported on 64-bit platforms. Given that the tools can be run from any XP client as well, this is not much of an issue unless you want to run a complete 64-bit server environment, and would like to distribute the tools with the DCs. One option is to have a virtual DC that runs Windows Server 2003 in 32-bit mode.

As only a handful of tools are necessary for Disaster Recovery, and you can run the tools from a client, it does not matter that much. The main point is that the tools should be available somewhere close to the DCs in every location. So, if you run them from a client, it might be a good idea to copy the tools onto the administration PC. A good option is to keep a CD copy of these tools stored with the Disaster Recovery Guide.

# Adminpack for Windows XP/Vista Clients

The Administrative Tools package (Adminpack) is the least-used administrator tool in most organizations. Although it is considered a best practice to install Adminpack onto the administrative PCs or the PCs of the IT department, this is rarely done. In several cases, a lot of the administrative tasks are performed via Remote Desktop, directly on the DCs. This, of course, means that you have to give all of the people who make even small changes in the AD access to log on to the DCs. This might not be a good idea from a security perspective and can lead to actions that could have been prevented, such as downloading things directly to the DC, and installing or copying/modifying settings on the DC directly.

As DCs are the heart that make AD work, these machines should be as secure and isolated as possible.

The Adminpack is actually a file called `adminpack.msi`, which can be found in the i386 folder on the 32-bit installation CD of Windows 2000 and Windows server 2003. It is also in the same directory on the 64-bit installation CD, but there it is called `wadminpack.msi`.

The Adminpack contains the necessary snap-ins for the Microsoft Management Console (MMC), and puts them into your Administrative tools folder. These snap-ins are the normal tools you would have on a DC in order to administer the AD (shown in the following screenshot). It is, however, possible to run them directly from your client instead of on the DC.

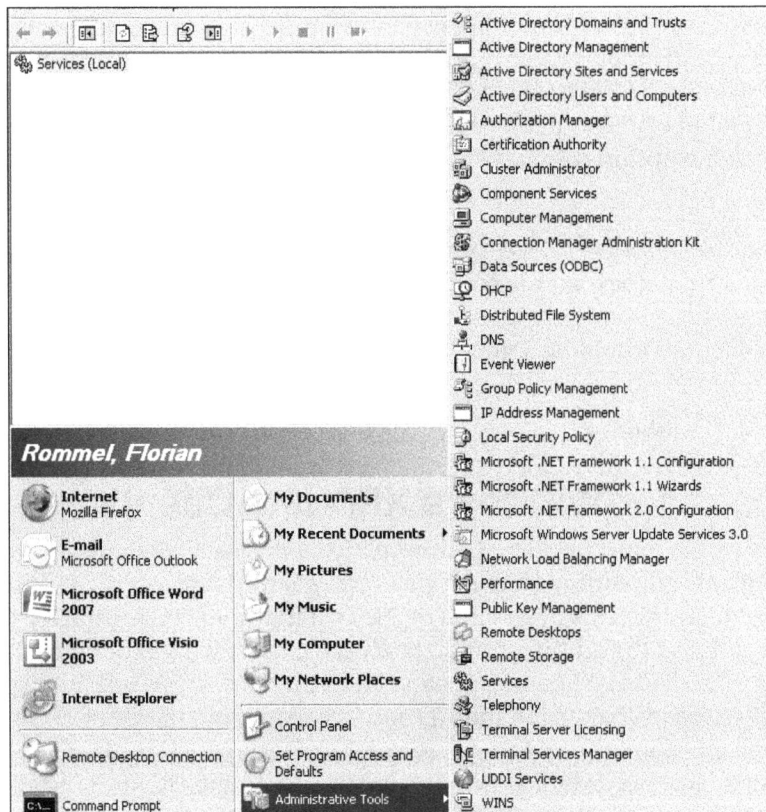

Using the Adminpack also allows you to re-target the tools to different DCs and you don't have to log on every time.

# Diagnosing and Troubleshooting Tools

In this section we are going through some of the more advanced uses and possibilities of three tools that will undoubtedly be of great help in diagnosing either AD problems or replication problems.

The three tools that almost every person who needs to perform troubleshooting on Windows Server 2003 should be familiar with are NetDiag.exe, DcDiag.exe, and Repadmin.exe.

All three are command-line utilities, which implies that they can be run from a Windows XP Professional or Windows Vista workstation, and that they are standalone executables that can be copied from one machine to another. A nice feature of these tools is that they connect remotely to the DCs via the Remote Procedure Call service (RPC) and therefore you do not need to log on to the DCs. The only requirement for most of them is that they need to run from a machine that is a member of the domain and has access to the network.

# DcDiag

DcDiag is the domain controller diagnostic utility. It allows you to diagnose a domain controller, and check if everything is ok. If it is not, then the tests will run until failure, and based on which tests fail, you can go about finding the cause. Even though this may sound rather simple, this utility, even if run without any flags or options, will execute a set of very meaningful tests, and based on pass or fail, you will have a very good idea of where to start looking. The tests performed are listed in the following tables:

| Primary tests | Descriptions |
|---|---|
| Connectivity | Tests whether or not the DC is connected to the network |
| Replications | Tests to ensure replications can be started, and are run on time |
| NCSecDesc | Checks that the security descriptors on the naming context heads have appropriate permissions for replication |
| NetLogons | Tests if the DC allows the appropriate logons to initiate replication |
| Advertising | Tests if the DC can advertise itself (DNS) |
| KnowsOfRoleHolders | Tests if the DC knows which servers hold the FSMO roles |
| RidManager | Tests if the DC can contact the RidManager |
| Machine Account | Tests if the DC has a valid Machine Account |
| Services | Tests if the necessary services are running on the DC |
| ObjectsReplicated | Tests whether or not the DSA and Machine Account objects have ever been replicated |
| frssysvol | Checks if the sysvol share is listed in the File Replication Service (FRS) |
| frsevent | Tests if FRS errors have been generated |
| kccevent | Tests if KCC errors have been generated |
| systemlog | Tests if there are system errors |
| VerifyReferences | Tests if AD FRS records are intact and correct for the replication infrastructure |

| DNS Partition tests | Descriptions |
|---|---|
| **Forest DNS tests** | |
| `CrossRefValidation` | Checks if the replication cross-references are intact in the forest DNS zone |
| `CheckSDRefDom` | Checks if the Security descriptors for the forest are intact |
| **Domain DNS tests** | |
| `CrossRefValidation` | Checks if the replication cross-references are intact in the domain DNS zone |
| `CheckSDRefDom` | Checks if the Security descriptors for the domain are intact |

| Schema, Configuration, and Enterprise tests | Descriptions |
|---|---|
| **Schema tests** | |
| `CrossRefValidation` | Checks if the replication cross-references are intact in the schema itself |
| `CheckSDRefDom` | Checks if the Security descriptors within the schema are intact |
| **Configuration** | |
| `CrossRefValidation` | Checks if the replication cross-references are intact in the current forest configuration |
| `CheckSDRefDom` | Checks if the Security descriptors within the configuration are intact |
| **Partition tests** | |
| `CrossRefValidation` | Checks if the replication cross-references are intact in the current application partition |
| `CheckSDRefDom` | Checks if the Security descriptors for the application partition are intact |
| **Enterprise tests** | |
| `Intersite` | Checks if the inter-site replication can be initiated |
| `FSMOCheck` | Checks that all FSMO roles are assigned and can be contacted |

As you can see, DCDiag performs a lot of tests. But bear in mind that most of these are run locally on the DC with the data held by that DC. This means that any error in the DNS, Schema, configuration or partition tests can be working on another DC. It is possible that only this particular replica of the DC is malfunctioning.

There are a few other helpful, additional tests that are not in the default set. These are important to know as well. To run the specific tests, simply type the following at the command prompt:

```
>dcdiag /test:TESTNAME
```

Where `testname` is the name of the test. You can see a list of these tests in the following table. The most notable tests are those in the DNS set. As the DNS is such an integral part of AD, testing its functionality will rule out, or at least narrow down, several things that could be wrong with the DNS.

| Additional tests | Descriptions |
| --- | --- |
| DNS | Tests DNS checks for the entire enterprise; subtests can be checked separately |
| DNS/DnsBasic | Tests the basic DNS functionality such as connecting and looking up records |
| DNS/DnsForwarders | Checks the forwarders and root hints for errors |
| DNS/DnsDelegation | Checks the DNS delegations |
| DNS/DnsDynamicUpdate | Checks if dynamic updates are working |
| DNS/DnsRecordRegistration | Checks if the DNS registration works |
| DNS/DnsResolveExtName | Checks if external names can be resolved |
| DNS/DnsAll | Runs all the subtests |
| DNS/DnsInternetName: | Can be used with /DnsResolveExtName with a URL to resolve |
| CheckSecurityError | Checks for security errors or potential security errors |
| VerifyReplicas | Checks all replicas on all replica servers for consistency |
| Topology | Checks whether the entire topology is fully connected |
| CutoffServers | Checks for servers whose partners are not available, and therefore can't receive replications |

Running DcDiag with the `/fix` flag will attempt to fix some minor problems it encounters. Some of the DNS-related issues, for example when the DC is not registered in the application partition, could quickly be fixed this way.

# NetDiag

NetDiag is another command-line utility that lets you perform tests with a lot of verbose output. It is also included in the Windows Support tools. While DcDiag allowed to you to test everything related to the DCs and DNS, NetDiag allows you to test everything related to the network stack of the machine.

NetDiag, by default, just like its cousin DcDiag, runs an extensive set of tests. These tests include checking network connectivity, checking which hotfixes are installed, whether the network card is configured properly and the network speed is configured correctly, what protocols and services are running, domain membership, and many more. A sample output from a working DC (DC1.nailcorp.com) is as follows:

```
C:\Documents and Settings\Administrator>netdiag

. . . . . . . . . . . . . . . . . . . . . . . . . . . . . . . . . . .

    Computer Name: DC1

    DNS Host Name: dc1.nailcorp.com

    System info : Microsoft Windows Server 2003 (Build 3790)

    Processor : x86 Family 6 Model 15 Stepping 8, GenuineIntel

    List of installed hotfixes :

        KB921503

        KB924667-v2

        KB925398_WMP64

        KB925902

        KB926122

        KB927891

        KB929123

        KB930178

        KB931784

        KB932168

        KB933360

        KB933729

        KB933854

        KB935839

        KB935840

        KB935966

        KB936021

        KB936357

        KB936782

        KB938127

        KB939653

        KB941202

        KB941568
```

```
        KB941569

        KB941644

        KB941672

        KB942615

        KB942763

        KB942840

        KB943460

        KB943485

        KB944653

        Q147222


Netcard queries test . . . . . . . : Passed

Per interface results:

    Adapter : Local Area Connection
        Netcard queries test . . . : Passed

        Host Name. . . . . . . . . : dc1

        IP Address . . . . . . . . : 10.0.0.50

        Subnet Mask. . . . . . . . : 255.255.255.0

        Default Gateway. . . . . . : 10.0.0.2

        Dns Servers. . . . . . . . : 10.0.0.50

        AutoConfiguration results. . . . . . : Passed

        Default gateway test . . . : Passed

        NetBT name test. . . . . . : Passed

        [WARNING] At least one of the <00> 'WorkStation Service', <03>
'Messenger Service', <20> 'WINS' names is missing.

WINS service test. . . . . : Skipped
There are no WINS servers configured for this interface.

Global results:
Domain membership test . . . . . . : Passed
NetBT transports test. . . . . . . : Passed
    List of NetBt transports currently configured:
        NetBT_Tcpip_{D8B5C232-8078-485D-8DE0-2F5C8C2FB480}
    1 NetBt transport currently configured.

Autonet address test . . . . . . . : Passed
```

```
IP loopback ping test. . . . . . . : Passed

Default gateway test . . . . . . . : Passed

NetBT name test. . . . . . . . . . : Passed

    [WARNING] You don't have a single interface with the <00>
'WorkStation Service', <03> 'Messenger Service', <20> 'WINS' names
defined.

Winsock test . . . . . . . . . . . : Passed

DNS test . . . . . . . . . . . . . : Passed

    PASS - All the DNS entries for DC are registered on DNS server
'192.168.0.50' and other DCs also have some of the names registered.

Redir and Browser test . . . . . . : Passed

    List of NetBt transports currently bound to the Redir

        NetBT_Tcpip_{D8B5C232-8078-485D-8DE0-2F5C8C2FB480}

    The redir is bound to 1 NetBt transport.

    List of NetBt transports currently bound to the browser

        NetBT_Tcpip_{D8B5C232-8078-485D-8DE0-2F5C8C2FB480}

    The browser is bound to 1 NetBt transport.

DC discovery test. . . . . . . . . : Passed

DC list test . . . . . . . . . . . : Passed

Trust relationship test. . . . . . : Skipped

Kerberos test. . . . . . . . . . . : Passed

LDAP test. . . . . . . . . . . . . : Passed

Bindings test. . . . . . . . . . . : Passed

WAN configuration test . . . . . . : Skipped

    No active remote access connections.

Modem diagnostics test . . . . . . : Passed

IP Security test . . . . . . . . . : Skipped

    Note: run "netsh ipsec dynamic show /?" for more detailed information

The command completed successfully
```

As you can see from this example output, there are several warnings and skips of tests. The warnings shown here occur because we do not have certain services running on the DCs. These are not critical services and we do not need them. However, NetDiag tested them anyway because, by default, it executes a standard set of tests which includes these. The Messenger Service, Workstation Service, and WINS names were not running because they are not needed in our domain structure.

Should you rely on these services, especially as many companies still have WINS servers running, these warnings should catch your attention because they should be running. As the WINS server address was not defined, the service test for WINS was skipped. We also have no current trust relationship with other domains, and therefore that test was also skipped. If we had one, the trust connection would have been checked to verify that it was working and the other end can be contacted. Lastly, we do not have any IPSec configured on our network cards, and no WAN or Remote Access connections, so this is why these tests were skipped as well. If you have a RAS connection configured, the test will try to use it and verify its state. This is particularly useful if you have modem or DSL-based backup lines that are used for replication should the LAN fail between the networks and DCs.

Just like DcDiag, NetDiag also has a set of extra switches and tests. The interesting ones are listed in the following table. And you can invoke the tests by typing:

```
>netdiag /OPTION /TESTNAME
```

The options in NetDiag are the ones that can give a lot of information on the verbose and debug flags.

| Netdiag switches | Descriptions |
| --- | --- |
| /q | This creates a quiet mode and only shows the errors and warnings encountered, if any |
| /v | Creates a verbose output for more information about each test result |
| /debug | Is the most verbose output; NetDiag can take quite a while to complete |
| /l | Creates a log file called netdiag.log in the same directory as executed |
| /d:NAME | NAME represents the domain name, and this option will find a DC in that domain |
| /fix | Like dcdiags /fix, this option fixes minor problems quickly |
| /DcAccountEnum | Enumerates all of the DC computer accounts within a domain |
| /test:Name | Name here is the name of the single test to run; for a full list, type netdiag /? |

If you have connectivity issues, NetDiag will almost certainly find them, and as with DcDiag, it is recommended that you always output everything to a log file, which is easier to read. The output of both utilities scrolls by rather quickly in the command line, and can be difficult to read.

# Monitoring with Sonar and Ultrasound

Monitoring your AD is something that needs to be done regularly, and there are many commercial utilities out there that will help you achieve this. However, it might be worth investigating tools that are available for free from Microsoft, and even from some other vendors.

## Introducing Sonar

Sonar and Ultrasound are two utilities that allow you to monitor the File Replication Service (FRS), and both utilities are good at detecting problems beforehand, or issues with replication from certain DCs. Sonar can be downloaded from the Microsoft Download Center at `http://www.microsoft.com/downloads`.

You will need to have the .Net Framework 1.1 installed on the machine where Sonar will run. Also, please be aware that if you have .Net Framework 2.0 installed, it does not include 1.1, and you need to install 1.1 as well.

Once installed, Sonar will not create a program menu entry, so you will need to search for it. For some reason, it will install itself into the Resource Kit folder (`C:\Program Files\Resource Kit\`) and it is called Sonar.exe. Once you run it, you will be presented with the following dialog box:

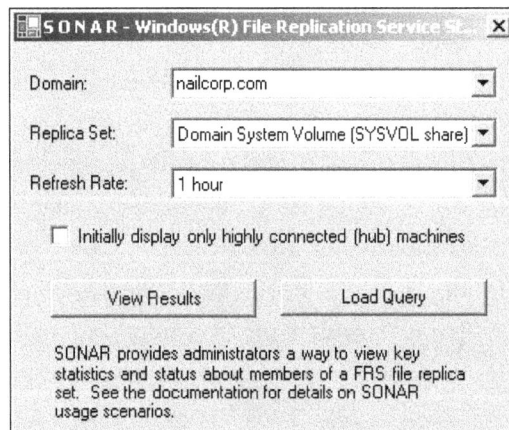

At this point, you can see two buttons, which can be used either for default querying (that is, all of the DCs within your domain) or for loading the settings with the **Load Query** button, if you have a specific query or setup saved. In our example, we will view the results and you will see the screen that you have seen in the previous figure. Also note the drop-down for **Replica Set**. This allows you to monitor DFS replications within your domain. So this tool is not just used to monitor the SYSVOL replications.

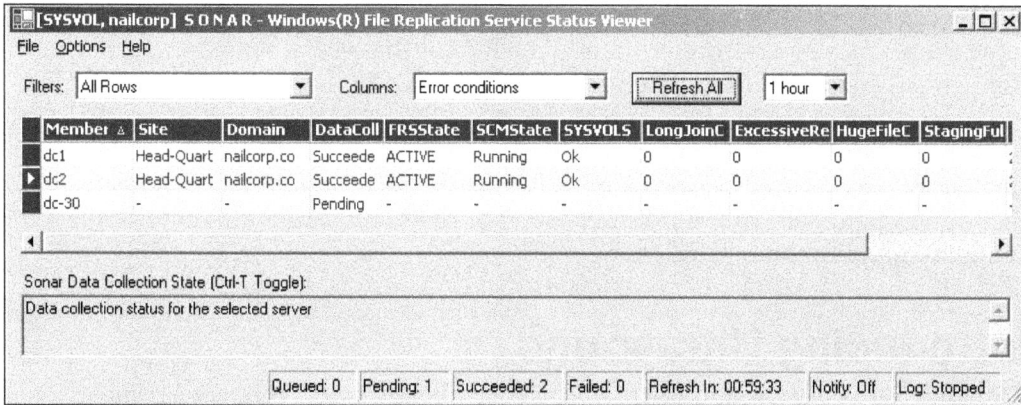

From the top part, you can easily select a very wide range of **Filters** via a drop-down list, and the **Columns** can be used to select the columns to be displayed. This relates to a *group* of columns, so there are more columns than just the ones selected from the drop-down. To illustrate the extent of information that you can get with this little utility, the following screenshot shows both of the menus expanded.

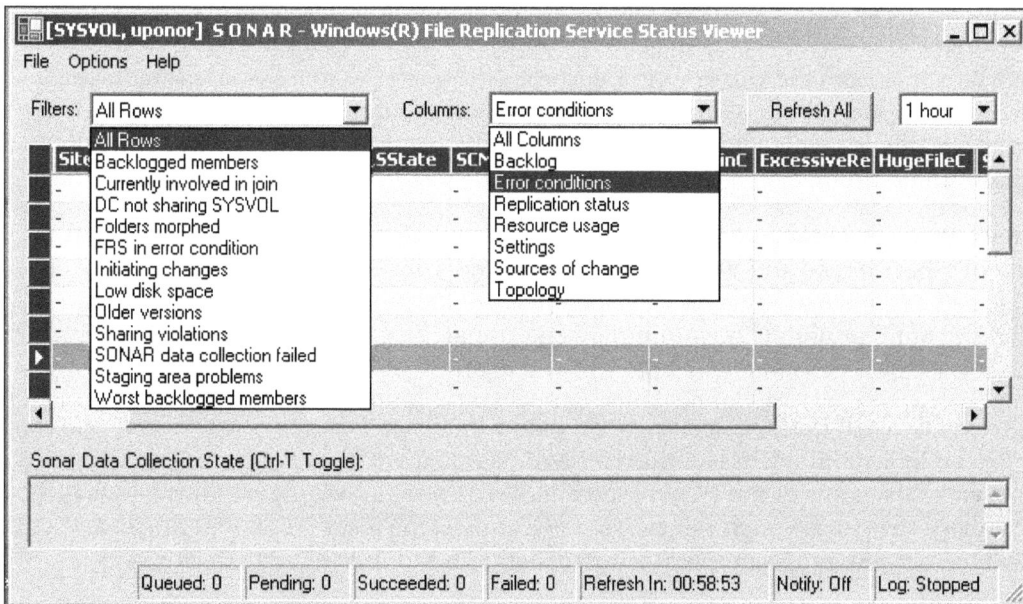

As you can see, you can use this tool to find out any information regarding the replication. Once you select the filters and columns that you want, you can click **Refresh All** and it will fetch that information from all DCs within your domain. You can see the disk usage of the AD database on all different DCs including any DC that has low disk space, is too slow, is backlogged with AD replications, and so on. This small utility, when used periodically, will help you to keep your AD in good healthy, shape and might help you find trouble-spots such as low bandwidth or wrongly configured replication schedules.

# Introducing Ultrasound

Although Sonar is a good utility that is small and does its job very well, some organizations either have many FRS points that they want to monitor, or want much more information.

This is where Ultrasound comes in. This utility is also a free download from Microsoft. However, it has much steeper requirements. Namely, it requires an SQL server as a backend. Even the SQL Server 2000 Desktop engine, or the free SQL Server 2005 Express Edition, downloadable from the Microsoft Download Center, will serve this purpose, but they would require a two-step setup and more resources. It also does collections periodically via agents that are deployed using WMI from within the Ultrasound interface. Although the free Desktop Engine has limitations, such as allowing only few connections, it does provide enough database functionality for Ultrasound. SQL Server 2005 Express edition will work perfectly fine with no problems.

If Sonar can be compared to a sonar on a boat, which gives you a lot of information about what's ahead and what's going on around you, then Ultrasound has all of the features of Sonar, plus an additional feature for radar and satellite surveillance. Getting familiar with Ultrasound may take some time. As Ultrasound is a Microsoft utility, it can be downloaded from the Microsoft Download Center.

Once you install the SQL server, or prepare a database on an existing server, you can proceed to installing Ultrasound. You will be asked which server to use and you can just enter the name of the PC where your SQL server is running. After deploying the database structure, which can take a few minutes, the installation will finish, and you will have a new program menu entry, called FRS Monitoring, where Ultrasound is located.

Once you launch Ultrasound for the first time, you will be asked to add an FRS replica to Ultrasound. At this point, you should click **Yes** and you will be prompted for your domain name and the available FRS replicas. In our case, this is similar to the example shown in the following screenshot. By simply clicking the replica set, and then clicking on **Add**, you can add it to the list of FRS replicas to the list of FRS replicas to be monitored.

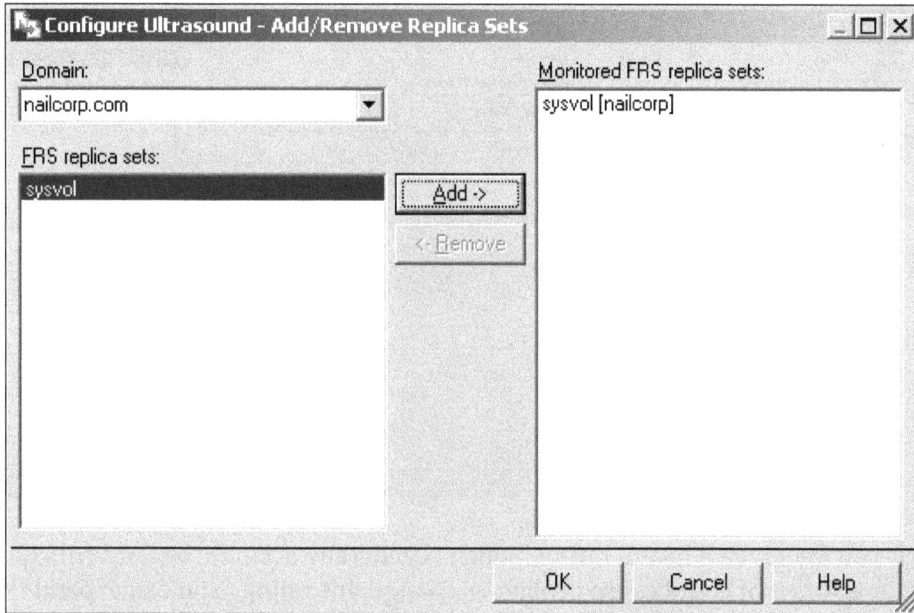

Next, you click **OK**, and Ultrasound will collect the Schema data from the selected replica set, and then ask you to add all Servers found, add only the highly connected, hub, servers or add none, and you will select your own. There is also an option to install the WMI collectors, which you want to do (shown in the following screenshot).

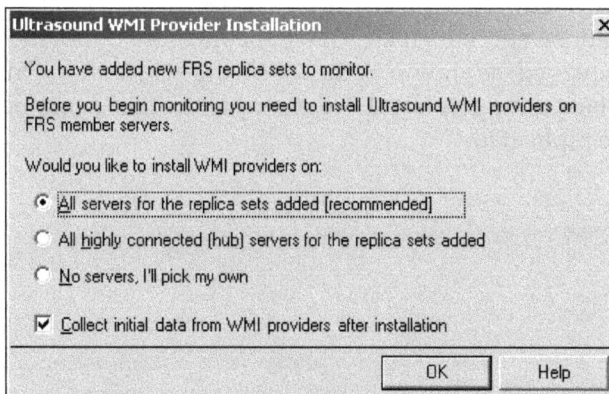

Once you have selected your approach, a whole world of information will open up. The tool may appear confusing simply because of the volume of information you can gather with it, but the learning curve quickly flattens, and the data that it provides becomes invaluable. After the initial WMI collector deployment is done, you can close the screen. Henceforth you will find that the screen shown in the following screenshot is always displayed when you start Ultrasound:

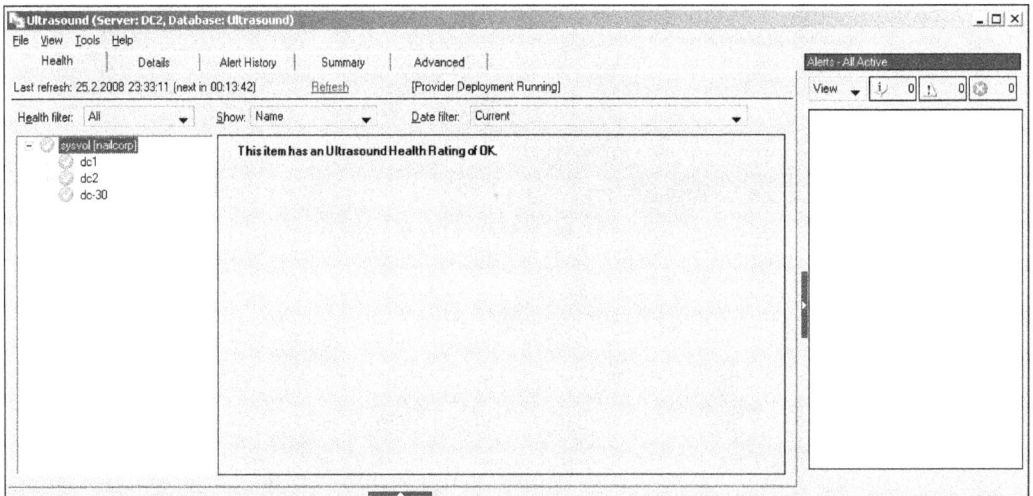

At first, you are given a health rating, which is generally accurate as only critical errors, or errors that could cause problems, change this rating. You can expand the replica set and see each server's health rating as well. This allows you to quickly identify any critical issues with the DCs.

# Details

On the second tab, **Details**, you will find information about the replications of the servers you have selected. We selected only DC1, DC2, and DC30, and details of the ongoing replications and which DCs have the most inbound and outbound connections are displayed, as shown in the following screenshot. On the top, you can also change the details to be displayed, for example the files contained within this Replica Set that are replicated.

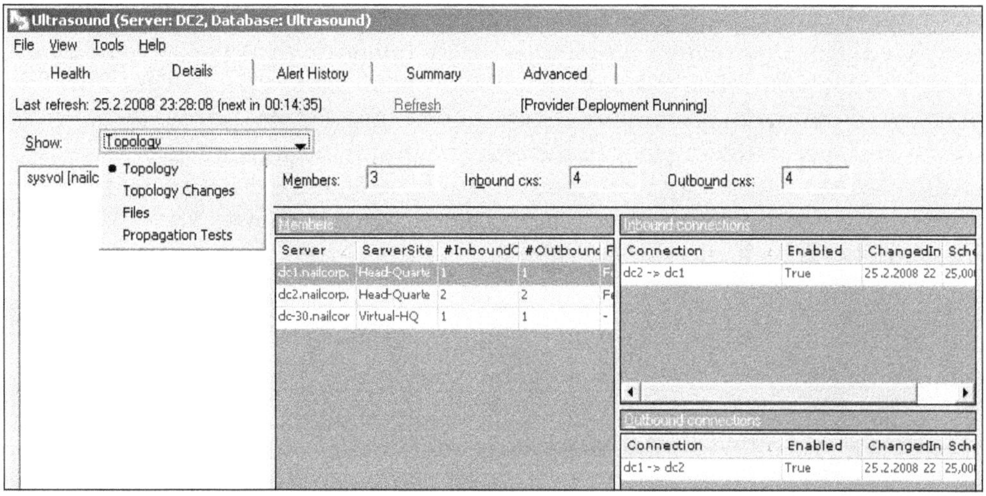

Right-clicking on a server opens up a context menu that either allows you to collect data from a specific server, or opens up the replica set and displays the details of the replica set for the server, depending on the context.

Right-clicking on the inbound or outbound connection windows will allow you to collect data, or see details regarding a specific inbound, outbound, or replica member.

# Alert History

The **Alert History** tab (shown in the following screenshot) contains all of the alerts caused by various actions or errors in the monitoring process, including failed WMI deployments, morphed directories, and other events. This is the power of Ultrasound. The detail-each error message contains is very surprising.

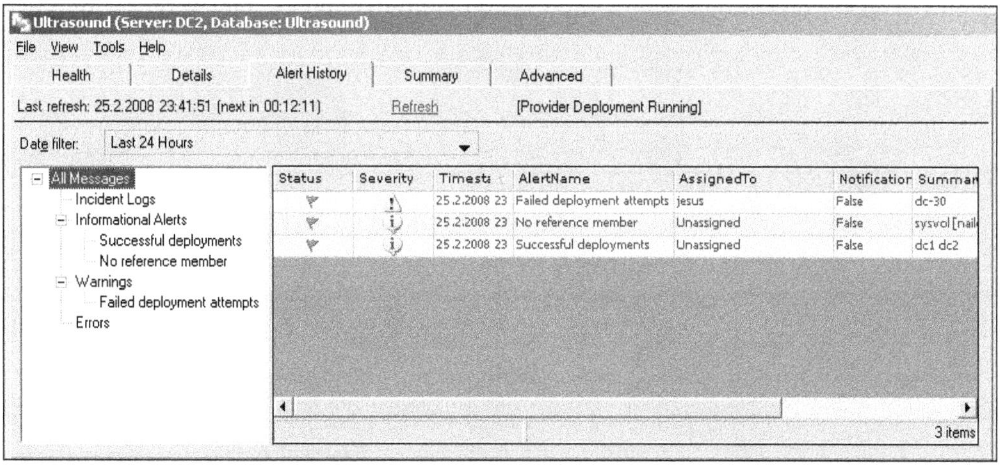

You simply double-click on an alert and the general view with all its information is displayed. This information contains the usual things, such as the date and time when the event occurred, a description of the problem, and so on. It also allows you to assign the error to a support person, and change the status from active to resolved and specify the urgency of the problem. But it the general view also has an **Advanced** tab where a lot more information regarding the error, such as what the actual error was, which server caused it, and so on, are shown. The following screenshot shows both tabs side-by-side:

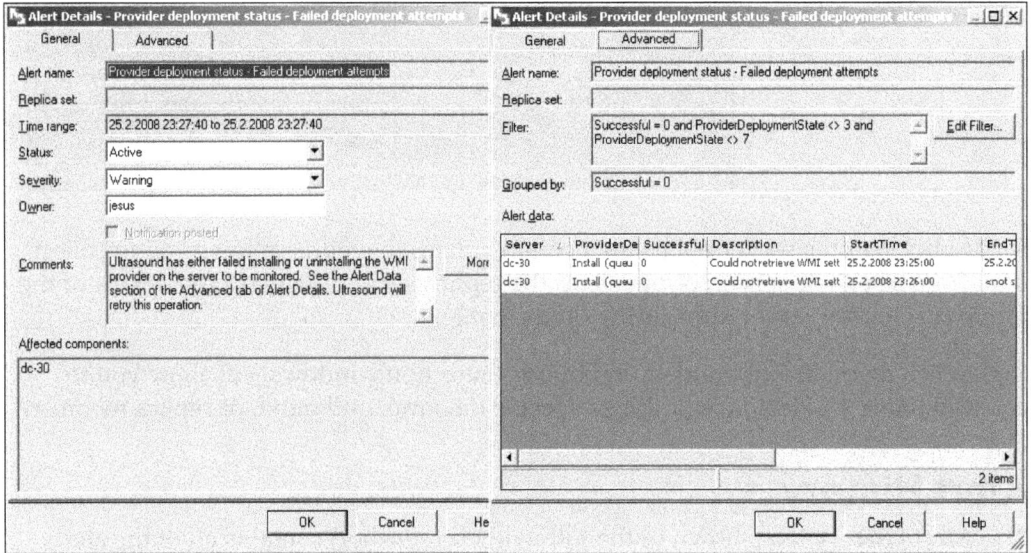

# Summary and Advanced Tabs

The **Summary** tab provides a full summary of your AD replications. It shows everything from every member, with the domain listed at the top. The domain view shows the number of files that are backlogged, the number of servers that have yellow connections, (that is, unhealthy ones) the servers that have a high connection count, and active notifications regarding the servers that are selected. All of these are illustrated in the following screenshot.

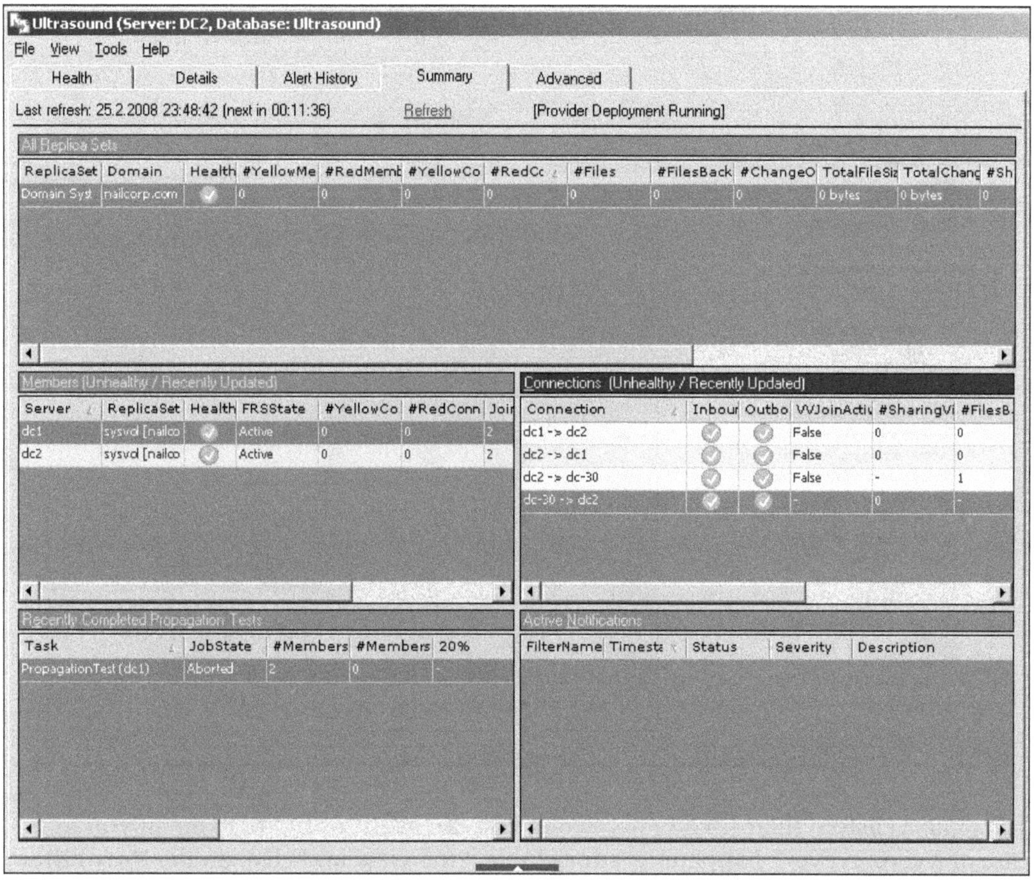

The **Advanced** tab extends the **Summary** tab, and all of the other ones. It allows you to query any information in the Ultrasound database. On the normal view, you can select pre-configured general view collections of your replica set, in the left hand pane. There are more views, such as **Failed AD updates**, than in any of the previous screens, although it is possible to easily create custom filters.

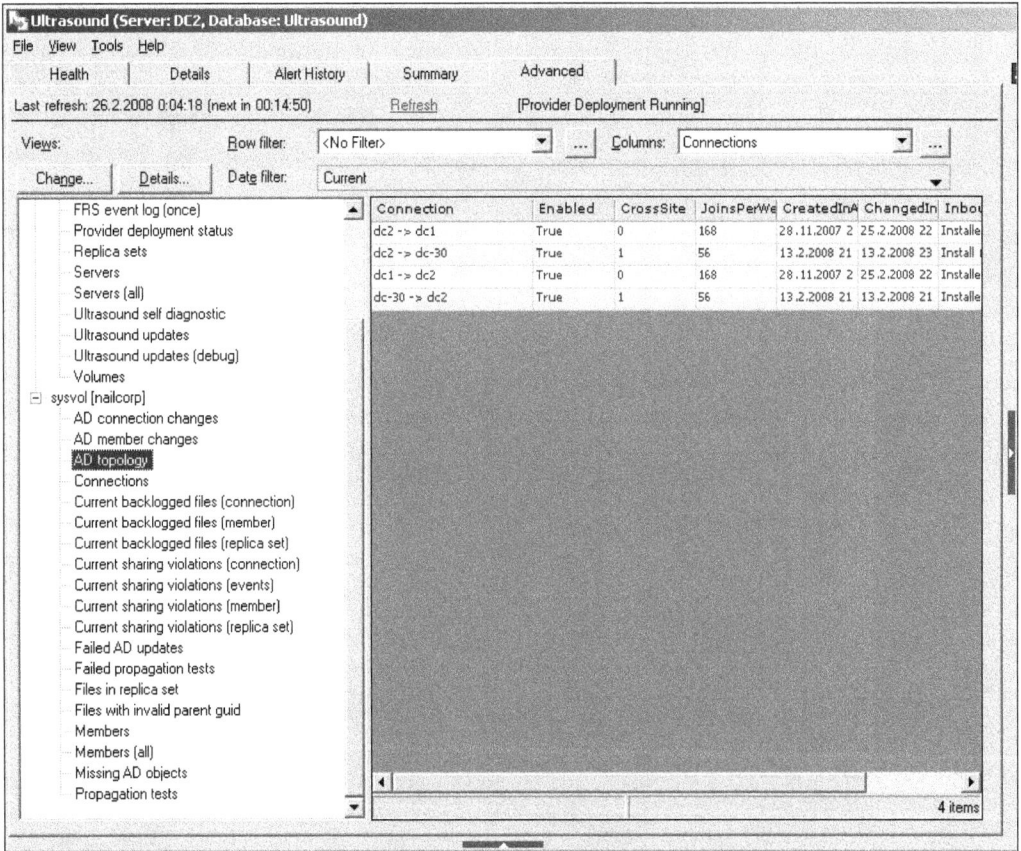

To create a custom filter for a view, which you can even configure to email you in case of a certain event happening, simply select the view and click on the **Row Filter** drop-down selection, and then click the "**...**" button, or leave it at **NO FILTER** and click the "**...**" button. You will be presented with a window that allows you to either change a filter by selecting it and then clicking on change, or to create a completely new one. In our case, we will edit the **AD Collection error** filter in the **Failed AD updates** view. Simply click on the second row with the Error 301 column, and click on **Change**.

We will change this filter to:

1. Notify us by email if a collection error occurs and

2. Set the health metrics for this filter to critical, as it then raises red flags immediately in the event of an AD collection failure.

This might seem a bit drastic as a collection failure can occur for a number of reasons, but unless these reasons occur a lot in your infrastructure, this should be a good way of identifying anomalies.

First, in the Change window, click on the **Alert** tab and select **Enable notifications**. Then, select the **Custom notifications** option. Finally, simply click on **ADD** on the right-hand side of the dialog box, and enter the email address to which you want the notification to be sent. You can only add one email address per notification, so, you have to add each email address separately. However, you can also log an event, even though you are receiving an email (as shown in the following screenshot).

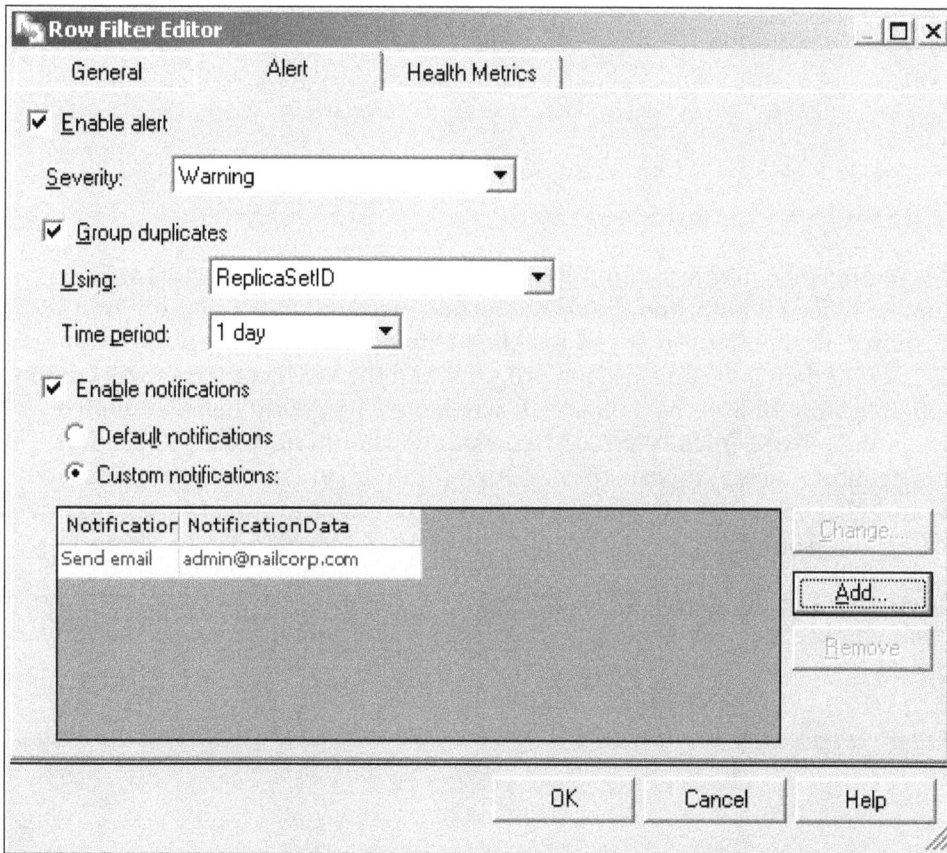

To set the health metrics to critical, first click on the **Health Metrics** tab, and click on **Enable health metrics**. Then, simply click on **ADD**, leave **Replica Set** selected, and select **Critical** from the bottom drop-down menu (as shown in the following screenshot). Finally, simply click on **OK** and you will be returned to Ultrasound.

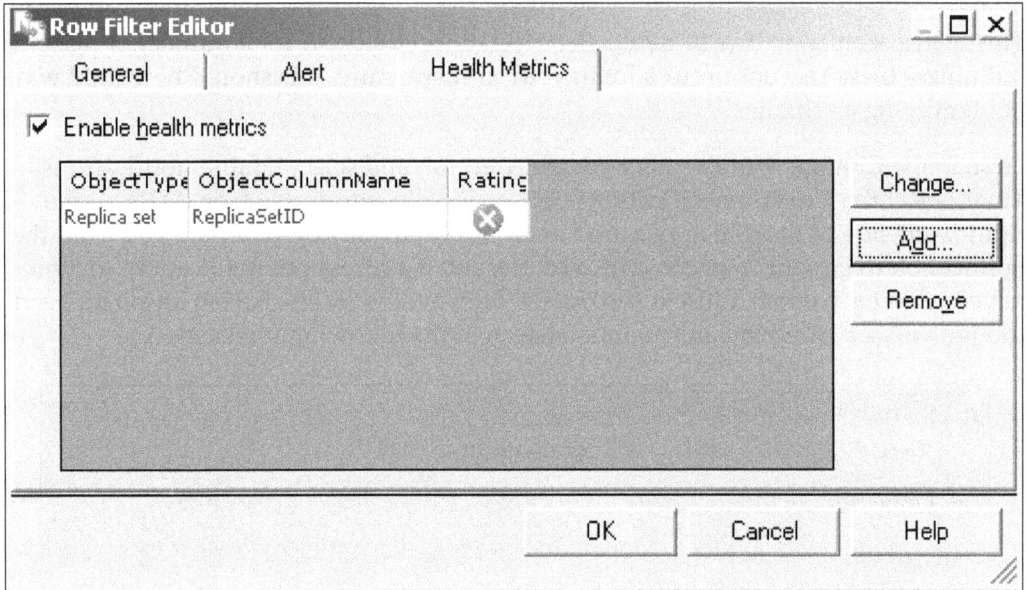

At this point, you could just minimize Ultrasound. The WMI collectors will continuously feed it data, and the AD collection alert will notify you for an AD replication collection failure. If you installed Ultrasound with a standard installation of SQL Server then you can close the program and the WMI collectors will continue to feed data straight into the database. If you have Ultrasound installed with a Desktop Engine, or SQL Server 2005 Express, you should have the application running continuously. You can, of course, configure many more notifications to make sure that you cover all your bases, and do not have to spend time continually watching Ultrasound.

Ultrasound is a utility that has a somewhat steep learning curve for a short time, but can help you keep a perfectly healthy, replicating AD, when deployed correctly and used well.

# Summary

In this chapter we discussed a few tools and utilities that will help you monitor and diagnose your AD. Although these might not be directly-related to disaster recovery, it is always good to have such important information at hand, as this can then allow you to find a problem before it becomes too widespread.

Also, small command line utilities such as DcDiag and NetDiag, together with the whole set of tools in the Resource Kit and the Support tools, are invaluable to have in the DCs, or at least on an administrative machine where they are available for use at any time. The output of these smaller utilities can be faster than sifting through event logs that also contain a lot of other things. Lastly, having tools such as Ultrasound deployed is useful. But if you have no processes defined for how and how often to monitor them, or the corrective course of action in to take case of a problem, its value decreases significantly.

# A

# Sample Business Continuity Plan

The following is an example Business Continuity Plan. If you have never written one, then you may want to use this one as a starting point and adjust it to your needs. This plan is comprised of several sample plans found on a variety of websites, including www.itil.org and www.drj.com (Disaster Recovery Journal). These websites contain extremely valuable information with regard to DSR and BCP in general. I strongly suggest that you check them out.

The following BCP is a proven design that has been used in larger corporations, and even though you may not need all of the sections, it is good to use as many as you can, and familiarize yourself with terms and formatting. This sample is geared towards Active Directory as an authentication service and the domain in question is nailcorp.com

## Nailcorp Business Continuity Plan

### PURPOSE

The purpose of this document is to provide a description of the continuity for the Global Authentication and domain logon service in case of server failure or other technical emergency.

The most important consideration regarding this document is that life comes before material assets. Human life is the first priority in any disaster or emergency situation.

# Description of the Service

Active Directory provides the back-end mechanisms to authenticate users and services throughout the nailcorp.com domain. With this authentication determines what rights a user has within the corporate environment.

The Active Directory backend runs on dedicated servers based on Windows 2003 R2 x64 (64-bit) Edition with Service Pack 2 installed. The following hardware specifications are the standard to use in the corporate DC environment:

| Component | Amount | Description |
|---|---|---|
| Processor(s) | 2 (dual core) | 64-bit x86 based dual-core processors |
| Memory | 4GB | Amount of RAM |
| Network Interfaces | 2, in teaming mode | Amount of network cards present and active |
| Storage | 2x76GB Raid 1 | Amount and configuration of the System Disks |
| Power | 2, redundant | Hot-pluggable, redundant power supplies |

# SCOPE

This Business Continuity Plan covers the global and site-specific strategy to continue the Active Directory service. Due to the distributed nature of Active Directory and its deployment within nailcorp.com, a global outage should never occur. However, some small sites might experience hardware failure AND network connectivity failure at the same time. This strategy will cover these cases as well.

# Responsibilities and Roles

This is a list of the responsible people involved in the execution of this plan.

John Doe – Account Manager from Service Provider

Jane Doe – Service Manager, nailcorp.com

Jim Doe – CIO, nailcorp.com

# OBJECTIVES

## What we are trying to achieve with this document is:

Maintaining continuous operations at the data centers that use the AD service on a 24x7 basis and, in the event of a disaster or interruption, to keep the downtime to a minimum.

# COMMUNICATIONS

This plan shall be communicated to all key personnel through orientation training, exercises, and by making this plan available for review.

Identify critical locations where copies of these documents are stored.

Copies of this Plan:

Managers and Team leaders

Business Continuity and Risk Management Group

Intranet, IT Section

# CALL TREE

In case of a disaster, the call tree structure is as follows:

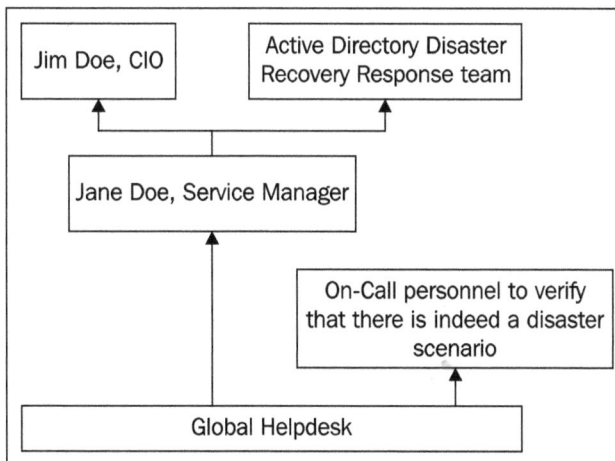

The service manager and delivery manager will be notified first. They will decide whether to declare a disaster or not. After that, the Team Leaders and the Active Directory specialists will be notified in order to recover from the disaster. Once the disaster has been overcome and the service is at an acceptable operational level again, the same structure goes backwards to declare the disaster situation over.

# Disaster declaration criteria for Active Directory service

Note: Based on the preliminary damage assessment, a determination will be made by the Manager(s) as to the level of the emergency/disaster (see Figure 1). This level will determine what actions we will take to recover.

Criteria used to determine if an emergency/disaster situation requires implementation /activation of the Business Continuity Plan.

EXAMPLE: If a site has two DCs and one fails, the service will still be available to users as Windows has automatic redirect if one logon server cannot be contacted. If the WAN connection fails, the users will still be able to authenticate via ADs stored on each DC. However, if both a DC and a WAN connection fails and the other DC a) cannot handle the load or b) have been used for something else, then no service is available to the user.

| Criteria (For Determining Potential Disaster Situation) | Date/Time Outage Occurred | Level of Outage | Assessment carried out by: | Comments (Include estimated outage) |
|---|---|---|---|---|
| Service is unavailable to all clients | | | | |
| Systems are offline and are not available to clients | | | | |
| Networking is offline | | | | |
| Major infrastructure problems (cooling, water, power) | | | | |

The following status levels should be applied

| LEVEL | DESCRIPTION |
|-------|-------------|
| 5 | Site is no longer functional (worse case) |
| 4 | Severe Impact (temporary move to another site) |
| 3 | Significant Impact (one or more applications or areas are unusable, but recovery is possible) |
| 2 | Moderate Impact (Application not available, or single area is affected) |
| 1 | Minimal Impact (Major application problems) |

# Functional restoration

REVIEW CRITICAL PLATFORM - SYSTEMS FUNCTIONS

Priority of Service: This list shows which service provided by a DC will have what priority.

Recovery Time Objective: Period from when a disaster is declared to recovery of critical functions.

Recovery Point Objective: The point in time at which Active Directory service must be returned to operation at the site.

# Recovery site(s)

Locations were Active Directory service is going to be recovered following a disaster is very distributed. If a complete hub site (Data Center) fails then the other sites will collectively take over the Active Directory service load automatically. This is done by

Windows automatically. Windows chooses the closest logon server based on the fastest reply.

| SERVICE NAME/ SITUATION | PRIORITY | RECOVERY TIME OBJECTIVE | RECOVERY POINT OBJECTIVE |
|--------------------------|----------|--------------------------|---------------------------|
| Active Directory (Authentication) | ONE + no down time | 1 hour | 4 hours |
| DNS Service on a DC | ONE | 4 hours | 8 hours |
| AD Replication failure | TWO 1-3 days | 1 day | 3 days |

# Necessary alternative site materials

Retrieve offsite materials

If an offsite vendor is used, coordinate requirements through the Operations Center. Verify that the location for delivery, and the name of the specific staff member designated to receive them, are correct

**Off-Site Storage Location for this service should be at any hosting facility that hosts Domain Controllers.**

[ ] Completed by _____ Date/Time _____ Note _____

# TECHNICAL RECOVERY STEPS TO RECOVER A FAILED DC

## 1. Functional Restoration of a Domain Controller

### 1.1. Single DC Failure - DC Recovery with same name

1.1.0. Notification Received by Manager

As a member of the Management Team, the Manager will receive notification that a disaster has been declared.

[ ] Completed by _____ Date/Time _____ Note _____

### 1.1.1. Seize FSMO roles

If the DC was holding any crucial FSMO roles, these need to be moved ("seized") to another DC as outlined in the Disaster Recovery Plan.

[ ] Completed by _____ Date/Time _____ Note _____

### 1.1.2. Clean Active Directory of old records

Because the recovery is attempted with the same name the Active Directory records of the "old" DC need to be removed first as outlined in the Disaster Recovery Plan.

[ ] Completed by _____ Date/Time _____ Note _____

### 1.1.3. Install new DC Hardware and OS

The new DC hardware and software should be installed and match the old one as closely as possible.

[ ] Completed by _____ Date/Time _____ Note _____

### 1.1.4. Promote DC and verify replication

When the new DC is installed it will be promoted to be an active DC within nailcorp.com. Once it has been promoted, someone needs to verify that the AD database is in fact replicated to the DC.

[  ]  Completed by _____  Date/Time _____  Note _____

### 1.1.4.1 Recover DC if no network connection is available.

If you have a site without a WAN connection, recover the DC from the last backup that has been made, following the steps outlined in the Disaster Recovery Plan.

[  ]  Completed by _____  Date/Time _____  Note _____

### 1.1.5. Delegate FSMO Roles

Once the DC has been verified as fully functional, re-apply the FSMO roles to it that it used to have.

[  ]  Completed by _____  Date/Time _____  Note _____

# APPENDICES

## Active Directory Service and support personnel

| Key Account Manager – Service Provider | John Doe | John.doe@service-provider.com | +1555448877 |
| --- | --- | --- | --- |
| Service Manager – NailCorp | Jane Doe | Jane.doe@nailcorp.com | +155588899 |
| CIO – NailCorp | Jim Doe | Jim.doe@nailcorp.com | +155588822 |
| AD Recovery Team lead – NailCorp | Jack Doe | Jack.doe@nailcorp.com | +155588811 |
| AD Recovery Specialist | Jill Doe | Jill.doe@nailcorp.com | +155588833 |

## Support documentation for the application/service attached to this plan

Disaster Recovery Plan for Active Directory

Full contact list of AD service personnel

## Shared Contacts

Include contact information for all vendors and supplier that would need to be contacted if there is an emergency or disaster that affects this application/service or site. This would include contractors and external contacts.

# Damage Assessment Forms

Damage Assessment Form - Recovery of Connectivity (Example)

Include a Damage Assessment Form for each platform.

| Activities | Resources Needed | Estimated Completion Time/Date | Completed By |
|---|---|---|---|
| **1. Assess Damage** | | | |
| On-site inspection to identify LAN and WAN network servers (services) affected by the disaster | | | |
| Arrange temporary power if necessary | | | |
| Ensure area around electrical equipment is dry and clear | | | |
| Test each LAN and WAN network server | | | |
| Prepare a record of all network components damaged or not working | | | |
| Ensure suitable safety levels | | | |
| Assess damage to network software through stringent tests | | | |
| Assess damage to ISP links | | | |
| Advise Continuity Group (they will Contact Risk Management Group) | | | |
| **2. Repair** | | | |
| Check to see if vendor maintenance support is available | | | |
| Have damage assessed by networks maintenance/repair engineer | | | |
| Identify back-up and recovery network tapes | | | |
| Obtain estimates for cost and period of repair | | | |
| Instruct vendors/maintenance partners to effect repairs | | | |

| Activities | Resources Needed | Estimated Completion Time/Date | Completed By |
|---|---|---|---|
| Maintain inventory of network components to be repaired | | | |
| Monitor that network components are repaired on time and tested | | | |
| Advise Disaster Recovery Manager | | | |

| Activities | Resources Needed | Estimated Completion Time/Date | Completed By |
|---|---|---|---|
| **3. Arrange Replacements** | | | |
| Prepare list of non-repairable equipment | | | |
| Ensure network specification is still suitable for organization's purposes | | | |
| Obtain vendor quotes or replacements | | | |
| Advise Continuity Manager | | | |

# GLOSSARY

Here are listed all continuity related terms used in this plan. Please do not remove them from this document as these are industry-standard, international definitions.

**ALTERNATIVE SITE:** A location, other than the normal facility, used to process data and/or conduct critical business functions in the event of a disaster.

**CONTINUITY PLANNING:** The process of developing advance arrangements and procedures that enable an organization to respond to an event in such a manner that critical functions continue without interruption or essential change.

**CONTINUITY MANAGEMENT:** The process of developing recovery timeline methodologies, documentation, procedures and instructions for use in restoring IT services. Continuity Management includes IT risk management, service continuity planning, and IT disaster recovery.

**COLD SITE:** An alternative facility that is void of any resources or equipment except air-conditioning and raised flooring. Equipment and resources must be installed in such a facility to duplicate the critical business functions of an organization. Cold-sites have many variations depending on their communication facilities, UPS systems, or mobility. SIMILAR TERMS: Shell-site; Backup site; Recovery site; Alternative site.

**COMMAND CENTER:** A centrally-located facility having adequate phone lines to begin recovery operations. Typically it is a temporary facility used by the management team to begin coordinating the recovery processes, and is used until the alternative sites are functional.

**DATA CENTER RECOVERY:** The component of Disaster Recovery that deals with the restoration, at an alternative location, of data centers services and computer processing capabilities.

**DATA SECURITY:** The securing and safeguarding of electronic equipment owned by an organization, using technology such as security software packages and data encryption devices.

**DAMAGE ASSESSMENT:** The process of assessing damage, following a disaster, to computer hardware, vital records, office facilities, etc., and determining what can be salvaged or restored and what must be replaced.

**DISASTER:** A sudden, unplanned, calamitous event causing great damage or loss. In the business environment, any event that creates the inability of an organization to provide critical business functions for at least a predetermined period of time.

**EMERGENCY:** A sudden, unexpected event requiring immediate action due to potential threat to health and safety, the environment, or property.

**EMERGENCY PREPAREDNESS:** The discipline that ensures an organization's, or community's readiness to respond to an emergency in a coordinated, timely, and effective manner.

**EMERGENCY PROCEDURES:** A plan of action to be followed, with immediate effect in the event of a disaster, to prevent the loss of life and minimize injury and property damage.

**HOT-SITE:** An alternative facility that has the equipment and resources to recover the business functions affected by the occurrence of a disaster. Hot-sites may vary in the type of facilities offered (such as data processing, communication, or any other critical business functions needing duplication). The location and size of the hot-site will be proportional to the equipment and resources needed.

**INTERNAL HOT-SITES:** A fully equipped alternative processing site owned and operated by the organization.

**NETWORK RECOVERY OBJECTIVE:** The time required to recover or fail-over network operations. Keep in mind that systems level recovery is not fully complete if associates cannot access the services via network connections.

**OFF-SITE STORAGE FACILITY:** A secure location, remote from the primary location, at which backup hardware, software, data files, documents, equipment, or supplies are stored.

**RECOVERY POINT OBJECTIVE:** The point at which data must be restored in order to resume processing transactions.

**RECOVERY TIME OBJECTIVE:** The time between a disaster being declared and the recovery of the critical functions.

**RISK ASSESSMENT/ANALYSIS:** The process of identifying and minimizing the exposure to certain threats that an organization may experience. SIMILAR TERMS: Risk assessment; impact assessment; corporate loss analysis; risk identification; hazard/exposure analysis; exposure assessment.

**RISK MANAGEMENT:** The discipline that ensures an organization does not assume an unacceptable level of risk.

**STRUCTURED WALK-THROUGH TEST:** An activity where team members walk through the Business Continuity Plan to identify and correct weaknesses.

**WARM SITE:** An alternative processing site that is only partially equipped (as compared to a Hot-Site, which is fully equipped).

# Bibliography

The following references were used as base for writing this book. Some material is also original work. For easier reading, they are grouped by chapter.

## Chapter 1

1. Microsoft Corporation, 2005. How Domain Controllers Are Located in Windows XP.[Electronic Knowledgebase Article].[Cited 29.2.2008]. Available at: `http://support.microsoft.com/kb/314861`

2. Microsoft Corporation, 2002. Support WebCast: Microsoft Active Directory Disaster Recovery.[Webcast].[Cited 28.2.2008]. Available at: `http://support.microsoft.com/kb/325560/en-us`

3. Wikipedia, 2008. Disaster recovery.[Electronic Document].[Cited4.3.2008]. Available at: `http://en.wikipedia.org/wiki/Disaster_recovery`

## Chapter 2

4. Microsoft Corporation, 2003. How DNS Support for Active Directory Works.[Electronic Technet Article].[Cited 26.2.2008]. Available at: `http://technet2.microsoft.com/windowsserver/en/library/9d62e91d-75c3-4a77-ae93-a8804e9ff2a11033.mspx?mfr=true`

5. Microsoft Corporation, 2007. FSMO placement and optimization on Active Directory domain controllers. [Electronic Knowledgebase Article]. [Cited 27.2.2008]. Available at: `http://support.microsoft.com/kb/223346`

6. Microsoft Corporation, 2003. Domains and Forests Technical Reference. [Electronic Knowledgebase Article]. [Cited 27.2.2008]. Available at: `http://technet2.microsoft.com/windowsserver/en/library/16a2bdb3-d0a3-4435-95fd-50116e300c571033.mspx`

7. Microsoft Corporation, 2003. 2007 Office system Administrative Template files (ADM, ADMX, ADML) and Office Customization Tool version 2.0. [Electronic Download]. [Cited 27.2.2008]. Available at: `http://www. microsoft.com/downloads/details.aspx?displaylang=en&FamilyID=92 d8519a-e143-4aee-8f7a-e4bbaeba13e7`

8. Microsoft Corporation, 2003. Determining Your Active Directory Design and Deployment Strategy. [Electronic Technet Article]. [Cited 27.2.2008]. Available at: `http://technet2.microsoft.com/windowsserver/en/ library/ff92f142-66ea-498b-ad0f-a379c411eb6e1033.mspx?mfr=true`

9. Microsoft Corporation, 2004. Windows Server 2003 Active Directory Branch Office Guide.[Electronic Document download].[Cited 27.2.2008]. Available at: `http://www.microsoft.com/downloads/details.aspx? FamilyId=9353A4F6-A8A8-40BB-9FA7-3A95C9540112&displaylang=en`

10. Microsoft Corporation, 2003. Windows Server 2003 Active Directory. [Electronic Document].[Cited 27.2.2008]. Available at: `http://www. microsoft.com/windowsserver2003/technologies/directory/ activedirectory/default.mspx`

11. Windowsnetworking.com, 2005. Managing Active Directory FSMO Roles.[Electronic Document].[Cited 27.2.2008]. Available at: `http://www. windowsnetworking.com/articles_tutorials/Managing-Active- Directory-FSMO-Roles.html`

# Chapter 3

12. Intel Corporation, 2007. The Spectrum of Risk Management in a Technology Company. [Published and Electronic Document]. [Cited 4.3.2008]. Available at: `http://www.intel.com/technology/itj/2007/v11i2/5-restricted- countries/5-methodology.htm`

13. MCI Corporation, 2002. IT Security Risk Management. [Electronic PDF Document]. [Cited 29.2.2008]. Available at: `http://global.mci.com/ca/ resources/whitepapers/pdf/Gerschefske1.pdf`

14. ComputerWorld.com, 2006. Five mistakes of vulnerability management. [Electronic Document].[Cited 27.2.2008]. Available at: `http://www. computerworld.com/printthis/2006/0,4814,107647,00.html`

15. Microsoft Corporation, 2004. Security Risk Management Guide. [Electronic Technet Document]. [Cited 3.3.2008]. Available at: `http://www.microsoft. com/technet/security/guidance/complianceandpolicies/secrisk/ default.mspx`

16. Microsoft Corporation, 2006. Windows Server 2003 Security Guide. [Electronic Document download]. [Cited 3.3.2008]. Available at: `http://www.microsoft.com/downloads/details.aspx?FamilyID=8A2643C1-0685-4D89-B655-521EA6C7B4DB&displaylang=en`

17. Microsoft Corporation, 2004. Security Risk Management Guide. [Electronic Document].[Cited 4.3.2008]. Available at: `http://www.microsoft.com/technet/security/guidance/complianceandpolicies/secrisk/srsgch01.mspx`

# Chapter 4

18. Microsoft Corporation, 2006. Best Practice Guide for Securing Active Directory Installations. [Electronic Technet Article]. [Cited 27.2.2008]. Available at: `http://technet2.microsoft.com/windowsserver/en/library/edc08cf1-d4ba-4235-9696-c93b0313ad6e1033.mspx?mfr=true`International Network

19. Services, 2005. Secure your Active Directory Environment. [Electronic PowerPoint Presentation].[Cited 28.2.2008]. Available at: `http://www.secureitconf.com/OLD/2005/presentations/Secure_your_Active_Directory_EnvironmentID194.ppt`

20. Microsoft Corporation, 2003. Windows Server 2003 Security Guide - Chapter 5: The Domain Controller Baseline Policy. [Electronic Technet Document]. [Cited 28.2.2008]. Available at: `http://www.microsoft.com/technet/security/prodtech/windowsserver2003/w2003hg/s3sgch05.mspx`

21. National Security Agency, 2006. The Windows Server 2003 - Security Guide, v2.1. [Electronic PDF Document].[Cited 4.3.2008]. Available at: `http://www.nsa.gov/notices/notic00004.cfm?Address=/snac/os/win2003/MSCG-001R-2003.pdf`

22. Microsoft Corporation, 2003. Windows Server 2003 Security Guide. [Electronic Document download]. [Cited 29.2.2008]. Available at: `http://www.microsoft.com/technet/security/prodtech/windowsserver2003/w2003hg/sgch00.mspx`

23. Microsoft Corporation, 2003. Best Practice Guide for Securing Active Directory Installations – Chapter 6: Securing DNS.[Electronic Technet Document].[Cited 27.2.2008]. Available at: `http://technet2.microsoft.com/windowsserver/en/library/cc1eff0a-3a9e-46d2-8a7d-6b2e16461c711033.mspx?mfr=true`

24. Blog.scottlowe.org, 2007. Delayed Replication DCs and Authoritative Restores. [Electronic Document]. [Cited 27.2.2008]. Available at: `http://blog.scottlowe.org/2007/07/20/delayed-replication-dcs-and-authoritative-restores/`

25. Microsoft Corporation, 2004. Step-by-Step Guide to Active Directory Sites and Services. [Electronic Tech Center Article]. [Cited 4.3.2008]. Available at: `http://www.microsoft.com/technet/prodtechnol/windowsserver2003/technologies/directory/activedirectory/stepbystep/adsrv.mspx`

26. Microsoft Corporation, 2005. Best practices for Active Directory Sites and Services.[Electronic Technet Article].[Cited 4.3.2008]. Available at: `http://technet2.microsoft.com/windowsserver/en/library/86417143-92b6-431b-8439-91f456e921dd1033.mspx?mfr=true`

27. Microsoft Corporation, 2004. Step-by-Step Guide to Using the Delegation of Control Wizard. [Electronic Tech Center Article]. [Cited 4.3.2008]. Available at: `http://www.microsoft.com/technet/prodtechnol/windowsserver2003/technologies/directory/activedirectory/stepbystep/ctrlwiz.mspx`

28. Searchwinit.com, 2005. Preventing Active Directory disaster: The replication lag site.[Electronic Article].[Cited 3.3.2008]. Available at: `http://searchwinit.techtarget.com/tip/0,289483,sid1_gci1086805,00.html`

29. Gilkirkpatrick.com, 2007. Restoring Active Directory data from a lag site DC. [Electronic Article].[Cited 3.3.2008]. Available at: `http://www.gilkirkpatrick.com/Blog/post/Restoring-Active-Directory-data-from-a-lag-site-DC.aspx`

# Chapter 5

30. Microsoft Corporation, 2000. Active Directory Diagnostic Tool.[Electronic Technet Document].[Cited 29.2.2008]. Available at: `http://www.microsoft.com/technet/prodtechnol/windows2000serv/reskit/distrib/dsfl_utl_nzzw.mspx?mfr=true`

31. Microsoft Corporation, 2003. Active Directory, Directory Services Maintenance Utility. [Electronic Technet Document]. [Cited 29.2.2008]. Available at: `http://technet2.microsoft.com/windowsserver/en/library/819bea8b-3889-4479-850f-1f031087693d1033.mspx?mfr=true`

32. Microsoft Corporation, 2006. Ntdsutil. [Electronic Technet Document]. [Cited 27.2.2008]. Available at: `http://technet2.microsoft.com/windowsserver/en/library/91559a2b-b666-442c-bdd2-df4b7c46983c1033.mspx?mfr=true`

33. Microsoft Corporation, 2007. How to remove data in Active Directory after an unsuccessful domain controller demotion. [Electronic Knowledgebase Article]. [Cited 27.2.2008]. Available at: `http://support.microsoft.com/kb/216498`

34. Microsoft Corporation, 2006. Using Ntdsutil.exe to transfer or seize FSMO roles to a domain controller. [Electronic Knowledgebase Article]. [Cited 27.2.2008]. Available at: `http://support.microsoft.com/kb/255504`

# Chapter 6

35. Microsoft Corporation, 2003. Replmon Overview.[Electronic Technet Document].[Cited 3.3.2008]. Available at: `http://technet2.microsoft.com/windowsserver/en/library/691910f2-a6a7-4ced-984e-972aec2cbdd21033.mspx?mfr=true`

36. Microsoft Corporation, 2003. Dcdiag Overview. [Electronic Technet Document]. [Cited 3.3.2008]. Available at: `http://technet2.microsoft.com/windowsserver/en/library/f7396ad6-0baa-4e66-8d18-17f83c5e4e6c1033.mspx?mfr=true`

37. Microsoft Corporation, 2003. Repadmin Overview. [Electronic Technet Document]. [Cited 3.3.2008]. Available at: `http://technet2.microsoft.com/windowsserver/en/library/24d8a2dd-2596-46cb-9b0f-179f977d434a1033.mspx?mfr=true`

38. Microsoft Corporation, 2007. How to use the Install from Media feature to promote Windows Server 2003-based domain controllers. [Electronic Technet Document]. [Cited 3.3.2008]. Available at: `http://support.microsoft.com/kb/311078`

# Chapter 7

39. Microsoft Corporation, 2007. Disaster Recovery: Active Directory Users and Groups. [Electronic Magazine Article]. [Cited 4.3.2008]. Available at: `http://technet.microsoft.com/en-us/magazine/cc162459.aspx`

40. Microsoft Corporation, 2008. How to restore deleted user accounts and their group memberships in Active Directory. [Electronic Knowledgebase Article]. [Cited 4.3.2008]. Available at: `http://support.microsoft.com/kb/840001`

41. Microsoft Corporation, 2004. Disaster Recovery: Step-by-Step Guide to Managing Active Directory.[Electronic Magazine Article].[Cited 4.3.2008]. Available at: `http://www.microsoft.com/technet/prodtechnol/windowsserver2003/technologies/directory/activedirectory/stepbystep/admng.mspx`

42. Microsoft Corporation, 2007. Lingering objects may remain after you bring an out-of-date global catalog server back online. [Electronic Knowledgebase Article]. [Cited 4.3.2008]. Available at: `http://support.microsoft.com/kb/314282/`

43. Microsoft Corporation, 2007. Event ID 1388 or 1988: A lingering object is detected. [Electronic Technet Article]. [Cited 4.3.2008]. Available at: `http://technet2.microsoft.com/windowsserver/en/library/77dbd146-f265-4d64-bdac-605ecbf1035f1033.mspx?mfr=true`

44. Microsoft Corporation, 2006. ADRestore v1.1. [Electronic download]. [Cited 4.3.2008]. Available at: `http://technet.microsoft.com/en-us/sysinternals/bb963906.aspx`

45. Microsoft Corporation, 2004. Group Policy Management Console with Service Pack 1. [Electronic download]. [Cited 4.3.2008]. Available at: `http://www.microsoft.com/downloads/details.aspx?FamilyID=0A6D4C24-8CBD-4B35-9272-DD3CBFC81887&displaylang=en`

46. Microsoft Corporation, 2008. Best Practice Active Directory Design for Managing Windows Networks.[Electronic Technet Article].[Cited 4.3.2008]. Available at: `http://technet.microsoft.com/en-us/library/bb727085.aspx`

# Chapter 8

47. Microsoft Corporation, 2007. Using the BurFlags registry key to reinitialize File Replication Service replica sets. [Electronic Support Article]. [Cited 1.3.2008]. Available at: `http://support.microsoft.com/kb/290762`

48. Microsoft Corporation, 2006. You cannot replicate files from a Windows Server 2003-based domain controller and events are logged in the File Replication Service log.[Electronic Support Article].[Cited 1.3.2008]. Available at: `http://support.microsoft.com/kb/925633`

49. Microsoft Corporation, 2005. Active Directory Recovery Planning.[Electronic PDF Document].[Cited 1.3.2008]. Available at: `http://download.microsoft.com/documents/australia/teched2005/SVR302_Chong.pdf`

50. NetPro Computing, 2005. The Definitive Guide to Active Directory Disaster Recovery. [Electronic PDF Document]. [Cited 1.3.2008]. Available at: `http://www.netpro.com/media/pdf/NetPro_ADDR_Guide.pdf`

51. Microsoft Corporation, 2003. Repadmin Overview.[Electronic Technet Article].[Cited 2.3.2008]. Available at: `http://technet2.microsoft.com/windowsserver/en/library/03b7fc47-e25c-4af8-822f-f856b565b76a1033.mspx?mfr=true`

52. Microsoft Corporation, 2003. Repadmin Syntax.[Electronic Technet Article].[Cited 2.3.2008]. Available at: `http://technet2.microsoft.com/WindowsServer/en/library/03b7fc47-e25c-4af8-822f-f856b565b76a1033.mspx`

# Chapter 9

53. Microsoft Corporation, 2007. How to move a Windows installation to different hardware. [Electronic Knowledgebase Article]. [Cited 3.3.2008]. Available at: `http://support.microsoft.com/kb/249694`

54. Microsoft Corporation, 2006. To Use the Backup Program to Back Up and Restore the System State in Windows 2000. [Electronic Knowledgebase Article]. [Cited 4.3.2008]. Available at: `http://support.microsoft.com/kb/240363`

55. Microsoft Corporation, 2007. How to perform a disaster recovery restoration of Active Directory on a computer with a different hardware configuration. [Electronic Knowledgebase Article].[Cited 4.3.2008]. Available at: `http://support.microsoft.com/kb/263532`

56. Microsoft Corporation, 2007. Netdom.exe: Windows Domain Manager.[Electronic Technet Article].[Cited 4.3.2008]. Available at: `http://technet2.microsoft.com/windowsserver/en/library/460e3705-9e5d-4f9b-a139-44341090cfd41033.mspx?mfr=true`

57. Microsoft Corporation, 2007. Initiating Replication Between Active Directory Direct Replication Partners.[Electronic Technet Article].[Cited 4.3.2008]. Available at: `http://support.microsoft.com/kb/232072/`

58. Microsoft Corporation, 2003. Replmon Overview. [Electronic Technet Document]. [Cited 3.3.2008]. Available at: `http://technet2.microsoft.com/windowsserver/en/library/691910f2-a6a7-4ced-984e-972aec2cbdd21033.mspx?mfr=true`

# Chapter 10

59. Microsoft Corporation, 2007. Windows 2000 Resource Kit Tools for administrative tasks. [Electronic Support Article].[Cited 4.3.2008]. Available at: `http://support.microsoft.com/kb/927229`

60. Microsoft Corporation, 2003. Windows Server 2003 Resource Kit Tools.[Electronic Technet Article].[Cited 4.3.2008]. Available at: `http://www.microsoft.com/Downloads/details.aspx?FamilyID=9d467a69-57ff-4ae7-96ee-b18c4790cffd&displaylang=en`

61. Microsoft Corporation, 2003. Windows Server 2003 Administration Tools Pack.[Electronic Technet Article].[Cited 4.3.2008]. Available at: `http://www.microsoft.com/Downloads/details.aspx?familyid=C16AE515-C8F4-47EF-A1E4-A8DCBACFF8E3&displaylang=en`

62. Microsoft Corporation, 2003.Dcdiag Overview. [Electronic Technet Article]. [Cited 4.3.2008]. Available at: `http://technet2.microsoft.com/windowsserver/en/library/f7396ad6-0baa-4e66-8d18-17f83c5e4e6c1033.mspx?mfr=true`

63. Microsoft Corporation, 2003.Dcdiag Syntax. [Electronic Technet Article]. [Cited 4.3.2008]. Available at: `http://technet2.microsoft.com/windowsserver/en/library/f7396ad6-0baa-4e66-8d18-17f83c5e4e6c1033.mspx?mfr=true`

64. Microsoft Corporation, 2003.Netdiag Overview. [Electronic Technet Article]. [Cited 4.3.2008]. Available at: `http://technet2.microsoft.com/windowsserver/en/library/f7396ad6-0baa-4e66-8d18-17f83c5e4e6c1033.mspx?mfr=true`

65. Microsoft Corporation, 2003. Netdiag Syntax.[Electronic Technet Article].[Cited 4.3.2008]. Available at: `http://technet2.microsoft.com/windowsserver/en/library/cf4926db-87ea-4f7a-9806-0b54e1c00a771033.mspx?mfr=true`

66. Microsoft Corporation, 2003. Sonar.exe: File Replication Service (FRS) Status Viewer.[Electronic download].[Cited 3.3.2008]. Available at: `http://www.microsoft.com/downloads/details.aspx?FamilyID=158cb0fb-fe09-477c-8148-25ae02cf15d8&displaylang=en`

67. Microsoft Corporation, 2005. Ultrasound - Monitoring and Troubleshooting Tool for File Replication Service (FRS). [Electronic download]. [Cited 3.3.2008]. Available at: `http://www.microsoft.com/downloads/details.aspx?familyid=61ACB9B9-C354-4F98-A823-24CC0DA73B50&displaylang=en`

68. Microsoft Corporation, 2003. Microsoft SQL Server 2000 Desktop Engine (MSDE 2000) Release A.[Electronic download].[Cited 3.3.2008]. Available at: `http://www.microsoft.com/downloads/details.aspx?FamilyID=413744D1-A0BC-479F-BAFA-E4B278EB9147&displaylang=en`

# Appendix

69. Disaster Recovery Journal, 2007. Business Continuity Planning Model.[Electronic Article].[Cited 3.3.2008]. Available at: `http://www.drj.com/index.php?option=com_content&task=view&id=753&Itemid=449`

70. Disaster Recovery Journal, 2002. Sample Plans. [Electronic Article]. [Cited 3.3.2008]. Available at: `http://www.drj.com/index.php?option=com_content&task=view&id=259&Itemid=298`

71. Disaster Recovery Guide, 2007. The Disaster Recovery Plan. [Electronic Article]. [Cited 3.3.2008]. Available at: `http://www.disaster-recovery-guide.com/plan.htm`

# Index

DSR 140
Dynamic Host Configuration Protocol.
    See DHCP

# F

Flexible Single Master Operation. See
    FSMO
FSMO 36
FSMO, roles
  about 36
  domain name master 37
  domain name master, changing 37
  failure consequence 39
  infrastructure Manager 36
  PDC Emulator 37
  RID Master 36
  schema master 37
  naming standard 32
full group control
  granting steps 71-73

# G

GC server 122
Global Catalog server. See GC server
Globally Unique Identifiers. See GUID
GPMC 149
GPMC used, GPO
  backing up 149, 150
  restoring 151
GPO
  about 22, 149
  ADM templates used 23
  restoring 149
GPO, restoring
  alternate option 152, 153
  GPMC used 149
Group Policy Management Console 149.
    See GPMC
group policy objects. See GPO
GUID 152

# H

HAL 174
Hardware Abstraction Layer. See HAL
hubsite 24

# I

IFM 113
implementing, disaster recovery plan
  about 56
  for AD 56
  presentation to management 57
  restoration order, defining 58
install from media. See IFM
IT infrastructure
  change management 75

# L

lag sites
  about 29, 90
  configuring 91
  creating 91
  establishing 30
  purpose 29
  replication, configuring 91
Lightweight Directory Access Protocol. See
    LDAP
LDAP 17
lingering objects
  about 137
  appearance 137
  checking 138
  checking for, event ID s 138

# M

manual operation, deleted objects recovery
  AdRestore tool 145
  steps 146, 147, 148
Microsoft Management Console. See MMC
MMMC 20
multi-domain forest
  uses 27
multi-forest
  images 28
  uses 28

# N

naming standard
  GPO's named 33
  group policies, naming 33

# [PACKT] PUBLISHING

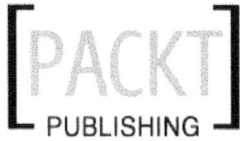

## Thank you for buying
# Active Directory Disaster Recovery

## About Packt Publishing

Packt, pronounced 'packed', published its first book "*Mastering phpMyAdmin for Effective MySQL Management*" in April 2004 and subsequently continued to specialize in publishing highly focused books on specific technologies and solutions.

Our books and publications share the experiences of your fellow IT professionals in adapting and customizing today's systems, applications, and frameworks. Our solution based books give you the knowledge and power to customize the software and technologies you're using to get the job done. Packt books are more specific and less general than the IT books you have seen in the past. Our unique business model allows us to bring you more focused information, giving you more of what you need to know, and less of what you don't.

Packt is a modern, yet unique publishing company, which focuses on producing quality, cutting-edge books for communities of developers, administrators, and newbies alike. For more information, please visit our website: www.packtpub.com.

## Writing for Packt

We welcome all inquiries from people who are interested in authoring. Book proposals should be sent to authors@packtpub.com. If your book idea is still at an early stage and you would like to discuss it first before writing a formal book proposal, contact us; one of our commissioning editors will get in touch with you.

We're not just looking for published authors; if you have strong technical skills but no writing experience, our experienced editors can help you develop a writing career, or simply get some additional reward for your expertise.

[PACKT]
PUBLISHING

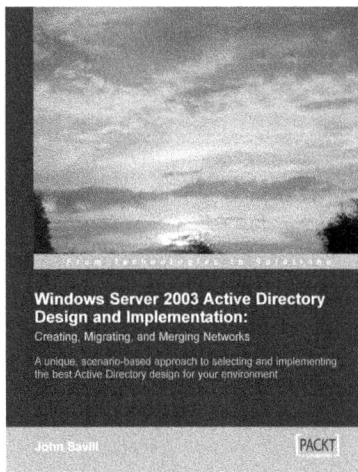

## Windows Server 2003 Active Directory Design and Implementation

ISBN: 190-4811-08-6    Paperback: 356 pages

A unique, scenario-based approach to selecting and implementing the best Active Directory design for your environment

Understand the principles of Active Directory design

1. Create new networks or evolve existing Active Directory installations

2. Create the best Active Directory design for a broad range of business environments

3. Implement your Active Directory designs

4. Migrate and merge Active Directory structures

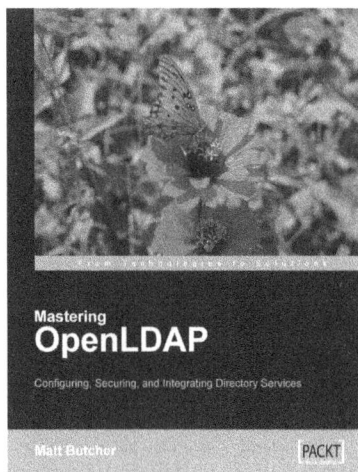

## Mastering OpenLDAP

ISBN: 184-7191-02-9    Paperback: 400 pages

Install, Configure, Build, and Integrate Secure Directory Services with OpenLDAP server in a networked environment

1. Up-to-date with the latest OpenLDAP release

2. Installing and configuring the OpenLDAP server

3. Synchronizing multiple OpenLDAP servers over the network

4. Creating custom LDAP schemas to model your own information

Please check **www.PacktPub.com** for information on our titles

[PACKT]
PUBLISHING

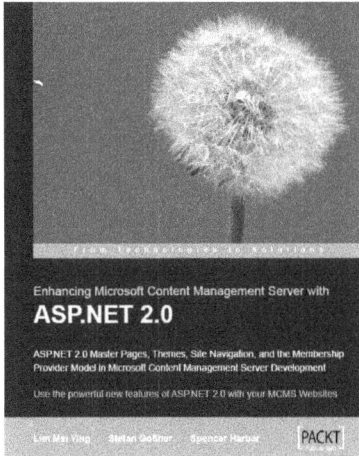

## Enhancing Microsoft Content Management Server with ASP.NET 2.0

ISBN: 190-4811-52-3          Paperback: 180 pages

Use the powerful new features of ASP.NET 2.0 with your MCMS Websites

1.  Get Microsoft Content Management Server Service Pack 2 up and running

2.  Use the most exciting features of ASP.NET 2.0 in your MCMS development

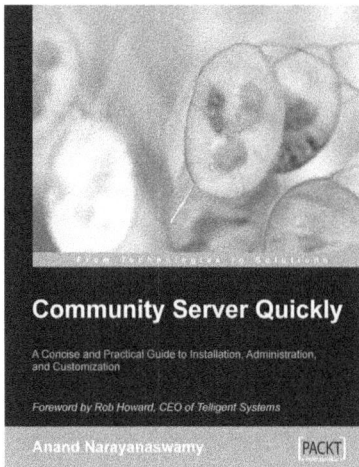

## Community Server Quickly

ISBN: 184-7190-87-1          Paperback: 300 pages

A Concise and Practical Guide to Installation, Administration, and Customization

1.  Get Community Server Express Edition set up and running fast

2.  Learn to manage blogs, users, forums, and file and photo galleries

3.  How to customize, market, and monetize your site

Please check **www.PacktPub.com** for information on our titles

www.ingramcontent.com/pod-product-compliance
Lightning Source LLC
Chambersburg PA
CBHW061404210326
41598CB00035B/6095

* 9 7 8 1 8 4 7 1 9 3 2 7 8 *